Charismatic Crisis-Prone Caribbean Leaders of Our Era

Charismatic Crisis-Prone Caribbean Leaders of Our Era

BY

Willie James

Ivy House Publishing Group
www.ivyhousebooks.com

PUBLISHED BY IVY HOUSE PUBLISHING GROUP
5122 Bur Oak Circle, Raleigh, NC 27612
United States of America
919.782.0281
www.ivyhousebooks.com

ISBN: 978-1-57197-504-1
Library of Congress Control Number: 2010929432

Printed in The United States of America

Table of Contents

Acknowledgements vii
Notation ix
Preface xi
Chapter 1: Castro 1
Chapter 2: Burnham 19
Chapter 3: Adams 59
Chapter 4: Gairy 77
Chapter 5: N. Manley 95
Chapter 6: Jagan 108
Chapter 7: M. Manley 126
Chapter 8: Williams 140
Chapter 9: Bustamante 166
Chapter 10: Price 176
Chapter 11: Bishop 183
Chapter 12: Bird 200
Chapter 13: Seaga 213
Chapter 14: Compton 222
Chapter 15: Barrow 240
Chapter 16: Bradshaw 250
Chapter 17: Joshua 259
Chapter 18: Pindling 277
Chapter 19: Douglas 286
Bibliography 299

Acknowledgements

I hasten to express very many thanks to Ms. Rosamund Stanislaus and other staff members of the Castries Central Library in St. Lucia, who for several weeks endured my presence and assisted me with some of the books from which the notes required to complete this writing project were taken. Your civility is hugely appreciated. Similarly, I am indebted to Tommy and Leular Kirnon, and Leathon and Sharon Anne Khan for a supply of notes on Jamaica—much obliged.

I do also owe a debt of gratitude to Austin and Pat Gittens and Grenadian and St. Lucian businessman Priestly Louison for their insight on conditions then in the Spice Isle. Profuse thanks.

Dates were vital to support the credibility of what was being advanced and Naula Williams, manager of the documentation and information center of the Organization of Eastern Caribbean States (OECS) exerted herself beyond expectations to find the required information. Thanks. Thanks to Sir John Compton and Earl Bousquet for their contribution.

And Shirley King, private secretary of the late, former Barbadian Prime Minister Tom Adams, and Clyde Griffith, former cabinet minister and general secretary of the Party during the Adams era, assisted enormously. To them especially I express boundless gratitude.

I must offer thanks unendingly to my colleague and friend of many years, editor of the St. Lucia *Mirror* newspaper, Guy Ellis, for his skilled editing of the manuscript and his criticism, advice and direction on publication. London or New York or Toronto? Suffice it to say I am eternally grateful.

However, this book could not have materialized into its present form without the invaluable assistance of my dear friend Angus Smith. I recognize that her typing of the manuscript was an enormous task. She pointed out repetitions, inconsistencies, and conflicting tenses. Angus, I am well aware that what was intended as mere typing assistance evolved into an imposition. You're wonderful and I am so fortunate to know that you are my friend. Eternally grateful to you.

My gratitude must also extend to Lisa Ferdinand for also absorbing a large percentage of the typing of the manuscript. She also supplied information from Trinidad and Tobago. The effort was commendable. Many thanks for your professionalism.

And to my lovely wife Annette who endured the many months of isolation—though not without some chiding—in the library at home, writing invariably from 7:00 AM to midnight or 1:00 AM the following day and to begin all over again later. But I am utterly grateful for your patience and understanding. And for the gallons of mauby, ginger beer, tea, rum punch and other beverages that you never failed to supply. May Jehovah bless you always.

—Willie James

Notation

If this Caribbean region were a one government controlled landmass of provinces through which anyone may travel to access information as on the subject chosen for this book, the exercise would have been less onerous than it has been. The sparse and nebulous information with few dates was daunting but this allowed observing what was missing and required for future attempts.

The finished material varied in length and this again was due to inaccessibility of personal histories on which an interesting biography could be compiled. Of course, I have been fortunate to have either interviewed or spoken to most of the Caribbean Leaders featured in this book here in St. Lucia, Guyana, Canada, Trinidad and Tobago and Barbados. As a former director of the St. Lucia government public relations and information services, I did perceive that it would be useful to interview these leaders, the aim being to incorporate them as features in both my GIS radio and television programs.

Most of these pleasurable encounters are memorable as though they were only yesterday. The most relaxed of these was with Premier Ebenezer T. Joshua of St. Vincent and the Grenadines. The most stressful, and perhaps it was more like a conflict of denials, was with Dr. Eric Eustace Williams, prime minister of Trinidad and Tobago. The most distasteful and hostile was with

Linden Forbes Sampson Burnham, former premier, prime minister and president of the Co-operative Republic of Guyana.

Of these many leaders whom I had been privileged to meet, the one who left an indelible impression as someone genuinely acquainted with that rare human quality described as "humility" was Ebenezer Theodore Joshua. Now how could this be best explained? An illustration would be that of the very many books I had read in my lifetime, the only opening paragraph that had remained vividly poignant with me, had been the Guyanese author Edward R. Brathwaite's novel, *To Sir, with Love.* It was, to my mind, the most fascinatingly descriptive introduction to a truly provocative social experience.

And anent the varying lengths of the features, the information of which had been eclectic in gathering, it should be appreciated that easy access as in the case of Sir John G. M. Compton, St. Lucia's first prime minister, for whom I had worked as P.R.O. and press officer on two occasions for about a decade, determined the length of what had to be told.

The notes on Ebenezer T. Joshua were not at all easy to come by. I am enormously grateful to my dear friend and brother, Peter Lewis, for the legwork employed to produce the notes he did. He searched, found something and posted it to me from Kingstown, St. Vincent and the Grenadines. But then, the seeming delay evidently served a purpose. Joshua must have been an intriguing personality to have influenced the just-elected prime minister of St. Vincent and the Grenadines, Dr. Ralph Gonsalzes. Several years ago, he produced his thesis on Joshua to earn his doctorate. It is hoped that this book will be more than adequate to assist other writers in their research for works of a similar nature.

—Willie James

Preface

Any attempt to compile solely an anthology of presumably the most charismatic leaders of our era would not escape a prompt charge of being invidious; hence the writer inevitably positioned himself wide open to the encroachments of challenge. It was accepted, however, that challenges in life were nothing novel. They were known to conduce to strength and hastened resolves that were considered an integral part of one's struggle for survival. Statistics extracted from the *Caribbean Junior Social Studies Atlas* indicated that in the Caribbean we numbered some 85 million. The English-speaking Caribbean may claim only some 6.5 million of that total.

The French speaking Caribbean, namely Martinique and Guadeloupe, were of especial interest to us. They were neither independent nations nor colonies. They were described, euphemistically, as Departments of the Republic of France in Europe though separated by the Atlantic Ocean some three thousand miles away. As such, their welfare at this time was wedded to that of the European economic community. These two Caribbean islands were classic vestiges of French overseas sugar and banana estates in this region. So much for France's watchword Liberty, Equality and Fraternity. Moreover, the meaningful words "liberty, beloved liberty," are a major element of "La Marseilles," the national anthem of France. Surely they must represent some significance to the French mind. Should they not be applicable to those colonized? Is it that they preach "liberty, beloved liberty," but sooner practice oppression? A considerable number of people consider the French posture ludicrous, anachronistic imperialism still active in this new millennium.

Historically, militarily the most defeated of the consummate plunderers, the French colonization precepts totally disagreed with the prevailing thought processes of universal liberation. They were supremely proficient in their unrelenting cruelty in the Caribbean, Africa and Asia. The past twenty years had witnessed numerous anti-colonial oppression clashes in all the French colonies. All were met with swift military suppression. Ironically, it was the noted French philosopher Jean-Jacques Rousseau in his *Du Contrat Social*, published in 1762, who declared: "Man is born free yet everywhere he is in chains."

Significantly, Rousseau also coined the slogan "Liberty, Equality and Fraternity" and this became the watchword of the French Revolution. And he also advanced that "civilization had corrupted our natural goodness and decreased our freedom."

Remarkably, France, one of the five principal imperialist nations of yesterday, had yet to come to grips with its past plunderings that constituted a bane to humanity. At the least, Britain had set free most of the lands plundered and colonized. Need we recall the boasts of our former years: "The sun never sets on the British Empire," and "Britannia rules the waves." And we can't help but remember in his *Memoirs of the Second World War*, Britain's most illustrious son, former Prime Minister Sir Winston Churchill, reflected on the fact that he had stated emphatically that he was not elected chief minister of Her Majesty's government "to preside over the liquidation of the British Empire."

In the circumstances, this writer's judgment was not unlike that of a submarine's periscope. It scanned the surface and revealed what it captured. It showed what it saw. Politics was a tumultuous occupation. And very many who loathed the behavior of many of its practitioners wondered why so many people of seeming integrity were attracted to that profession! We assumed that we knew why. They fell victims to, or became casualties of, the power syndrome. But greed or economic well-being appeared to be fundamental. It lent to corruption. Experience had taught that no politician admitted to being corrupt until he was caught and there was the evidence from which he could not divorce himself.

At this very moment, the former president of the Philippines, Joseph Estrada, was under arrest for alleged corruption. And some years before, President Ferdinand Marcos. Need we mention the former president of Indonesia, Sukarno, who was forced out of office for mismanagement in 1966? In July 2001, the incumbent Abdurrahman Wahid was impeached for corruption and mismanagement. Over the past twenty years some six Japanese prime ministers have been forced to resign as a result of "no confidence," and similarly some eight Italian prime ministers have been forced out of office, and not because they were suitable. It should be concluded that universally corruption was endemic in politics. And perhaps it was as good a reason as any that impelled the greatest man who ever lived, Jesus Christ, to admonish his followers in "the need to be different from the power-hungry rulers of the world" (Luke 22: 24-27).

Here in the Caribbean, Premier Patrick John of the Commonwealth of Dominica was forced to leave for misconduct and Premier Cheddi Jagan of Guyana failed to accept that he had lost at the polls. He was removed but regained the presidency some twenty years later.

As it was, the law was an instrument or device that both sheltered and indicted lawyers, considered clever devils, very many of whom—like trade unionists—were irresistibly attracted to politics.

The Webster New World Dictionary defined politics as, "the science of government; political affairs; political opinions, principles, etc. Factional scheming for power." This last definition seemed to victimize many politicians to stigmatize that profession. Politics then, it should be understood by nature, had an inbuilt self-destruct element that very many of its practitioners were unable to resist. It could be described as an occupational hazard. Politics demanded—from keen observation—an almost precise, critical judgment, cunning, intellectual vitality, sincerity, credibility, congeniality and resistance to self-indulgence. To summarize, it demanded only two words: unquestionable integrity. The failure rate then was appreciated. As I saw it, politics was a dichotomous journey in the struggle for survival. It was a risk, but the choice to proceed on the route should be taken. The motivation then, it would seem, was fundamentally a quality of life, irrespective if it were self-first driven or genuinely to contribute to bringing about a change that should improve the quality of life of others.

The honest politician—and very many do struggle to remain honest—entered that profession to make a difference to society. Perhaps unknowingly, the approach was, from the inception, ambivalent. This politician intended to give but must take, being afflicted with a self-compensatory fever. Time was vital. It should not be wasted. Of necessity, it was a give-and-take world. Consequently, taking was not improper. This, apparently, was the working philosophy of most politicians of presumed integrity. History bore evidence that the politician universally was seemingly sincere. That was, until the virus of either greed or power assumed control. He was infected. And he changed as he assumed an air associated with celebrities. Now, progressively, he overestimated himself. And at this juncture he forgot that he had begged to serve. Now somewhat chameleon, in attitude he brashly considered himself confident. Not merely to serve but to control. And it was really astonishing how man changed with power. It was a paradox! Though the onus rested with the electorate, too many people who consisted of the electorate were naïve, stupid, poor, ignorant, subliterate and illiterate, greedy, selfish and generally uneducated. The politician recognized this. And there were many facets of service to offer. What with a multiplicity of tastes to accommodate the errant politician. Now he found himself, though, seemingly in a province of unending harvest.

Incidentally, even this weather-beaten democracy—embraced and practiced by the western world—was terribly suspect. Very many will swear that it was defective. A politician was voted into office by the most fatuous, naïve, uneducated, indecisive, criminal and unbalanced people in society. He was unconcerned. The numbers counted, not their quality. He considered himself a legitimate winner as it served a purpose. It will perhaps be recalled that one of the most celebrated of statesmen, Sir Winston Churchill, said, "Democracy was beyond doubt a reprehensible system but it will suffice until another evolves to replace it."

Then we have presumably gravitated from feudalism on to capitalism, to socialism. They were competing ideologies that affected the lives of so many people. Significantly a former president of the United States of America, Ronald Reagan, defended the capitalist system in his autobiographical book *An American Life* (Pocket Books - Simon and Schuster, Inc.). According to him:

> The competitive free enterprise system has given us the greatest standard of living in the world, produced generation after generation of technical wizards who consistently lead the world in invention and innovation and has provided unlimited opportunities enabling industrious Americans from the most humble of backgrounds to climb to the top of the ladder of success.

This, in essence, was a reality but it was handicapped and severely questioned by a diametrically opposite reality as pointed out by Charles A., Mary R., and William Beards in their book *Basic*

History of the United States (Double Day Company Inc.). It succinctly stated, "Gross inequalities in the distribution of wealth, have long been the subject of populistic, progressive and socialistic criticism."

And this was ably supported in the same book by the Beards' *Socialist Platform Denounces the Capitalist System* (1912). The representatives of the Socialist Party in national convention at Indianapolis declared that the capitalist system had outgrown its historical function, and had become utterly incapable of meeting the problems now confronting society. They denounced this outgrown system as incompetent and corrupt and the source of unspeakable misery and suffering to the whole working class. It stressed:

> Under this system the industrial equipment of the Nation has passed into the absolute control of the plutocracy which exacts an annual tribute of millions of dollars from the producers . . . . Multitudes of unemployed walk the streets of our cities . . . . The farmers in every State are plundered . . . . Capitalist concentration is mercilessly crushing the class of small businessmen. It is the capitalist system that is responsible for the increasing burden of armaments, the poverty, slums, child labor, most of the insanity, crime and prostitution, and much of the disease that afflicts mankind.

As this writer saw it, the crux of the crevasse between the two conflicting ideologies was that both possessed advantages and disadvantages and acceptance of which depended on one's early cultural indoctrination; one either accepted or rejected it. The hysteria over socialism was the obvious abuse at the top with the seeming endemic State-controlled regimentation that ensured there was full employment. Conversely, the other bred inequalities, injustices and abrasive unemployment. It begged for uncommon initiative, creativity and industry to excel and become rich and invited the control of the less industrious. But another point of view by a well-known international personality who spent some twenty-eight years in prison with ample time to think—former South African President Nelson Mandela—was expressed in his book *Long Walk to Freedom* (Little, Brown and Company). What will it be, feudalism, capitalism or socialism? "My approach was not ideological, but it was biased in favor of socialism, which I saw as the most advanced stage of economic life then evolved by man," declared Mandela.

This debate will persist until the end of this system of things.

In an excellent compilation of the thoughts of Simon Bolivar "the Liberator" of South America, he, a brilliant soldier and powerful intellectual, pointed out:

> The continuance of authority in the same individual has frequently meant the end of democratic governments. Repeated elections are essential in popular systems of governments for nothing is more perilous than to permit one citizen to retain power for an extended period. The people become accustomed to obeying him, and he forms the habit of commanding them; herein lie the origins of usurpation and tyranny.

This sufficed to suggest why Dr. Walter Rodney swore to usurp Forbes Burnham in Guyana. George Odlum was so obsessed with the idea of replacing John Compton in St. Lucia; Tim Hector intended to run Vere Bird into the ground in Antigua. And why the late Maurice Bishop usurped Sir Eric Gairy in Grenada.

The democratic system can hold. The Constitution, however, housed the flaws that allowed a leader to remain uninterrupted in office. This abrogated democracy as dictatorship or oligarchy stepped in. The Constitution should be rewritten to ensure that no leader remained in office for more than eight years at any one time. The Republic of Venezuela permitted one four-year term in office. The leader stepped aside and, if he wished, sought re-election after a hiatus of ten years. The United States of America's Constitution allowed for two terms of office of four years each if re-elected. However, after two terms, a president was not allowed to return.

This constitutional arrangement freed us of a dictatorship and usurpation within the democratic system. It should be adopted and made mandatory by all Caribbean States. Of course, many politicians, or most of them, here in the Caribbean would not hesitate to oppose this view as the indignity of obedience to a leader is of less importance and concern than the power to manipulate the conditions that keep the people subservient. But then, most Caribbean politicians were self-indulgent and no Simon Bolivar.

The verity was that we were seemingly fated not to be free of politics, as the exercise in itself was found in many forms in every spectrum of the society where people socialized, even within religious persuasions where so-called Christians viciously flayed their brothers under the pretext of imparting direction and knowledge. The excuse appeared to be that these politics were consistent with the human imperfection. We were reminded that, as an entity, politics was "the science of government; factional scheming for power." Fact was "power" in this context should be for personal gain.

France had resisted—upwards to this juncture of the new millennium 2001—granting freedom to Guadeloupe and Martinique, St. Bartholomew in our region with French (Cayenne) Guiana in South America. At this time it seemed that the freedom fighters were regrouping underground, hence were temporarily silenced.

This was not the case in Vietnam or in Algeria. And not in what the French had described "the world's best colony," Haiti. It was expected that as the sun rose, there would be a resurgence of freedom activities. It was not at all difficult to sustain the aversion we nursed relative to France's colonization's persuasion. It was the Cuban revolutionary Dr. Fidel Castro who declared, "How can the rope and the hanged man understand each other or the chain and the slave? Imperialism is the chain. Understanding is impossible."

France did not understand this language and logic and it would be superfluous to state there was a distinct difference between colonization a la France's territories, irrespective of the euphemism "departments" or "provinces" of France. That imperial state colonized and continued its oppression veiled in modern paternalism, and in language, communication semantics had become all too prevalent. For instance, the citizens of Martinique are not Martiniquans as we are St. Lucians and Dominicans. They are France's overseas "Creoles" from its colonies of Martinique, as Emperor Napoleon's wife Josephine was described. The debate still raged relative to where she was born. Was it in Martinique or was it in Paix Bouche, St. Lucia? France's posture bred terrorism! And according to the *Awake* Magazine of May 22, 2001 in its feature on terrorism:

> The causes and history of terrorism have proved the truth of the biblical statement: "man has dominated man to his injury." (Ecclesiastes 8:9) The Bible even foretold the traits that have nurtured terrorism. It says: "In the last days critical times hard to deal with will be here. For men will be lovers of themselves . . . having no natural affection, not open to any agreement, slanderers without self-control, fierce, without love of goodness, betrayers, headstrong, puffed-up with pride." (2 Timothy 3:1-5)

Pay some attention to historian Eric Williams' observation on colonization and independence. This concerns the inalienable right of man's freedom. And it was excerpted from the book *Forged From the Love of Liberty* compiled by Dr. Paul K. Sutton. It was published by Longman Caribbean. Williams pointed out:

> Independence also meant the prospect of comprehensive reform, especially of those institutions which as fashioned under colonialism could no longer serve the needs of the free people. This meant the direct reform of the public service and of the economic system.

Positively, there were psychological realities to independence that upwards to this point cannot be experienced to be enjoyed by the still-fettered French Caribbean colonies as Martinique and Guadeloupe, St. Bartholomew, Marie-Galante, one half of St. Maarten and Cayenne. Overseas colonies suffer psychological institutionalized repression. *Liberte, Equalite et Fraternite* as a philosophy was a palpable misnomer. And Barbara Ward, the noted English economist, philosopher, journalist and environmentalist, in her book *Nationalism and Ideology* declared:

> Today we are going through such a phase on a scale the world has never seen before. We are witnessing all round the world the disappearance of Western colonial control. This control, if we look at it collectively, created the largest single imperial system in man's history. We do not know yet what is going to take place. The world's power relationships are all being either subtly or brutally changed. We cannot rely on any status quo, and every change is doubled with risk that it may lead, by way of declining solidarity, to the less understanding and further divisions between communities to the ultimate catastrophe of nuclear annihilation.

France may probably respond to that: "Who cares?" And there was a fascinating anecdote regarding Guadeloupe and Canada. It occurred during the period of murderous rivalry between France and Britain. Bruce Bliven wrote in his article "The Incomparable Ben Franklin" in the book *Great Lives Great Deeds* (Readers Digest Association, Ltd.):

> The British had captured Canada from France in 1760. In the subsequent peace settlement, the English negotiators hesitated as to whether they should keep the vast unexplored northern wilderness or the rich, sugar producing island of Guadeloupe in the West Indies. Many favored the latter. Franklin argued that Canada would ultimately be the greater prize.

Canada's geography was the second largest in the world—3,831,033 square miles, second to Russia. Canada had since been an independent nation while France had brutally suppressed the several attempts for self-determination in the comparatively small

687-square-mile Guadeloupe. Canada attained its independence from Britain in 1867. Hitherto, it was still not understood how one imperialist nation could seize already-inhabited land and claim it as its own. Isn't that burglary or larceny of some form? It was brutal theft.

Geographically, it would be folly to exclude Cuba in this dissertation. It was the largest island in the Caribbean with a population of some thirteen million people. And how did Trinidadian C. L. R. James—"the black Plato" as the *London Times* once described him—refer to Cuba in his best selling novel *The Black Jacobins*? He opined, "Cuba is the most West Indian island in the West Indies."

This was indisputable. It may not have been through altruism, Christian love, morality and decency or humanitarianism; Britain was not just being noble. It could have been sheer economics but whatever; Britain saw the need to give freedom through independence to plundered lands. True, most of them were released plundered and, in that condition, better and more acceptable than still being owned. France had, for too many years, touted the claim that its citizens enjoyed the precept of *Liberte, Egalite et Fraternite.* Perhaps this related only to the residents of France. French Philosopher Montesquieu did put it into proper perspective, "It is harder to release a nation from servitude than to enslave a free nation."

Again, perhaps this represented the French experience relative to its colonies. Anent race relations though, France did display an infinitely better record than the USA, which touted itself as "the land of the free." However, it was Voltaire, perhaps France's most celebrated philosopher and most incarcerated by the French government for his writings on its unchristian-like unscrupulousness, who wrote: "People awake! Break your chains."

And according to writer Donald Culross Peattie in a piece titled "He Started the Age of Reason" in the book *Great Lives Great Deeds* (Readers Digest Associates, Ltd.):

> A quarter of a million people pressed forward between the long lines of the guards to pay homage to his [Voltaire's] remains before they were taken to the Pontheon where the great of France lie buried. As the procession moved forward a banner unrolled in the wind. It carried these words: "He gave wings to the human mind. He prepared us to be free." The freedom fighters in the colonies will not disregard Voltaire's championing of their cause.

While it was our God-given right to disagree with perhaps some of Dr. Fidel Castro's methods—influenced doubtless by succeeding brutal events—he had survived nine hostile and despairing American presidents. Castro and Cuba continued to be of immense significance to our world. We should recall also the statement made by that historian Dr. Eric Williams in his book *Inward Hunger.* He stated, "The role of the politician wrapped as it is in expediency and survival is a very different one."

Evidently Williams was attempting to justify being an historian and philosopher and at the same time assume the sometimes dubious character of the politician. The two former were disciplines that pursue truth and knowledge. The latter was sustained on half-truths and deception of necessity. Castro was the trained lawyer, dedicated soldier and purposeful politician. However, to arrive at a conclusion that a leader was charismatic, though based on leadership and accomplishment, it could also be likened to a person choosing other persons to be the most beautiful of persons! Was it not claimed that "beauty was in the eyes of the beholder?" Fact was, we tended to see things, even beauty, differently. Every one of us. And try as we may, invariably we were forced to prove or justify that we were unequivocally, mere creatures of disorder.

Chapter 1

Dr. Fidel Castro
Prime Minister and President of Cuba

In this utterly stormy ocean of politics within our Caribbean, this writer's periscopic view of the undulating surface picked up the most charismatic of our leaders. The overwhelming image was that of Dr. Fidel Castro of Cuba. He had seemingly defied man, guns and time. The debonair, articulate attorney, soldier and statesman had established an enviable, colorful and eventful record that stood still incomplete. So far at this juncture, the impact he had left on this world was indelible and stupendous, that was historic. The tall, dashing and attractive Fidel Castro Ruz was born in Oriente Province in Cuba. Clever and studious as a youngster, he progressed academically to the University of Havana in 1950 where he attained his doctorate in law.

The young Castro courted strong views on nationalism. He became involved in several adventurous exploits. Ill fortune visited him. He was captured and incarcerated in the process. As a result he was jettisoned into international prominence on July 26, 1953. He attempted an assault against the then-dictator Fulgencio Batista's government. The Moncada Army barracks in Santiago de Cuba was the chosen target. The attack was effectively repulsed and foiled. Many of his 170-guerrilla force perished. He made an-

other attempt in 1955. This fearless rebel leader Castro was captured and following his trial, he was sentenced to fifteen years in prison. It seemed ineffable, but after serving two years of his sentence, Batista was supposedly touched by a rare attack of liberality. He pardoned Castro to his subsequent detriment. Castro, the soldier-turned-rebel who on two previous occasions had attempted to overthrow Batista's government, was gifted with unexpected leniency. It was presumed that Batista was confident and convinced that Castro, with his negligible small gang of rebels or mercenaries, was no match, hence no serious threat to his powerful and ruthless security machinery.

Castro was exiled to Mexico where he wasted no time regrouping and recruiting a reliable force. They were called the 26th of July Movement; this title was perhaps less inspiring than psychological. It was on that date they were last defeated. The training camp was reported to be only a short distance away from Mexico City, the capital. And upwards to today, the dictator's decision to release Castro remained a conundrum. Why that wicked and immoral regime failed to live up to its reputation by executing Castro for treason was a major political mistake of the twentieth century in the Americas. Castro by then was perceived as a modern day combination of Robin Hood and Simon Bolivar merged into one fearless man.

The Batista government failed to anticipate another attack! At that period, the capital, Havana, was an exotically captivating city with fascinating boulevards, and tree-lined spacious streets conducive to a Caribbean-American aura that left a lingering sense of delicious intoxication. Havana was the fun city that the American hedonists especially adored. Seemingly felicity was Havana's oxygen and it pervaded as though there would be no end. This writer visited Havana in 1953 just after Castro's first attempt to usurp Batista. It was totally Americanized and punctuated with night clubs, daytime strip-bars, hotels, gaming casinos and all the concomitant elements supportive of hedonistic adventures. That city was ideally the weekend haven to which Americans must escape.

At that time, I recall distinctly that many Caribbean nationals who had immigrated to Cuba—and had been working and residing there for many years legally or illegally—were apprehensive they would be deported to their various islands. Americans then owned substantial properties such as oil refineries, sugar and tobacco estates, ranches and numerous other holdings. And one could perhaps presuppose that the hatred for the military dictatorship of Fulgencia Batista was unquestionably pervasive. How else could such a ruthless regime, insulated by a powerful force of sycophants, parasites and firearms be so complacent such as would allow a small force, however well-trained, to overthrow the might of Batista? It's a paradox! The operatives were perhaps then assisted by divine guidance, and in a manner not unlike the biblical David and Goliath. In addition, that ever present well-earned disloyalty contributed to the successful overthrow.

Castro and his rebels made another assault in December 1956. Tragically, most of his men were killed but he and eleven others managed to escape to the Sierra Maestra mountains. Throughout 1957 and onto the middle of 1958, Castro and his rebels had gained considerable ground, as most Cubans seemed to be voluntary recruits of his revolution. He could not have succeeded without their assistance. Castro eliminated the odds. He overthrew the Batista regime!

The Americans were devastated. Their hegemony was considered evil. That was in 1959. The American behavior reflected a message that they could ill afford to lose Cuba. It was a neighboring independent state. They did not own it! And one marveled at the gall of such an enormous country as the USA shamelessly displaying one of their self-indulgent traits of hegemony.

If anyone were to gaze at the map to find the United States of America in North America, no one could miss its location and its monstrous size next to Cuba. The geography of the USA could be likened to one horrendously malformed turtle, with one eye near the top of its head that is menacingly close to its prey. The head is the state of Florida that is perennially washed by the Caribbean Sea. By comparison, Cuba seemed a tiny, disoriented, helpless lizard—as though waiting for the inevitable—to be devoured. It is inconceivable why such a gigantic country would be so obsessed in commandeering and staking out a claim within its neighbors' property. It was so clearly morally wrong. And all the U.S. presidents, save Roosevelt, appeared irresistibly attracted to doing wrong as it suited them. How could they identify with and justify qualities as decency, respect, charity, integrity, love, compassion and justice?

Now, it would only be a matter of time before they would begin an egregious Central Intelligence Agency (CIA) strategy to destroy Castro. Batista had fled to Panama. He fled and thereafter consigned—with his millions of American dollars in a Swiss Bank—to oblivion.

From then, the valiant Castro became an American disease. He represented an unforgettable and unforgivable bane to each succeeding and merciless American administration. In fact, the American posture had been for the past forty years, as though Cuba's indomitable leader were an incurable disease to be scorned. Previous to the advent of Castro, Cuba had been the last century's modern Babylon, an immoral and corrupt state for the pleasure of Americans. This offended Castro's sense of decency and integrity. This was not chauvinism but a genuine disgust for American domination. Castro and an untold number of Cubans had lost their self-respect, being dominated by "your neighbor in your own country!" This generated a sentiment of intolerance that impelled physical action.

Remarkably, Castro had survived nine American presidents, namely Harry Truman, John F. Kennedy, Lyndon B. Johnson, Richard Nixon, Gerald Ford, Jimmy Carter, Ronald Reagan,

George Bush, William Jefferson Clinton, and their reasoning on Cuba remained unswervingly one of the enigmas of the twentieth and twenty-first centuries. Notwithstanding, Castro and Cuba had prevailed though absorbing the cruel and seemingly unending blast of a senseless American hostility. And the pretext had been Castro's ideology. He was said to be communist. But so was China! So was Russia. So was North Korea. So was Vietnam. Relative to communism, the Americans were helplessly paranoid. They could not suffer to know that a smaller neighbor they once controlled was now Communist! Was the fear one of infection? Was it not a fact that if communism were applied, as it should be—free of administrative abuse in the dispensing of privileges to those in power and their friends—the potential of the realization of an egalitarian society would be more swiftly accomplished than the cultivation of capitalism? Did capitalism conduce to an egalitarian society? Never in this lifetime. Capitalism was sustained on the calculated exploitation of the indigent masses.

C. L. R. James in his book *The Black Jacobins* wrote, "The Caribbean is now an American Sea. Puerto Rico is their showpiece."

That island was earlier annexed by the USA on July 25, 1898. Though the island had been allowed internal self-government, Puerto Ricans also shared U.S. citizenship. In retrospect, history will show that America today could be likened to Ancient Rome in its declining years. Moral decay with a disintegration of integrity. It was authoritarian with a tendency to dictate rather than solicit. Evidently the role was supremely enjoyed and it was described as positive, forceful leadership. But this was perhaps esoteric. The USA, during two passages of its existence, did rule Cuba from 1898 to 1902. Eric Williams, in his book *History of the People of Trinidad and Tobago*, wrote that it should be noted that in 1904 an American assistant secretary of state declared, "No picture of our future is complete which does not contemplate and comprehend the United States as a dominant power in the Caribbean Sea!

This 'Caribbean Sea' the Americans have described, 'the American Mediterranean.' "

And on the subject of sovereign control: the Americans again controlled Cuba from 1906 to 1909. That the control of Cuba became an American behavior was really not too difficult to comprehend. Soon after the overthrow of the Batista regime, the Americans attempted to lend support to the Castro effort but his senior colleagues rejected such advances that they considered opportunistic and parasitical. Rather, the administration confiscated all oil refineries then later sugar refineries, tobacco and other businesses on the island. Ironically, Cuba's principal trading partner was its huge neighbor. The USA suspended trade with Cuba. Rapid events ensued. Now that that country had instituted an economic war on Cuba, what was it expected to do? To keel over and perish? In this self-indulgent and wicked world, one must devise methods of survival. Of necessity one must be innovative. Fidel Castro's logical choice was to solicit aid from America's adversary. This was representative of the human behavior. He turned to the Soviet Union. Castro and his men were suspicious of the American attitude. They tried to import arms from the states in Western Europe. Under pressure from the powerful USA they all declined to sell arms to Cuba. Today, all these countries will concede they ought not to have allowed their sovereignty to be that subservient to the U.S. government. Their stand was an error of judgment in history. To aggravate the situation, the American government allowed Cuban exiles and the CIA to use Florida as a base from which American planes flew to Cuba dropping firebombs and anti-Castro leaflets. This intensified the Cuban hostility to the American administration. In fact, they feared an all-out invasion. The Castro regime appealed to Russia and that country responded with alacrity. Here was an opportunity; perhaps a miraculous opportunity had presented itself to be legitimately close up to the bad, big bully's backyard. An agreement of economic and military aid was signed in February, 1960 by the two countries. The year 1961 witnessed an avenging American government allowing approval for an invasion of Cuba by Cuban exiles and American military advisers and CIA observers. This invasion of Cuba failed fatally and was an international embarrassment to the United States. Most of the invaders were captured but were later exchanged for "non-military merchandise."

The next year, 1962, will long be remembered as a crucial year in which World War III came to the brink of explosion. The Russians had sent military assistance to Cuba to defend that country from an assumed invasion. Missile sites were constructed from which to launch assaults into the USA. When it was learned by the U.S. administration that these sites physically existed, the USA proceeded to set up a naval blockade of Cuba to halt any shipping into the island. A compromise was arrived at. The Russians agreed to remove the missile sites if the Americans pledged not to invade Cuba. The weapons were removed though Castro protested angrily.

And in his book, *A Thousand Days,* which was a dissertation on the thousand days in the office of U.S. President John F. Kennedy, author Arthur Schlesinger, Jr. (Special Advisor to the president) wrote that Kennedy was not at all unsympathetic to Castro. As it related to this Castro and Kennedy conflict, Schlesinger, opined:

> Cuba was not a new issue for Kennedy nor had his view of Fidel Castro been wholly negative. Early in 1960, writing of the wild and angry, passionate course of the Cuban Revolution in *The Strategy of Peace* he described Castro as "part of the legacy of Bolivar, part of the frustration of that earlier revolution which won its war against Spain but left largely untouched the indigenous feudal order." He had no doubt, as he said later in the year, that "the brutal, bloody, and despotic dictatorship of Fulgencio Batista had invited its own downfall, and he freely declared his sympathy with the motives behind the revolution and with its expressed objectives." He even raised the question in *The Strategy of Peace* whether

> Castro would have taken "a more rational course" had the United States government not backed Batista, so long and so uncritically, and had given Castro a warmer welcome on his trip to Washington. But he had no question now that Castro had betrayed the ideals of the Cuban Revolution and transformed Cuba into a hostile and militant Communist satellite.

Kennedy had need to blame himself for the Cuban debacle. Schlesinger's writing suggested that the American government supported and condoned a ruthless dictatorship "so long and so uncritically." They were supportive of improper ideals so long as they redounded to the interests of the Americans. Kennedy's staff members were suggesting that he should lend support to Cuba's exiles who intended to invade Cuba to unseat Castro. They were trained and financed by the CIA. At first he resisted. Then, as though irresistibly, he relented; "Alright, but how would we have saved Cuba if we had the power?" According to Schlesinger, "Then he paused, looked out the window and said, 'What the hell, they never told us how they would have saved China.' In that spirit he began to succumb to temptation."

Obviously the temptation referred to here was the subsequent Bay of Pigs invasion by American zealots and Cuban exiles. It was an absolute disaster. And in a lamentation on *Who Lost Cuba?*, Schlesinger's book *A Thousand Days* begged the question:

> Was all this inevitable? Or was it the result of mistaken United States policy which left Castro no alternative? No legend is more enduring than the notion that Washington "forced" Cuba into the arms of Moscow. In fact, the Revolution was very popular in the United States in the early months of 1959. When Castro visited this country in the spring, his journey had aspects of a triumphal procession. I met him at the Harvard Faculty Club in Cambridge, jaunty in his olive green fatigues and heard him speak that evening to several thousand students in the Harvard Stadium. He gave a fluent

> harangue, memorable chiefly for a disarming ability to make jokes in English. The undergraduates were delighted. They saw him, I think, the hipster who in the era of the organization man had joyfully defied the system, summoned a dozen friends and overturned a government of wicked old men.

As early as January 25, 1962, Castro emphasized philosophically anent the U.S.-Cuba relationship:

> How can the rope and the hanged man understand each other or the chain and the slave? Imperialism is the chain. Understanding is impossible. We are so different that there are no bonds between us. Some day there will be links—when there is a revolution in the United States.

Suffice it to say that notwithstanding the adverse super-powerful force, USA's economic embargo on Cuba for the past forty years, that island state had progressed splendidly, while also contributing enormously to the welfare of most Caribbean states through education. Most importantly this enlightenment should accrue rewards of effective leadership free of the many ills of capitalism now endemic in both developed and underdeveloped or developing states universally. Castro was held in such high esteem; a Norwegian official nominated him recently for the Nobel Prize for Peace. On May 13, 2001, the first and highest ranking American government official Secretary of State Colin Powell of the incumbent Bush administration conceded that "Castro has done a great deal for his people but he had remained trapped in time." While this was all nonsense, it was indicative that at best Powell had a conscience and at worse a subtle admission that Americans were unjust to Castro and Cuba. Nonetheless, what appeared to be still wanting was an American conscience that appeared still trapped in delusion relative to its occupation of Cuban territory under the subterfuge of an indefinite treaty. And it should be noted here that some 3,000 years ago a wise ruler declared, "Man has dominated man to his injury." This truth persisted without let-up.

To the then inordinately proud American regime—and nine succeeding regimes—the seizure of American properties was unforgivable. This was perhaps the obtuse American rationale behind the seemingly unending hostility and oppression of Cuba. Not astonishingly, the USA did not use its power with authority; that nation abused it. The USA exemplified the philosophy of *might is right* as Rome did.

Doubtless, Castro's enemies were numerous—but so were those of the greatest man who ever lived, Jesus Christ—a large percentage of whom would be capitalistic Americanized Cubans who fled Cuba to the USA, most based in Florida. As may be expected, several assassination attempts had been made on the ingenious and indomitable Castro. He survived them all. Remarkably, two of my favorite human beings, Canada's former Prime Minister Pierre Elliott Trudeau and Jamaica's former Prime Minister Michael Manley were among Castro's closest colleagues. And an illustration of his affection was seen when Castro defied the specter of the vengeful Cuban exiles and the American CIA to attend Trudeau's funeral ceremony in Montreal in 2000. Manley had passed away years earlier. Castro was reputed for loyalty.

The Castro regime had repeatedly demanded that the USA vacate the occupation of Guantanamo Bay in Cuba. The USA had established a naval base there and would not be dislodged. The claim was that the USA will remain in Guantanamo Bay consistent with an old treaty tenable indefinitely. This treaty—the Platt Amendment—was drawn up when the Americans in 1901 were effectively in control of Cuba with the specter of Spain proposing to recapture Cuba, which it had earlier plundered. Spain had colonized Cuba for 400 years. That treaty was an imperialistic imposition. To maintain a military base in your neighbor's yard when the neighbor disapproved was a most ruthless and violent ongoing conflict in peacetime. *Might is right.* I want it, I take it. What can you do about it? Wasn't that the epitome of imperialism? In 1964, Castro cut off the fresh water supply to the Guantanamo Bay naval facility. The USA hastily installed a desalination plant that converts seawater to drinking water. But as regards treaties of friendship, it is interesting to note that what existed between the Americans and the British stood the test of time. And following two World Wars, Churchill in the epilogue of his book, *The Memoirs of the Second World War* explained:

> But for the immediate future and the long term I had urged the continuation of the special Anglo-American relationship which has been one of the main themes of my political life.

He emphasized:

> Neither the sure prevention of war nor the continuous rise of world organization will be gained without what I have called the fraternal association of the English-speaking peoples. This means a special relationship between the British Commonwealth and Empire and the United States.
>
> It should carry with it a continuance of the present facilities for mutual security by the joint use of all naval and air force bases in the possession of either country all over the world. . . . the United States has already a permanent defense agreement with the Dominion of Canada. This principle should be extended to all British Commonwealths with full reciprocity. The next three years were to see the unfolding of a design that approached but has not yet attained this ideal.

As impartial observers we dared not ignore the dominant Anglo-American violent role at this juncture of our history. Was it a verification of Daniel's Bible prophecy? Since the September 11th World Trade Center episode in the United States of America, the British Prime Minister Tony Blair evidently had taken over the leadership of "War on Terrorism" from the U.S. President George

W. Bush. His pronouncements were infinitely more belligerent and frequent as he paraded the world stage soliciting empathy, approval and support for raining bombs on Afghanistan to kill a terrorist Osama bin Laden and the regime that sheltered him.

Can it be conceived of an American occupation of China or Russia or North Korea or even Vietnam where they were taught an unforgettable lesson? But positively, some people never learned. There was not a shred of decency and moral fiber that supported that ludicrous American claim of a treaty that lasted indefinitely. Treaties by nature were intended to be reciprocal. Doesn't this remind us of the biblical King David taking possession of another man's property, Bathsheba, and he abused his power to have the man removed definitely? Oh the American conscience! The occupation of Guantanamo Bay in Cuba was a palpable manifestation of the posture *might is right*. That occupation was unequivocally predatory. Can the Americans justify the occupation of Guantanamo Bay? There was no moral basis. A wrong cannot be right! Every American administration since 1901, save Franklin D. Roosevelt's, had perpetuated this Cuban infamy.

However, during any period of unrest, seizure of properties was the norm. Castro had confiscated all American owned properties in Cuba. This was what conquerors resorted to for years immemorial. There was a difference, however. Castro seized properties in his own country. Not on foreign soil. But Castro's legal claim of billions of dollars for American crimes against Cuba may never result in the American government conceding guilt followed by a willingness to pay the billions. Castro, however, could register a moral victory at the World Court in the Hague if ruling tipped in his favor. Don't expect it to tip in his favor. Universally though, more nations were empathetic to Castro and Cuba than not. A widespread view was that this American authoritarianism was the antipathy of compassion, humility, love and good relations. And succeeding American administrations had demonstrated little or no respect for world opinion. All the American psychopathological pharaohs had been diseased with stupid vengeance and pointless wickedness. Not even the hypocritical Bible-toting Bill Clinton—who seemed a glimmer of hope to veer away from ruthlessness—made a difference in posture to Cuba. And the British—that other half of the Anglo-American epochal domination—had searched their cause-and-effect fund to determine the American behavior, but failed to identify any sort of justification. British companies had been trading with Cuba for many years.

Human beings thrived in societies and everyone struggled to improve one's well-being. Could Cubans, in view of the historical circumstances, consider the USA a good neighbor? There was a distinct difference between "the good neighbor" and "the straight imperialist version." And factually there had been only one American president to have repudiated the imposition of this predatory Platt Amendment protectorate clause on Cuba. He was Roosevelt in the early 1930s. In the book *Basic History of the United States*, the Beards wrote of the president's appeal to the American Congress: "He induced Congress to free Cuba from the protectorate Platt Amendment of 1901 imposed on her." President Roosevelt, according to the Beards, "signed with commendation an Act of the Democratic Congress under which the imperialist experiment in the Philippine Islands was to be liquidated by granting independence to become effective in 1946."

This had materialized but not the revocation of the Platt Amendment. Could this not be similarly liquidated? It appeared ludicrous, but why must any American administration insist on its control of Cuba as they do Puerto Rico; only the Americans possessed intelligence on that malaise. Obviously Congress frequently paid little attention to the president. And then it was also a Democratic Congress. Hitherto that appeal had been disregarded. Why? Should Americans be considered unscrupulous? Could they not distinguish the difference between right and wrong? Where was the American conscience?

Celebrated British author H. G. Wells in his book *A Short History of the World* (Watts and Co., Fleet Street, London) looked at the phenomenal growth of the United States of America:

> The growth of the United States was unprecedented in the world's history. It was a new kind of occurrence. Such a community could not have come into existence before, and if it had without railways it would certainly have dropped to pieces long before now. Without railways or telegraph it would be far easier to administer California from Peking than from Washington. But this great population of the United States of America has not only grown outrageously. It has kept uniform.

In brief, time and circumstances fashioned the USA into the dominating nation it had evolved into.

Lest it be misconstrued that this writer is anti-American, I should like to deny this. Rather, I write free of hypocrisy. Unequivocally, I express horror at the gruesome terrorist strike on New York City and Washington, DC on Tuesday, September 11, 2001. That act was the epitome of barbarity. And even those who suffered the terror and ruthlessness of the American behavior could not hesitate to publicly deplore and loudly condemn the attack on the American people. So many perished senselessly. For instance, Dr. Fidel Castro, who nursed multiple reasons to hate succeeding American administrations, was loud in his condemnation of his barbarous awakening for America that physically occupied a section of his country and refused to be dislodged. Castro's expression of sympathy and goodwill to the American people exemplified the character of the man.

Many nations throughout the world had stated unequivocally that the USA as a nation was a "bully" that convinced itself that it was invincible. Haughty statements as "those who attacked the

United States have done so at their own destruction" and "if you are not with us you are against us," among others are cases in point. The Bible that gave guidance to humanity had been disregarded. It stated, "Man has dominated man to his injury." However this may be translated, the sentiment is a fact.

The verity is Castro and Cuba, like the world and governments especially, are facing unprecedented challenges of survival. The *Awake* Magazine of March 2001 pointed out, "Another challenge facing modern societies is the sheer speed of change," says the book *A Green History of the World.* Ed Ayres, editor of *World Watch* magazine writes, "We are being confronted by something so completely outside our collective experience that we don't really see it, even when the evidence is overwhelming. For us, that 'something' is a blitz of enormous biological and physical alterations in the world that has been sustaining us."

But according to *Awake* Magazine historian Pardon E. Tillinghast: "The directions in which society is moving have become infinitely more complex, and for many of us the dilemmas are terrifying. What guidance can professional historians offer to confused people today? Not very much it seems." But the former U.S. Secretary of State Henry Kissinger gave his insight: "Every civilization that has ever existed has ultimately collapsed." He added, "History is a tale of efforts failed, of aspirations that weren't realized. So, as a historian, one has to live with a sense of the inevitability of tragedy." And it should not be insignificant to note here that universally, sentiments of empathy and sympathy were freely expressed relative to the September 11 American tragedy, and the St. Lucia *Mirror* was no exception. It declared my thoughts exactly, only in milder form. Here is an excerpt:

> Suddenly, the powerful Pentagon—the U.S. Ministry of Defense that enforces America's might all over the world—could not defend itself against a rogue commercial jet on a hideous mission. It went up in flames while lucky bureaucrats

> and security staff ran for cover, leaving their less fortunate colleagues entangled in a huge fireball. The Mighty Central Intelligence Agency (CIA) could not forewarn itself of danger and had to be evacuated. The White House had to be "emptied" and members of Congress went into hiding.
>
> These were not scenes from a Third World backwater; they were from the United Sates. In the twinkling of an eye the "Home of the Brave" with all its sophistication, technology, money and influence was helpless.

The perception of freedom and democracy had changed and Castro conceded recently that these times proved less than liberal.

In spite of America's forty-year-old animosity directed at Fidel Castro during which Cuba suffered untold deprivation, that island-state—some ninety miles south of Florida and the American mainland—had progressed enormously in health and agriculture especially; on the surface modernity seemed to have bypassed Cuba. This was significant. But if one had good health and could feed self and family, survival was more endurable. Doubtless, the nation Cuba missed some adventures in capitalistic materialism, but according to King Solomon, "that's all vanity." Cuba's successful survival was a manifestation of the breathing of the reputable academic and former Prime Minister of Barbados, Errol Barrow: "True personal development cannot take place if the political leaders of a country believe that the masses were therefore manipulative." He had characterized these leaders as "bandits."

Castro's Cuba had given scholarships to perhaps every English Caribbean territory. Many practicing doctors, architects, agriculturists, engineers, teachers, computer technologists and several other professionals owed their good fortune of their training and education to Dr. Fidel Castro. That he had survived repeated hitmen attempts must be ascribed to the protection of divinity. Castro must accept the embrace and kisses as the most charismatic and effective of Caribbean leaders. There was no second or third or last of them all. The rest of the Caribbean leaders were charismatic leaders. They followed his bountiful and productive example though several expressed disapproval of his regime. Dr. Fidel Castro proved to be the synthesis of exemplary leadership in spite of unrelenting American adversity.

Chapter 2

Linden Forbes Sampson Burnham

Former President of the Co-operative Republic of Guyana

The other image that loomed large and appeared to follow Dr. Fidel Castro in political tenacity and intrigue was that of Linden Forbes Sampson Burnham, former premier, prime minister and president of the Co-operative Republic of Guyana. Tall, handsome, pompous, a brilliant orator and attorney, Burnham took British Guiana into independence then proceeded to ruin Guyana. A territory of 83,000 square miles—larger than England—and located on the Atlantic Northern side of South America, Guyana in this writer's view will someday recover to a degree such as to be the breadbasket of the Caribbean. Abundantly endowed with deposits of gold, gypsum, bauxite, water, cattle, fish, timber and other resources, Guyana was the richest of CARICOM territories. Bordered by Suriname to the east, Brazil to the southwest and Venezuela to the west, that was the absolutely beautiful and bountiful country which Burnham assumed control of from the United Kingdom in 1966.

Gifted from childhood, indications were that given the opportunity, young Burnham would be a powerful force with which to reckon. While his well-meaning sparse salaried school princi-

pal father from Barbados pushed him to excel, the boy Burnham displayed the positive symptoms of a genius in the making. That his life would be punctuated with tumult was not then predictable. Born on February 20, 1923 in Kitty, a community just on the fringe of Georgetown, the capital of Guyana (later to become British Guiana), Burnham was the second of five children. He loved reading and developed a thrill in being studious as a pastime. At twelve he was already attending Queen's College, the premier secondary school in that country.

Doubtless Burnham was the sort of son every struggling parent would hope to have; that was, relative to being bright and acutely receptive. First he had won an internal scholarship and later two more. His parents need not have bothered. He completed his secondary education brilliantly. The school report to his parents indicated: "He is a natural leader. He is diligent and studious but not aloof. A great favorite with others in the class."

The young Burnham won the Guiana Scholarship in 1942. This was the brightest student award, which would allow him to further his studies at a university in the United Kingdom. The University of London accepted him, but World War II held up his departure. Undaunted, he did not hesitate. He took the course from long distance and attained his Bachelor of Arts degree. Interestingly, the young scholar Burnham was sociable. The girls adored him and the boys envied but admired him. A few just hated him as a bombast! Then he was the epitome of savoir faire. Impressed with his cerebral level, the administration at Queen's College engaged Burnham as an assistant master. He excelled and according to Martin Carter, who later gravitated to being Guyana's leading poet, "Burnham was acceptably the most intellectually gifted of the Masters of Queen's College."

Several who assessed him critically claimed that from his young student days, he nursed an air of superciliousness about him that infuriated. And many years later, his sister Jesse openly expressed her disdain of him—her brother. Jesse and this writer worked as reporters at the *Guyana Times* magazine. According to her, "He cannot be trusted. And he is dishonest," she declared. "He appears to be suave and articulate. That is a façade. He deceives people and does it without remorse. I should know. He is my brother," she insisted.

When any sane sister so condemns her brother, there must be a defect somewhere—in one or the other. Like her brother, she was a member of Cheddi Jagan's People's Progressive Party (PPP). Nonetheless, Burnham appeared to have been conditioned by the encomiums that never ceased to rain upon him. He sensed that he was extraordinary. At that period of his life Burnham had already decided on law as a career.

In 1945, the young and energetic Burnham arrived in London. He was already associated with the University of London. There he won the Best Speaker's Cup of the law faculty. This was no surprise to those who knew, liked or disliked him and followed his academic ascendancy.

In 1947, he added the accomplishment of LLB (Hons.) to his list of achievements. He was called to the Bar at Gray's Inn one year later, 1948. Now a qualified barrister with a stimulating power of expression, Burnham could not fail to impress those associated with him. His marvelous command of the English language, his seeming sincerity, his charm, all jelled to thrill and attract the majority. The students, also in 1947, voted him president of the West Indian Students' Union.

Burnham became utterly active in demonstrations supporting African and Caribbean student issues. These dealt fundamentally with oppression in the British colonial territories and their struggle to be free of the yoke of colonization. The ultimate struggle then was for independence.

Burnham, not unlike most academics from the oppressed Caribbean especially, had read and studied Karl Marx. He was fascinated by that German's thoughts, some aspects of which he adjudged as quite ponderous. Marx's and Engels' efforts, as he understood them, were designed for the German peasantry fundamentally, but rather fortuitously caught the situational interest of the Union of Soviet Socialist Republics (USSR). The Soviet Union and her partners federated with a German ideology that helped to attract the proletariat. Burnham reasoned that it could work to the benefit of the oppressed majority that populated the world. He held his reservations very closely concealed.

The new president of the West Indian Students' Union openly discussed Marx's theory and his eloquence recruited more followers. Now there was no better person to lead a West Indian Students' Union delegation to attend the World Youth Festival being held in Prague, Czechoslovakia. Burnham led the delegation and registered a successful conference in Prague. As most overseas students did after graduation, Burnham the attorney-at-law returned home to British Guiana in 1949. Conditions there were still pathetic. The country still was to gravitate to the control of its own destiny. Neighboring French Guiana claimed that British Guiana was still fortunate. The colonial office in London was prepared to listen to arguments soliciting self-determination; the French would not listen. France had adopted the policy of "finders-keepers." Theirs was never to return anything stolen. It was obvious that independence was never given. It had to be earned or taken by force. But the best route to self-determination would be through the political process. And there was one common thought that perhaps may not have been that salient had they not traveled, educated themselves and lived abroad to see civilization in progress. They were educated in civics but a return to the territories fired one with anger as people's lives were controlled by people of a different ethnic group who failed to demonstrate they held the best interest of a colonial people dearly. The educated returnees were appalled by the white foreign domination. The course of their lives was being fashioned and dictated by the colonial office. The situation demanded an urgent mobilization of the Guianese people. As the days and weeks and months succeeded each other, increasingly the desire to radically change the status quo became urgent.

Here we have no doubt that the motivation to enter the political arena was propelled by a fervent desire to bring about a change to secure a better quality of life for the people of British Guiana. Noticeably from the late '40s and succeeding years, the British West Indies had arrived at the point of being politically conscious. That powerful consciousness appeared to have infected, disturbingly, the entire region.

Appearing at different periods, George Price in British Honduras whipped up interest in Adult Suffrage; Lynden Pindling took on the Bahamas and to the north, Jamaica found agitation in Norman Washington Manley. The west would cheer the political clinics of Robert Llewellyn Bradshaw in St. Kitts, Nevis-Anguilla and Vere Cornwall Bird next door in Antigua and Barbuda. The east Caribbean Dominica boasted salwarts as Edward LeBlanc and Patrick John. And St. Lucia was led by John George Melvin Compton and Maurice Mason.

Only sixty miles away across the channel, St. Vincent and the Grenadines were being dominated by Ebenezer Theodore Joshua. And ninety-six miles east of St. Vincent and the Grenadines, Barbados, the most easterly of the Caribbean states, found leadership in Grantley Adams, later his son, Tom Adams, and Errol Barrow.

The volatility continued south to Grenada where Marryshow and then Eric Matthew Gairy and Maurice Bishop revolutionized politics that affected the entire region. Trinidad and Tobago, the largest and most cosmopolitan of the eastern grouping, found unquestionable control in professor turned politican, Dr. Eric Eustace Williams.

Historically, the Caribbean was incomplete without British Guiana. Dr. Cheddi Jagan, his wife, Janet, and Forbes Sampson Burnham struggled for political control of that territory. This created an obnoxious racial division that must be considered the most despicable in the world.

A political metamorphosis was affecting the Caribbean and remarkably, not excluding Cuba. Fidel Castro was imprisoned for thirty-three years for his attempt to violently change the status quo. Britain's prime minister, Harold MacMillan was subsequently to make his immortal statement about "the wind of change" in South Africa. That wind of change was evidently universal, especially in the Caribbean and it was not avant-garde. Federation of the West Indies was imminent. The prospects then seemed glowing.

In British Guiana, a young dentist of East Indian heritage—a soi-disant Marxist—had returned several years earlier from the U.S. with his fiery American-born wife Janet. They were vociferous in their condemnation of the prevailing conditions in British Guiana. Considered Communists, the Jagans had dedicated themselves to opposing and fighting the British authorities whom they had deemed Imperialists. Their struggle was described as anti-imperialism. Inevitably, the dentist and the attorney of like mind would meet.

Burnham, as fate would have it, joined forces with the activist Cheddi Jagan, whose wife Janet was enthralled by Burnham's power of language. She persuaded Cheddi to enlist Burnham. They would make a splendid team. However, from the inception, their ideologies did not appear to harmonize. Cheddi and Janet Jagan were inveterate Communists, but not Burnham. He was more capitalistic, though certain elements that affected the poor bothered him. Yet capitalism was unable to prosper free of poverty. Joining the Jagans then made sense. They already commanded a political power base. He controlled an incredible following in the rural districts. They consulted and formed a political alliance. Unavoidably they founded the People's Progressive Party (PPP). This name was attributed to Burnham's genius. The meeting accepted the name as it had immense appeal. Originally, this grouping was first known as the Political Affairs Committee. Now it evolved into PPP with Cheddi Jagan as the leader. The PPP then became the first politically organized national party in the sole South American British territory.

The Party's manifesto was publicized and it found ready acceptance with the people from all walks of life. It was tantamount to a new beginning, an awakening that should eventually evolve into controlling one's own destiny in British Guiana. Throughout the capital city, Georgetown, every Guianese seemed energized by the PPP's zealous campaigns. The chairman of the Party was perhaps Guiana's most exciting orator, Burnham. Janet Jagan was the general secretary of the Party. It should be appreciated that the average Guianese citizen was never given the privilege to vote. The Party was anti-colonialism and the people supported that Party. Adult suffrage would soon be introduced. Anyone twenty-one years of age would be eligible to vote. Moreover, the political consensus was a demand for internal self-government that would unavoidably lend to a better or higher standard of living.

The political machinery was in positive motion throughout British Guiana. The Jagan-Burnham team was totally embraced. They were headed for the polls and an overwhelming victory was anticipated. In and around Georgetown were a few independent politicians. Since they did not support this new radical PPP proposition, it was then presumed that they were stooges of the British government. Nonetheless, they could not stall or circumvent this whirlwind of change.

The audacious orator Burnham was in demand, and the highlight at all meetings. He overwhelmed the crowds and even amassed considerable support within the Trade Union Movement. On this summit of popularity he was, in 1952, elected president of the British Guiana Labor Union. Being the president of the West Indian Students' Union was some responsibility but to head and lead a labor union was another proposition.

All the elections' trappings were in place. The year was 1953. The PPP won overwhelmingly, capturing eighteen of the twenty-four seats in the then Legislative Council. As dictated by the Constitution, Cheddi Jagan as leader of the Party and having the confidence of most of his elected members, became the first chief minister of the colony of British Guiana. Evidently, the then Governor Sir Alfred Savage found the new militant ideological posturing to be unacceptable. He was obviously intimidated. Anti-communism in the Western World propelled by an antagonistic USA was rampant. The public relations or propaganda machinery pushed to its limits the deprivation of freedoms and civil liberties under communism. This Anglo-American alliance accepted and proposed to convince colonials this was gospel. They intended to repel communism at any cost.

The new chief minister of British Guiana was an openly declared Marxist, vigorously supported by his wife, Janet, who helped to influence him during his student days in Chicago. The PPP then was tainted Communist; as a result, British Guiana would be as well. This could not be condoned by Governor Savage. Remarkably, the Burnham-Jagan team was enjoying phenomenal popularity, save for some anachronistic and unswerving Guianese colonials who could not accept change. They had accepted the British dependency way of life. British Guiana was PPP. The statistics broke down this way. Burnham's power of language made him a star with very many admirers. In addition, he was the president of the British Guiana Labor Union. The members of African, Chinese, Portuguese, and East Indian and Amerindian descent were enamored of him. Moreover, journalists, printers, teachers and the professionals including university graduates were solidly behind him. On the other hand, Jagan controlled the East Indian following. This was some 50 percent of the 750,000 of British Guiana's population.

On October 9, 1953, a mere six months after the swearing-in ceremony in April 1953, the Jagan government was thrown out of office. That was, the Winston Churchill conservative government in London suspended the British Guiana Constitution. An executive *Interim Government* was set up by the British.

Governor Sir Alfred Savage had convinced his superiors in London that Marxist Cheddi Jagan was in the throes of transforming British Guiana into a Communist state. One was known by the company one kept. Though Burnham was known or believed to be Capitalist by his copious breathings, however eloquent, he was considered to be Jagan's articulate accomplice in his quest to accommodate the Soviet Union. This view was inaccurate as Jagan had not established any direct link with the USSR. He perhaps could have been characterized an iconoclastic idealist.

The suspension of British Guiana's Constitution and the subsequent incarceration of the government leader and his ministers with other associates were condemned throughout the British Commonwealth and also in Britain itself; not throughout the Caribbean, however. Norman Manley and Alexander Bustamante of Jamaica, and Grantley Adams of Barbados applauded the suspension of the Constitution and the arrest of the leaders. Duncan Sandys, the British Secretary of State for the Colonies, then impressed upon the House of Commons on October 22 that the government of Cheddi Jagan was displaying unquestionably pro-Communist leanings and these, in his judgment, were a potential threat conducive to disorder and instability. The approach was a clever plan to indoctrinate the citizens of British Guiana to communism.

The British government attitude even from the British Parliament was considered savage and wicked. Despite the opposition, the government won approval by a small margin of thirty-eight votes. The government also took a beating from the British press. Burnham and Jagan journeyed to the British capital, London, to advance their case. According to Burnham's point man Sydney King, "Burnham was already disgusted with Jagan's unwavering commitment to communism. He prioritized it over the commitment to British Guiana, his land of birth. Moreover he had questioned Jagan's love for British Guiana and considered it a means to an end."

Incidentally, King later changed his name to Eusi Kwayana, and also served as editor of Burnham's People's National Congress (PNC) newspaper, *New Nation.* Later he was made managing director of the Guyana Marketing Board. Interestingly, though Burnham and King were seemingly colleagues who had endured hardships and joyousness together, Burnham appeared to have established a distance between them—the Napoleon-Chauvin type of relationship. King was fawning and would address Burnham as "Mr. Burnham." Once, in 1959, I was in the PNC office discussing the third part of a short story, "Our Erma," which I had written for the *New Nation.* Burnham came by. "Sydney," he snapped. Sydney jumped up from his chair, almost knocking it over. "Yes, Mr. Burnham," he responded too enthusiastically. I considered this undue display of fawning to please somewhat disgusting. The discussion was brief. When Burnham left the office, I asked King, "Why do you have to call him Mr. Burnham? I thought you were friends of long standing being jailbirds together."

He replied with a smirk, "Well, you must know the man. He likes to be elevated. That's the way he is."

I interrupted, "And you are comfortable in such company?"

"Well, I don't mind; it doesn't trouble me," he remonstrated.

"I guess it takes all kinds to make this world what it is," I said.

I knew then that Burnham was a man who gave no consideration to the fact that he was made of dust and the obsequious King, not unlike Chauvin, served with unquestionable loyalty. I had also concluded that as a human being Jagan made and respected friends and acquaintances. Conversely, Burnham collected followers to serve his self-indulgence. This was saying he lived up to the perceived reputation of the typical politician. His intention to serve was honorable when he first entered politics. It was to remove oppression and elevate the underprivileged. Along the way, he discovered that life would be more meaningful controlling the lives of those whom he sought to liberate. He epitomized Errol Barrow's theory of "masses manipulation."

Vividly, I recalled having been assigned by my editor Richard de Corum at the *Evening Post* to interview Burnham. He was president of the British Guiana Bar Association. He had also been made a Queen's Council (Q.C.), president of the British Guiana Trade Unions, leader of the opposition and leader of the People's National Congress. I met him at his chambers. He said to me, "Mr. James, you may not believe it, but I have no time for reporters. I have work to do. I am too busy to idle."

"You consider being here to get an answer to a couple questions as being idle?"

"Believe it. For me it is," he smiled cynically and walked away.

On another occasion I was sent to get a clarification from Premier Dr. Jagan. He told me, "I am on my way to the Parliament building. Walk with me and let's talk." He was a pleasant man.

This established the difference between the two dynamic leaders of British Guiana.

Only the naïve or those who paid scant attention to British Guiana's politics could claim surprise that Dr. Jagan and Burnham parted company. At the inception there was no doubt that they needed the strengths of each other. But experience revealed their contrasting personalities must inevitably ignite and an explosion would occur, the damage of which would be irreparable.

The ideologies of communism and capitalism were diametrically opposed to each other. Burnham in this respect was the opportunist. It was only a matter of time until he seized the leadership of the party from Dr. Jagan, who was a rather clever politician. And with the cerebral wife Janet behind him how could Forbes Burnham succeed? He did. Why? The man was immensely gifted with charm and the aesthetics and the power of language. It was my view that, save for perhaps Sir Winston Churchill, no other government leader—British prime ministers or American presidents—of the twentieth century could match Burnham's power of language. Perhaps the former USA President Bill Clinton drew up a distance away. Expression of the English language was his forte. And when he became prime minister of British Guiana, British Prime Minister Harold Wilson fell victim to his caustic breathings in an exchange at a Commonwealth Leaders Conference held in Jamaica. It was said that the British prime minister advanced that the British Guiana prime minister's viewpoint gained its strength from the fact that he possessed a trained legal brain. Burnham replied with a huge measure of bombast and sarcasm that, "legal training has not the remotest relationship with the command and expression of the English language." I think it should be pointed out here that perhaps most unusually, Burnham's memory was almost phenomenal. Most or every leader of government was required periodically or regularly to deliver speeches, and most did employ speechwriters. Not Burnham. He may have jotted down some notes but his frequent addresses had always been extemporaneous. His extraordinary skill with words served him to ad-lib every address which must be considered unique in politics. He was truly a powerful orator, the most powerful in the Caribbean. In this writer's view, noted examples as Dr. Eric Williams, Tom Adams, Norman Manley, Errol Barrow and Michael Manley were left behind in his wash.

If anyone had to study Burnham's general posture then, it would have been discovered that someone as capable and inordinately ambitious as that rising political star could not continue to accept subservience or even junior partnership. He perhaps knowingly was headed, relentlessly, to the summit of consummate dictatorship. Had he not been black, and given the right conditions, Burnham could have pursued the leadership of Britain or the United States of America and won. Abundantly, he possessed the brain, the style and over all savoir faire.

Many internal irritations never surfaced. This period in 1955 was untimely for a breakup, but the differences were stretched to their limits. Burnham and his supporters designed it. At the internal party elections for leadership confidence, the audacious Burnham unseated Dr. Jagan. Though it was the usual democratic procedure, Jagan found his loss to be unacceptable. He could never suffer losing. Angrily, he stormed out of the meeting devastated. Perhaps this was unprecedented in the world of politics—a political party with two leaders and two powerful followings. This wrangling waged for two years. Burnham would, after the elections, wisely rename his party for distinct identification. A meeting termed "crucial" was called to replace the PPP sobriquet being used and was in conflict with the PPP being accommodated by Dr. Jagan's faction. The dominant and creative Burnham presented the name People's National Congress for perusal and approval. In fact, a report from the meeting indicated that Burnham had already tested the name on several of his associates and followers. Everyone had agreed to its acceptance and adoption. The meeting was a mere formality and a brand new party with a new name People's National Congress (PNC) was born. They celebrated and toasted the PNC that was expected to transport them on to victory and political power. This was the conclusive split of the two PPPs. Now it was to each his own.

This pried open what could be described as the Pandora's Box. The virulent latent racial animosity was soon to surface. Up until this time, Blacks and East Indians were simply Guianese. Jagan's supporters consisted of some 50 percent of the population. They were of East Indian descent. Burnham controlled some forty-one percent, and this was of African descent. In the circumstances, Burnham was perturbed about this situation as he was at the disadvantage. This was potentially dangerous as both parties' membership boasted a percentage of the other races. The PNC had a number of East Indians and the PPP also had among them a number of Blacks. This gauche situation introduced the element of being disloyal to one's racial heritage. This was a vicious, unsavory and unwise ethnical debauchery the colony of Guiana would countenance and endure with its resonating effects for an untold number of years.

These two charismatic leaders were clever politicians. Universally, politicians extend themselves to the limits, embracing even impropriety to win. Politics was not a profession of saints. My reliable information was that it was the trouble shooter Janet Jagan who made the suggestion that their supporters should be told to embrace the elections as a racial issue. They were numerically superior. The idea was swiftly approved though with some reservations as this concept excluded Blacks. For instance, the deputy leader of their party, Brindley Benn, was black and so were many members of the party. This could have been counter-productive! The slogan would be *Apen Jhaat.* Translated in Hindi it meant, "Vote for your own." Clearly, because it would be to his disadvantage, Burnham appealed to all at a public meeting that danger lurked within this racial division. He'd sooner have voters support him because of his beliefs and not because of his race. This was interpreted by many to mean that he was less concerned about the damage of racial division than losing the elections. However, *Apen Jhaat,* that seemingly innocuous germ of an idea, gave birth to the racial disease that prevailed forty-six years later in the year 2001. That conflict had intensified.

The British sat and observed this political scenario being played out. Neither one of the two leaders was favored. New elections would be allowed but the condition of the exercise limited the Constitution to the status of internal self-government. Britain would be responsible for foreign affairs. The call for independence was being disregarded by Britain at this time. This was the crucial election to decide which one of the political antagonists would emerge the chosen leader by the people of British Guiana. It was called in August 1957. Not unexpectedly, Dr. Jagan and his PPP won. East Indians, like most other races—save Blacks—were loyal to their heritage. Some Blacks would quite likely vote against Burnham, but East Indians would not vote against Jagan. This was a conundrum of sociology. Jagan won 47 percent of the overall vote and nine of the fourteen House seats. It was estimated that 40 percent of registered voters failed to vote, the majority of whom were supporters of Burnham. A small percentage of East Indians feared and resisted Jagan's communism. They preferred the Capitalist system that allowed them to become rich if the skill permitted. Their votes were withheld.

Three years later in 1960 and still agitating for independence, both PPP and PNC influenced the British to call a constitutional conference in London. It would seem that Burnham nursed an electoral boundary problem. He claimed that it offered a clear advantage to Jagan's PPP. Burnham advanced that a change of the electoral system that reflected a Proportional Representation would be fair. It had long been known that imperial Britain may listen but acted as it pleased within its own time factor. It had not been a practicing imperialist all these centuries to be moved by rhetoric. The British appointed an electoral commission. Thirty-five new constitutional boundaries were demarcated. Observing that his advantage had been eroded, Jagan yelled that there was gerrymandering of the boundaries and all rigged to remove him from office. Amidst all this tumult in 1961, another political party, the United Force, emerged. Led by Peter D'Aguiar—a powerful businessman of Portuguese descent—the United Force had captured the interest of the middle class, the wealthy and the Amerindian community. The situation suggested that Burnham would inevitably lose some valuable support from the middle and upper middle class. This United Force, though on the surface appeared to be a device to further fragment Burnham's support base, later would fortuitously become his savior and a leverage into office. As expected, the Capitalist D'Aguiar campaigned vigorously against Dr. Jagan's communism and then assailed the PNC as the PPP's accomplice to divide and ruin British Guiana.

Reports suggested that D'Aguiar's vicious assault on Burnham's PNC was the direct result of the rejection of a proposal to form an alliance with the PNC. Burnham found the proposal unacceptable. While Burnham failed to disclose this, several around him revealed that D'Aguiar's condition was that he be appointed premier and minister of finance. The elections in 1961 were held and, again, Dr. Jagan's PPP won, but not free of damage to its base. They captured twenty of the thirty-five seat House of Assembly. The People's National Congress won eleven seats with 41 percent of the vote. This translated to mean that Burnham's PNC did infinitely better than expected. The statistics, however, indicated clearly that many voters stayed with the PNC as PPP lost the majority vote. This was an ominous turn for the party. The United Force Party won only four seats, a mere 16.3 percent of the votes cast.

It was obvious at this time that Premier Jagan could not suffer that the work force of British Guiana was being controlled by his adversary Burnham. He could not contain himself. His government rashly introduced a burdensome tax-on-the-underprivileged budget on January 31, 1962. In character, it gave easy expression to an unfair and radical and illegal control of the Trade Union Movement. What ensued could have been obviated. But man must have his way, and life's survival constituted constant warfare, and experience had taught that man's self-indulgence clouded his sense of reasoning until it was too late. Then, he must suffer the consequences of his folly. Life and politics especially were punctuated with this widespread want of self-control. Up until this period of our history, the inordinately ambitious politician had no clear definition of democratic rights and human liberties. He, if necessary, would abrogate the rights of the majority to secure his position of total control. The trade unions called for and initiated a protest demonstration in Georgetown. Most unions and workers came out in full force. Both leaders of the PNC, Forbes and Burnham, and the United Force's Peter D'Aguiar were in attendance. Supportive of them were children and housewives. They demonstrated against what they claimed was an oppressive budget.

The ominous presence of gas-masked police in riot gear did not deter the demonstrators. They seemed confident that this show of force would not endanger them. Moreover, the marching was peaceful. The area around the Parliament building was declared restricted, though it was a favorite place of protest in Georgetown. In an earlier protest, this writer distinctly recalled that both Burnham and a shadow minister of culture, Winifred Gaskin had prostrated themselves across the entrance to the assembly. They were forcibly lifted and removed to allow the governor's vehicle to proceed to the building. It was the job of the police to be present when there was potential for disorder. The demonstrators miscalculated. Premier Jagan had given the order to tear gas the marchers. Unavoidably, on February 16, 1962, what was intended to be a peaceful protest, as exercised in all democratic societies, erupted into total disorder. Rioting ensued and the result was considerable damage to the many businesses and properties in the city of Georgetown.

Jagan's unduly severe action, supported by his wife and advisor, Janet, should be a lesson to those who aspire to power. Evidently, Burnham did learn. Years later when he took control—with his specially trained to be loyal security forces, as in totalitarian states—he unequivocally ruled with an unyielding iron fist. Jagan and his party were kept in the wilderness for some twenty years until after

Burnham had expired. The aftermath of this disturbance, in which British troops were brought in by the governor at the request of Jagan, was a Commonwealth Commission of Inquiry chaired by Englishman Sir Henry Wynn Parry, assisted by two jurists, of African and Indian descent. Dr. Jagan had contended unendingly that the disturbance was calculated and designed to overthrow his PPP government. This was not the finding of the inquiry. They found that events rapidly succeeded each other and got totally out of hand. It could be likened to "spontaneous combustion."

At this period the appalling ethnicity situation continued to foment. It became a wicked centrifugal force and it grew proportionally too huge to contain. Then and now—though both men were removed from the scene—the legacy of this malaise had festered to such a degree it militated against the core centripetal fabric of nationalism. British Guiana then, in the '50s and '60s and hitherto 2001, an independent Guyana was unchanged. It was one of the most pathologically, racially divisive countries in the world. The East Indians who supported Jagan were numerically superior. They openly detested blacks who supported Burnham. The shower of insults were ceaseless. The Indians identified Burnham's support as the black man and they called Jagan support the coolies. This fatuous, racial hatred remained unrelenting.

How politicians presumed to lead and engender prosperity and stability in a country that was being shredded by racial conflict was truly a conundrum! At this juncture, both Burnham and Jagan were agreed on the demand for independence. While Jagan advanced that he had a mandate for independence, Burnham suggested that election was necessary first. Following general elections with proportional representational independence was of necessity. Significantly, Jagan's two political adversaries whose views were not sharply different, save for political expediency, eventually came together as it could not fail to benefit their self-interests. The unspoken aim was to unseat Jagan. And what was the rationale behind this ongoing vicious political conflict? Thomas More in his book *Utopia*, edited by H.V. S. Ogden, University of Michigan advanced,"Men and animals alike are greedy and rapacious from fear of want. Only human pride glories in surpassing others in conspicuous consumption."

Doubtless this vice was rampant and insatiable in democratic societies everywhere. Greed was the propeller. Very many deluded themselves that extravagant living was the ideal. A quality of life!

A constitutional conference was held in London in 1962. The three political leaders, Dr. Jagan, Burnham and D'Aguiar, contended for independence, but from varying perspectives. Burnham advanced his cause along the route of Proportional Representation. His sole approach was to defeat Jagan at the polls. Jagan argued against Proportional Representation, while D'Aguiar feebly held on to a middle of the road determination. The British listened, but seemed unmoved. Duncan Sandys, secretary of state for the colonies, did not seem impressed. It was obvious that he felt that a nation gravitated in stages to independence. And arguments, however persuasive, would not alter this process. The leaders of British Guiana were in conflict, and all propelled by self-interest. There was absolutely no cooperation. No give and take. The three leaders were grasping inflexibly. Sandys ended the conference and sent them back to Guiana.

The next year, in 1963, the three leaders were summoned to another conference in London and some progress was made. But this was imposed by the secretary of state. He accused them of wasting precious moments by non-cooperation and indecision. Then he threatened to suspend the talks indefinitely. He presented them with a document that gave him the freedom to initiate new elections. Reluctantly, they signed. The conditions were:

1. The election exercise would be British supervised
2. The system would change from the existing to Proportional Representation (as Burnham required)

3. There would be a fifty-three-member unicameral House of Assembly
4. There would be a new voters list
5. Following the elections a conference will be arranged to set a date for the attainment of independence

It was a virtual triumph for Burnham. It will be recalled that the British had noted and acted on the advice of the American administration. They had told the British that Burnham was intelligent, but "an opportunist," yet he would be more acceptable than Jagan, who was flirting with communism.

"Proportional Representation would be the recommended approach to pursue." This was the American recommendation to Sandys.

Persistently, Burnham had been arguing for Proportional Representation elections before independence. Jagan felt disadvantaged. At a press conference he declared, "I do not feel bound to accept Sandys' decision." He gave to understand: "They are only inviting trouble and I cannot be responsible for what will happen." Doubtless this was an innuendo.

Guianese people were now bitterly divided, especially the two largest racial groups, the East Indians and Blacks. The country slipped into turmoil. In the capital city, Georgetown, homes were being arbitrarily bombed and razed to the ground. Jagan attributed this disorder to the British imposition of Proportional Representation. The violence was rampant. Even in the Bauxite community of Mackenzie there were several eruptions. If one were to take the time to review this Guianese tragedy, it will be found that politicians everywhere, if given the circumstances, would not hesitate to exploit race or any other stratagem to triumph at the polls. The legacy was appalling. Will today's Guyana ever find an antidote to heal its disease? The tragedy was that the politicians who were guilty of a crime that yielded horrendous implications had both passed on. One wondered how man could wreak such havoc to the detriment of succeeding generations with impunity.

British Guiana was being torn apart racially. Most East Indians unswervingly supported Jagan. They were the largest faction. Similarly, most Africans or Blacks gave support to Burnham's PNC. The other factions of the Guianese population (i.e. Whites, Portuguese, Chinese and Amerindians) voted for the United Force Party of D'Aguiar. After all, it was a racial exercise and emotions from it were powerful. Universally people were sooner prone to do wrong than right.

Remarkably, during the ongoing disturbance, Jagan's deputy premier, a black, Brindley Benn, was among those from the two parties arrested on the order of the new Governor Sir Richard Luyt, who had replaced Sir Alfred Savage. Again, a state of emergency was declared with British troops being brought in to restore order. That was the year 1964. Elections were scheduled to be called later on December 7. New boundaries were set and approximately 250,000 voters were registered.

The three political parties were joined by two other seemingly opportunistic parties. They were exploiting the racial division but failed in the process. The parties were of East Indian heritage. The elections system had changed from the first-past-the-post to Proportional Representation. The campaign was on, and it intensified. Jagan declared that the British imperialists were against him. More money was expended on radio and newspaper ads, pamphlets and posters than at any previous campaign.

Polling day arrived and ended. Speculation was rife. The PPP couldn't lose. Though Jagan knew that the odds at this election were against him, his party amassed 45 percent of the votes. The PNC got 40.8 percent votes and UF 12.5 percent, some 4 percent less than what had been anticipated. It was inconsistent with the percentage of the racial support figure. Earlier it was understood that, in the event of the present circumstances, the minority parties would pool their resources to form a coalition government. The election results were an upset that did not fail to unsettle Jagan. He lost to the coalition and he refused to resign when it was revealed that the Constitution did not offer accommodation for the premier's resignation. Governor Luyt accepted the coalition of the two parties. He declared Burnham the new premier of British Guiana. This was the eventuality from where the decline of Guyana began. Burnham was asked to form the next government. However, an Order-in-Council had to be made to dislodge Jagan from office. It was always so humiliating when a politician was unable to accept defeat. One won and the others lost until possibly the next elections. Unavoidably this was the political system.

The foremost business entrepreneur-turned-politician in British Guiana, D'Aguiar, was appointed the minister of finance. If anyone were acquainted with him and Burnham, it could not take one very long to sense and predict that this alliance was doomed to failure. The problem then would be to predict when. This was a form of political corruption of which both Burnham and d'Aguiar were guilty. But aren't politicians by character guilty until proven otherwise? There was an absence of fondness for one another. But there was respect for the power each held over the other. They depended on each other to realize their individual objectives. Burnham's was to control the lives of the Guianese people. He had it within a grasp that was precarious. Any false or rash action could scuttle the attainment for which he struggled in the wilderness for almost a decade. He was rather familiar with the sentiments associated with repeated failure. Now it was his turn to court some measure of success. Seemingly, though, this success was pyrrhic; the victory that inflicted enormous pain. Nonetheless, both Burnham and D'Aguiar held on in an attempt to delay the inevitable.

D'Aguair proved himself a competent minister of finance, but this was not unexpected. He had accumulated a fortune from his company's distillery and associated businesses, and it was by sound management. Immediately following six months in office, Premier Burnham announced that British Guiana had been enjoying a delightful recovery. It was responding with a vibrancy that promised total resuscitation at most economic levels.

At that time no one could accuse Burnham of insincerity. He was totally focused on leading British Guiana and the Guianese people into an unprecedented economic growth and development that would prove a model of recovery from political turmoil. Burnham then enjoyed the goodwill of other Caribbean leaders. Many had hoped for several years that he would wrest leadership of British Guiana from the Marxist Jagan. His ideology was alien to them. The Caribbean leaders were hoping to bring British Guiana into the community. Earlier, Jagan had resisted all efforts to be a member of the ill-fated West Indies Federation. Other attempts to recruit him into the Caribbean grouping had failed.

In retrospect, one evening in 1958, Jagan held a meeting in Kitty just outside the city of Georgetown. I then lived only a block away. As a reporter at the *Evening Post*, I had learned that there was always an interesting story whenever Jagan spoke. And he was loquacious, complacent, modest, considerate and courteous, unlike Burnham. Jagan failed to draw a crowd that evening. Only eight of us were in attendance. He declared that the British government and the Caribbean leaders were trying to recruit Guiana to join in a federation. He declared emotionally:

> They are cunning. Their aim is to open Guiana to the people of African descent to immigrate here. Why? To tip the racial balance. We are numerically superior. They want to change that advantage. But I have a surprise for them. We won't be coerced or dragged into any West Indies Federation. We will be pursuing a continental destiny with our neighbors Brazil, Suriname and others.

Jagan failed to mention Venezuela. That republic had repeatedly claimed two-thirds of British Guiana as its own.

Burnham, on the other hand, was inclined towards the British West Indies. They shared the same heritage. He would open his comparatively huge South American country to them. And Jagan was correct. If people from the islands were allowed freedom to enter British Guiana, this would be to Burnham's advantage. That was a factor that could not be discounted. Burnham needed the friendship and goodwill of the leaders of the British West Indies. The premier of British Guiana and the leader of the opposition and their delegations were invited to London for talks. Independence was imminent. The Constitutional Conference would be convened in October 1965. Finance Minister D'Aguiar accompanied Burnham. The differences between them had enlarged. They differed on too many issues, as though they were adversaries rather than teammates. While D'Aguiar was not really opposed to the attainment of independence, he displayed a lukewarm approach in contrast to Burnham's positive zeal. Moreover, it was no secret that he did not share Burnham's desire to have British Guiana become a republic at independence.

Jagan, on the other hand, repudiated the conference. Palpably, he could not get over having lost the premiership of the country. He was bitter as though he did not understand that in politics one must win while the other would lose. And it was a paradoxical condition that every political leader faced universally. The independence conference was not unlike a forum that struggled to resolve unresolved bitter conflicts. Cut and thrust, then press on. Burnham, the orator whose expression of language was impeccable, his flow of words emitted unhesitatingly like oil from a container onto a smooth surface that influenced controlled speed and saturation. Like a statesman of civility, he conceded a delay to change to the new status to a republic until after the next election. Nonetheless, he won a date for independence, May 26, 1966.

Independence was attained and the appendage "British" was dropped from the new nation's name. In addition, the spelling of the name "Guiana" was changed to "Guyana." This new nation now begged for peace, appreciation, cooperation, industry, stability and love, not unattainable qualities, but exceedingly difficult in Guyana's atmosphere. Even at this time of writing in April, 2001, political and racial disorder still prevailed in Guyana. Both Jagan and Burnham had expired, but their adversarial opportunism was a legacy of incredibly obtuse racial turmoil. When will it die? Jagan's PPP won the elections of 2001, but the PNC, led by Desmond Hoyte, was unwilling to accept the defeat. Thirty-five years after independence, the conflict continues unabated. It is ironic. Guyanese are some of the most intelligent groups of people in this Caribbean region.

The love, cooperation and tranquility perceived, emanate from the cabinet of the new nation Guyana. Unfortunately, this coalition government's existence was ephemeral. There were open dissentions at cabinet meetings between Prime Minister Burnham and Finance Minister D'Aguiar. The latter's rebellious attitude suggested that he should have carte blanche to perform as he pleased, as though he were accountable to no one. He appeared to contend that he had it within his power to bring down the government. That was a factor. This he used to intimidate the prime minister and voiced public criticism of their differences. It was generally felt that it was only a matter of time before the coalition government would self-destruct. Conversely, the bombast Burnham struggled to hold on to his government. In the National Assembly, PPP and UF members were crossing the floor. The PNC had gained some degree of respectability and increasing support nationwide. But the sore in the coalition continued to fester and the differences were irreconcilable. They failed to heal. In the circumstances, the coalition survived longer than expected. Gradually, it spiraled to asunder. Almost one year after that unholy alliance was formed to remove

Premier Jagan from office, D'Aguiar resigned from the government, but other UF members of the coalition failed to follow their leader. They stayed with the PNC government. And not long after it was discovered that Jagan and D'Aguiar had been seeing each other, the intention being to work out some sort of cooperation between the two parties. This in essence validated the expediency of politicians!

Elections were due to be held. Burnham appealed to the nation to give him and the PNC a clear mandate to continue to lead the country on towards peace, tranquility and economic prosperity for Guyana. He was given that mandate with an overwhelming triumph for him and his PNC, registering 55.81 percent of the votes polled. This gave him thirty seats in the National Assembly. And for the very first time, Jagan's PPP was reduced to 36.48 percent with nineteen seats. D'Aguair's United Force gained 7.42 percent and only four seats, which should be considered a rejection of what he represented politically. Some men were intended to offer service to their community, not as politicians but as entrepreneurs, but this was never understood.

Linden Forbes Sampson Burnham had struggled relentlessly to gain total control of Guyana. This success epitomized the adage that "if at first you don't succeed try, try and try again." Now he was given control on a platter. What would he conceive for Guyana? Would he introduce his Co-operative Republic ideology to his people? The glowing prospects seemed unlimited for this beautiful, young and mineral rich country. Within a decade, Burnham had so consolidated himself, that perhaps imperceptibly, he was transformed from the charming debonair, articulate attorney who sincerely intended to mold a new destiny for Guyana, but lost his way! First, most of the Guyanese professionals whom he induced to return home could no longer suffer his society. They fled Guyana. He gravitated from being autocratic to being tyrannical. It would seem that the transition from being prime minister to president altered his perspective of serving the Guyanese nation. Now he owned them. He surrounded himself with a powerful security force similar to the Tonton Macoutes of Papa Doc's Haiti. Moreover, his police force operated as though Guyana was a police state. The country was terrified by Guyana's security forces. It was true that the other brilliant son of Guyana, Dr. Walter Rodney, could be accused of stupidity—as everyone periodically visits this province—for having publicly stated that he had dedicated himself to rid Guyana of Burnham. This was a positive threat. Perhaps the president disregarded it, but his associates did not. Ridding Guyana of Burnham was tantamount to removing the source of excellent livelihood for many. They were committed to defending their president. Dr. Rodney was murdered, and the man allegedly responsible for handing him that walkie-talkie bomb was allowed to flee the country.

The precept of Burnham's Co-operative Republic established that everything consumed in that republic must be produced there. This supposedly ingenious ideology appeared to be superb in theory only. It proved a dismal failure in practice. Guyana declined tragically. A positively industrious people and nation brought to economic ruin by an obstinate, narcissistic dictator. Some have even characterized him as satanic, with a wicked following, many of whom existed like suckers living on the external microorganism of a shark.

While some or many may have enjoyed Burnham's generosity, his insensibility knew no bounds. He decreed that Guyana should be self-sufficient. This was superb thinking in the right direction. Billions of dollars in foreign exchange would be saved on the imposition of goods and services. But even a vast and enormously industrialized country such as the USA with a population of 300 million people recognized that it was folly to exist in isolation. Indubitably, the exchange of goods and services offered immense advantages. The result was that the USA was one of the wealthiest countries in the world. At this juncture of our history it was the largest industrialized economy. Burnham's concept for the growth and development of Guyana was wise and commendable on one hand, and inordinately ambitious on the other. Both the expertise, resources and mechanism were in short supply. And, gradually, the method of implementation was totally inflexible and fatuous. Burnham, by any measurement, miscalculated. Either his advisors were incompetent or he followed his own senseless counsel. He was an attorney and an orator, but positively no Sir Arthur Lewis. The English economist, philosopher, and journalist Barbara Ward in her book, *Spaceship Earth* (Columbia University Press), wrote adumbrating the economic limitations with which micro-states were unavoidably burdened:

> If even a state on the scale of Russia cannot feed itself, if the United States is not in control of its balance of payments, how can one measure the economic limitations of the micro-states? Their limits must be seen to be almost as total as the sovereignty they claim. But economics are secondary. Survival comes first. The present organization of mankind in a lawless assembly of competing sovereignties deprives every state of security, great and small alike.

The Guyanese, who were a fiercely patriotic people, commenced an exodus that was only matched by that of the East African State of Uganda, which was involuntary. There was the difference. The then dictator Idi Amin had ordered the expulsion of thousands of Southeast Asians. In the case of Guyana, it was a move by Guyanese of their own volition. They were escaping a ruthless tyrant. People did not run away from freedom, comfort and stability. Scarborough was a suburb on the eastern end of the city of Toronto, Canada. There will be found some one hundred thousand East Indians from Guyana. Today, thousands of Guyanese—some of the smartest people in the Caribbean—are now dispersed not only throughout Canada, the USA and Europe, but also in every territory in the

Caribbean. They were permitted to leave if they wished, but with no more than a reported eighteen dollars. Many Guyanese trekked the wilderness that bordered Suriname, French Guiana or Brazil, then to emigrate from there to elsewhere. It was one of the most grotesque phases of Guyana's history. Guyana was stripped of its dignity. Ironically, Burnham's original intention was to struggle for Guyanese to cultivate a strong sense of dignity.

At this crucial point, no opposing political party in Guyana could hope to win an election, and Cheddi Jagan and his PPP would be confined to the opposition for the next twenty years. Jagan and his wife had exacerbated the already egregious condition of Guyana by lending fodder to the vicious racial conflict. This was being less politically strategic than idiotic. This was considered a means to an end—one of desperation. Remarkably, the alleged assistance of the CIA was identified during the 1964 elections, which exited the PPP from office. Both the PPP and the UF were decimated. Never was such an abundance of publicity materials distributed in Georgetown and throughout the country. Posters, pamphlets, billboards, buntings with inscriptions incessant, radio and print advertisements, and money all contributed to an effective campaign and victory. Burnham never lost another election.

The devious Americans seemed to have miscalculated again, as they did with Castro's Cuba. They had hoped to earn the cooperation and favor of a Burnham PNC government. This failed to occur. The Guyana president had always resented imperialists. A specialist diplomat, and as perhaps no living soul commands words as he does, he was perhaps successful in receiving technical, military and economic aid from both Washington and Moscow? But neither got anything out of him. As he stated in one of his many eloquent and forcefully candid speeches, "The East and West are the same, six and a half dozen." He contended that they, the imperial powers, gave, though not out of altruism or humanity but rather out of expediency. And this is saying that Burnham had always been wary of the USA and Britain and the USSR.

Precisely twenty years after Burnham assumed office, I wrote a feature that chided his posture in the picture news monthly magazine, *Teller*, which I edited and published from Castries, St. Lucia. The story was headed, "Burnham, A Most Impressive Failure."

> One Caribbean politician, certainly the most impressive failure as a head of government in this region—who would not be expected to relinquish his office, not even if God begged him to—is the inscrutable President Forbes Burnham of Guyana. The paradoxical irony of the Burnham tragedy on Guyana is that he replaced Marxist Premier Dr. Cheddi Jagan with the blessings of both the British and the USA.
>
> The rationale behind the cultivation of Burnham by the British and American Intelligence was simply one of expediency aimed at staggering or effectively stunting the communist growth in that sole English-speaking territory on the South American mainland. Regrettably, that is from the American point of view. University of London graduate Burnham turned out to be an even more complex proposition than Marxist Cheddi Jagan.
>
> An unholy alliance formed after the 1964 election between the Forbes Burnham People's National Congress and Portuguese businessman Peter D'Aguiar's United Force shot Burnham into the Premiership of Guyana. Peter D'Aguiar was given the minister of finance portfolio.
>
> In an attempt to fulfill his vision of a Cooperative Socialist Republic for Guyana, Burnham instituted some austere measures unprecedented in the history of the region. His philosophy was that of a tyrant's. Precisely the antithesis of the splendid leadership Simon Bolivar struggled to discourage in this region. Guyanese found themselves severely repressed. His style of economics trammeled a rather sensible people who then decided to run for it, rather than remain and be regi-

mented by Burnham's regime. His politics were thought to be original and refreshing in theory but when translated in to practical form they were abysmally unrealistic.

The exodus from Guyana began and has not stopped; not even when the Regime prevented the very many desirous of leaving from taking their life's earnings with them. Just now, there is no government policy more repressive in the entire Caribbean than Guyana's, and neither the state nor the people prosper in any way. Indeed, of the front line states in this region, Guyana is foremost in registering negative results.

President Burnham has entrenched himself and is insulated both by the army and the police. In essence, Guyana is not unlike a totalitarian state and the militarized element represents the president's insurance to hold on to power. Incidentally, as it concerns power he is on record as having pointed out: "We politicians want power. The politician who tells you he does not want power is either a fool or a rascal."

Everyone knows Burnham is no fool. What is he? His honesty is moving! Guyana in this region is incomparable in terms of natural and mineral resources. It is richer in resources than all the CARICOM Member States combined. It possesses large deposits of gold, diamond, gypsum and bauxite among minerals of this nature. Cattle, forestry, rice, sugar, water and so on. Yet year after year since the advent of Burnham, that state's economic performance proved repeatedly disgraceful, the obvious reason being perfect mismanagement. On management and development, economist George Theophilus said, "The quality of management determines the quality of development."

Burnham contended when he sought to lead Guyana, "This country will never get off its feet if you try to toady to America. This country will never get on its feet if you want to make a satellite of Russia. This country, we contend, can never get off its feet unless the People's National Congress philosophy prevails."

The PNC philosophy prevails and economic decadence with it. President Burnham's conception of managing a country is inextricably wedded to error. And along the way over the years he has methodically dismantled a peaceful, friendly and free society to introduce an inflexible estate-type of regimentation that is hideous.

Since he assumed power, he proceeded to become an amazingly skilled trapeze-artist-style politician balancing between the United States of America and the Soviet Union while he struggles to maintain a non-aligned posture in his foreign policy.

Simon Bolivar said, and it is a fact, "The most perfect system of government is that which results in the greatest possible measure of happiness and maximum of social security and political stability."

The Burnham government cannot be associated with "the greatest possible measure of happiness and maximum of social security and political stability." People do not run away from happiness, security and stability as they have been forced to do from Guyana. Earlier during his struggle for power, President Burnham eloquently declared that: "We wanted a constitution which would have given the majority of people in this country a feeling that they were secure, a feeling that they were supporters or members of the governing party, their basic rights would not be trampled upon, their aspirations and attitudes would not be ignored and that they would live with a certain feeling of security, that acceptance of government of the day, there is found to be instability which instability cannot be removed by recruitment of political armies. If there is instability, it will mean that the prerequisite for economic progress will be lacking."

What prevailed in Guyana today is an obscene contradiction to the above statement. President Burnham tailored out an authoritarian administration that was propped up by a political army. There was instability therefore progress was lacking.

Obviously his troubles are many. And they stem from political unrest which he keeps a lid on with the guns of his military. He seems little troubled, but to compound his domestic discomfort he is severely burdened with the Venezuela claim to two-thirds of Guyana. Venezuela is superior in size and military might and, therefore, poses some terrors of invasion for him. And that's the crux of his condemnation of the American led invasion of Grenada. The events in Grenada saw Burnham directing a tactical Anti-American war in which he and his archrival Cheddi Jagan are in agreement.

The Organization of Eastern Caribbean States (OECS), Barbados and Jamaica had, without ceremony, totally discounted his stand not to resort to military action: he ought to have considered his standing in the region. No one respects him nor gives credence to his views, as no one respects a failure. Burnham's anger exploded and reverberated throughout the region and to back that up, he ordered the sponsoring of a motion along with Nicaragua in the U.N. Security Council, condemning the October 25 American invasion.

The consensus among the heads of the Eastern Caribbean states—save Trinidad and Tobago—is that, Burnham the tyrant has betrayed their cause. He voted against them. That's unforgivable.

Today, relations are strained and it is assumed—mind you, not feared—that Guyana may opt out of CARICOM.

On October 27, Burnham held a Mass Solidarity Rally with "Free Grenada" being the theme at the Sophia Auditorium in Georgetown and there he gave his version of the Grenada experience.

He impressed upon the Guyanese people that the Americans had plans to invade Guyana. As he termed it, "Today Grenada! Tomorrow Guyana? Next day???"

> That man has now engaged himself in a psychological war, but his expectations are difficult to determine. He proceeded further to declare that he will not recognize any new administration in St. George's, Grenada.
>
> Does Grenada really need any sort of recognition from Guyana for its survival? Not really. Guyana is no exemplary model of a progressive nation-state to emulate.
>
> Directing a diplomatic war against Grenada is hardly a pinch to hurt the bottom of the USA, as that is clearly Burnham's intention. We bleed for Guyana as Burnham continues his autocratic and repressive rule. We must hold resolutely to one consolation; that is, Burnham can't survive forever. He will be usurped.

Guyana was of some significance to the Caribbean. Moreover, the element *forthright* being a part of Burnham's character, it was inevitable that he would assail the posture of some administrations within CARICOM. The verity of human behavior was such that we treasured the propensity to see the flaws of others, while we luxuriated in our own unsavory habits. The president of Guyana was no model of virtue and rectitude. But realistically, if Burnham would not hesitate to grapple with the likes of the USA, Britain, the United Nations, and the European community, it would be dumb to presume that such a volatile character would play a reticent role in an action-packed Caribbean. Burnham had disapproved and as a result, resented the American invasion of Grenada. The prime minister of the Commonwealth of Dominica, Eugenia Charles, was then chairman of the Organization of Eastern Caribbean States (OECS). After consultation with member states and some leaders of the wider Caribbean, Charles made a crucial journey to Washington to meet U.S. President Ronald Reagan. This infuriated Burnham. He claimed that he was not consulted. Perhaps he was not. And for no other reason than he had been adjudged untrustworthy. Indications were that he had leaked the intention of the

CARICOM forces to be deployed in Grenada. He had disagreed with the decision.

Burnham the consummate intellectual was always very stimulating even when he employed innuendos to assault the USA, Britain and Russia. For instance, on March 21, 1967 during a foreign policy debate in the National Assembly, Georgetown, he eloquently articulated the distinction between neutrality and neutralism. He argued:

> Neutrality, to my mind connotes an unwillingness to come to a decision and remaining completely neutral on many, if not all, important international questions; giving no opinion; coming to no decision and voting neither way. Not only is such an attitude cowardly, but also I would submit, it is unrealistic.
>
> Neutralism, on the other hand, connotes that there is no commitment to come out or make a decision on either side in a dispute before the facts are ventilated and the mind applied to such facts. Neutralism, I would describe as a pursuit of an independent foreign policy, the exercise of an independent judgment on any international question. A country, which pursues a foreign policy of neutralism, is one which neither of the super powers or great blocs can depend on automatically to support on any issue.
>
> Countries like Guyana, which have experienced the colonialism of a Western country and which are anxious to confirm, establish and advertise their independence, are frequently led into a position where the emphasizing and confirmation of that independence takes the form of a constant anti-Western posture. On the other hand, there are some developing countries, newly independent who pursue an equally disgusting, if not more disgusting series of postures, believing that the West is richer, believing that the West is more generous, that commit themselves to primitive adulation of everything Western and to automatic support of the West, even in cases when the West does not have right on its side and in circum-

> stances which sometimes draw the contempt and surprise of those they support.
>
> This was not a written speech. He spoke extemporaneously. And in this respect he was exquisitely skilled.

President Burnham's candor, with a mixture of arrogance and confidence, was superbly documented and his capacity to stay in power was notorious. He practiced the art successfully for some twenty years. However, there was the saying "the longest rope has an end." This remained undisputed. And though death was never in dispute, as we were educated to the fact that it is inevitable, some men seemed to disregard the fact that life was unpredictable. He died in 1984 during a minor throat operation. It shocked Guyana as that operation was not at all life threatening. I sensed that only the minority, some members of his immediate family and relatives and those who benefited from his office, might have mourned his loss. This was saying that President Linden Forbes Sampson Burnham, the dictator, was not the all-consummate evil. However, the record shows that he had brutally disrupted the lives of an untold number of Guyanese who perhaps did not, and would not ever have the opportunity to, forgive him.

Will he be mourned? This was a subject for easy debate. I wrote the following at the news of his passing away. "A Dictator Passes On."

> It takes much more than mere will to disregard such a significant event as the passing away of the hugest Caribbean political enigma of our time, Guyana's President Linden Forbes Sampson Burnham. And it would not be unfair to say that while many Guyanese—like members of the defense force and the police whom he paid very well to insulate him against reality—will miss his presence and accompanying favors; there are infinitely more who are jubilant that the "tyrant" has ended his marathon tight control over the Guyanese people in his singular attempt to mold their destiny.

Forbes Burnham was loved by as many people who loved Idi Amin of Uganda and conversely, hated by considerably more. It will be recalled that Henry VIII was also mourned when he passed away.

In my view, Burnham despoiled rather than developed Guyana, an absolutely beautiful, comparatively vast country—larger than England—with eighty-three thousand square miles of gold, diamond, bauxite, water, cattle, timber, the Kaieteur Falls, sugar, rice, rum among those that spring to mind and an incredible array of talented people.

However, we need to look at what that indisputably brilliant man Forbes Burnham could have been, and could have done for Guyana, the region and the world, had he not been devoid of humanity, altruism and empathy. His brilliance dazzled his People's National Congress (PNC) fanatical followers. They became a chauvinistic, myopic, follow-my-leader Burnham gang whose servility proved rich fodder in which he exalted himself beyond their levels for any objective, sensible and Socratic communication. They made him a God. And they were slaves to him, most of them save his sister, Jessie. As far back as 1958 Jessie and I wrote for the same magazine in Georgetown, the *Guyana Times*, if my memory serves me accurately. She said, "Forbes is brilliant, but this brilliance overwhelms him. He can't handle it to the extent that it will not benefit the many who surround him. From a child at home he took everything. He never gave. What beats me is that no one else seems to recognize that he has all the traits of another Hitler. Actually, he hates other people, but loves himself." Jessie Burnham opposed him vigorously for many years.

Tall, dashing, debonair Forbes Burnham generated both admiration and fear. He was the perfect black intellectual who used the English language better than everyone else. Many Englishmen could not match his fluency and power of language that was later to include the former prime minister of Britain, Harold Wilson. Compared with other leaders in the

Caribbean, perhaps only the deceased Dr. Eric Williams of Trinidad and Tobago and Tom Adams of Barbados could match, but not better him in fluency of language. He was an immense orator.

Like Martin Luther King, Burnham had a dream to mold the destiny of the mineral rich Guyana. His Co-operative Republic concept was excellent in theory but its application in practice failed. While his regime was not Communist, he was not inclined to make favorite of the Americans. He was strong in authority and his ideas were hardly ever challenged, and when they were he was always proven the victor.

His elevation to the premiership of British Guyana soon found him surrounded by an impressive force of brilliant professionals. Unfortunately, conceit and self-righteousness, the major flaws in politicians of his breed, eroded and subverted the love, admiration, respect and confidence his colleagues had bestowed upon him and which had helped to sustain him. He alienated these talented people. Men and women of self-respect, they all deserted him and are now in the USA and Canada. He did not suffer sacrifices with the working people, which is a tenet of the Communist and Socialist systems.

Burnham's Co-operative Republic concept was marvelous, but inflexible, if not almost ruthless elements of application brought about not a dissimilar failure to that of the "Nyerere experiment" in Tanzania in East Africa. That gave rise to an astonishing exodus of some of the most talented people from any one country in this region. Today Guyanese—an intensely nationalistic people—are now scattered involuntarily throughout this region in every territory and also in the USA and Canada. People do not flee from comfort and happiness. The lot of the average Guyanese was painfully distressing.

Burnham's vision of a cultural renaissance for Guyana is still perfect in the mind; but such a project that courts with utter stringency to adversely affect traditional lifestyles

> can only lend to totalitarian methods of application, which suppress a people and militarily enslave them to obedience. Inevitably, while many, like parasites, lived acceptably on, or through his goodwill, very many more will give evidence to posterity that when tyrant rulers are being numbered, Linden Sampson Forbes Burnham will not escape being included on that list.
>
> Burnham's greatest achievement in my view was that he was undoubtedly a Caribbean integrationist. And he opposed the American influence and domination throughout this region. As a result, Guyana ensured and maintained a healthy political balance within CARICOM. Given his brilliance and the utopia into which he could have transformed mineral rich Guyana, Burnham was a pathetic failure. To state otherwise would be indulging in an exercise of hypocrisy. I extend sincere sympathy to his family.

That man—an enigma to most—who evidently somewhere on his journey to procure power believed that he was not accountable to anyone, passed away as everyone did. He was not ill, per se. The operation was considered minor and not at all life threatening. In death, controversy attended him. To embalm him like Lenin or not? Linden Forbes Sampson Burnham was perhaps the only leader in the Caribbean whose death was no shattering loss to the majority in Guyana and the Caribbean. Was his premature death in question? Was it suspect? Not unlike the wisest of leaders, King Solomon, who almost at the end of his sterling journey had lost his way, perhaps Burnham did in his efforts contribute materially to the welfare of many; but to the majority of displaced Guyanese and Guyana, he represented a disaster damage that even time may prove inadequate to repair.

Chapter 3

The Right Honorable
John Michael Geoffrey Manningham Adams
Former Prime Minister Of Barbados

Perhaps only a few would hazard to give some sort of explanation why some nice people of integrity entered politics. Everyone, or almost everyone, contributed to a consensus that the profession of politics was really compatible with our wicked world that it sought to fashion. The history of politics bore evidence that supposedly decent people entered its province well intentioned, but the strength of character was later enfeebled. They fell victims to self-indulgence. The mission of honest and dedicated service retreated and got lost.

Man was imperfect. He would not and cannot serve a multitude and not incur the displeasure of a few or more. But some politicians notwithstanding endeavored and succeeded in giving sterling service to the people and nation and region they begged to lead. One such politician was John Michael Geoffrey Manningham Adams. Need anyone speculate why he was popularly known as simply Tom Adams? His background sensitized and prepared him to eventually become the leader of the Barbados Labor Party (BLP), founded by his father, Sir Grantley Adams, former premier of Barbados and then prime minister of the ill-fated West Indies Federation. Sir

Grantley must have known that his only son followed admirably in his footsteps.

Born September 24, 1931 in Barbados, Adams, then as a child in a prejudiced Barbados, was privileged. However, his father, a highly esteemed attorney up until the fifties, was not permitted to enter, for instance, the Aquatic Club. His mother Grace, being English and white, would visit there. This gives an idea of the racist colonial system then. But young Tom was half-caste, and the fair-skinned person was the next best to white. They got the best jobs where and when whites were not available. Barbados was predominantly Black.

Barbados was unique in that its British status was never challenged. The British took possession of this totally flat coral island that was the most easterly of the chain of Caribbean islands in the year of 1624. It was unlike its neighbors that exchanged hands between French and British, or Dutch and French or British and Spanish. Britain, France, Holland, Spain and Portugal were Imperialists that plundered and murdered unarmed inhabitants of far away countries as a way of life. They were expanding beyond their shores. Even today, France was an obscene example. While Barbados was not overtly a South Africa or Rhodesia that was government institutionalized, strong elements of racial discrimination were imposed on the Black offspring of African slaves. For example, hundreds of poor, uneducated convicts from Scotland, considered social misfits in Britain, were exported to Barbados. From there, they were dispersed to the neighboring islands of St. Vincent and the Grenadines and Grenada. They were of the Caucasian heritage and were more privileged than those of African ancestry who were born on that island. Suffice it to say that Tom Adams was aware that his mother could socialize at the Aquatic Club, but not his father.

Tom Adams, like most scholars, was studious. He attended Harrison College in Barbados where he excelled academically. He enjoyed life as most boys of his age did irrespective of conditions. Cricket, football, track and field, and girls. It was no surprise to anyone when he won the island scholarship for 1950. He departed for London where he met his English relatives. Very little about this association with them was revealed. Was it comfortable or uncomfortable? Nevertheless, this was the past. Tom Adams earned his B.A. and later M.A. in 1957 at Magdalene College, Oxford University.

About this time there were remarkable political stirrings back home in the British West Indies. There was social and political turmoil throughout—strikes and rioting in Barbados, Guyana, St. Lucia, Grenada, St. Vincent, St. Kitts among others. His father was associated with the oppressed workers. He was a part of vociferous demonstrations with papa Grantley toting placards with hammer and sickle, the symbol of socialism. Positively, he struggled assiduously to become premier of Barbados and then suspended this office to assume the position of prime minister of the West Indies Federation with headquarters in Port of Spain, Trinidad. At Oxford the articulate Tom Adams was elected president of the West Indies Students Association and vice president of the West Indian Students' Union, London. During these student days, he engaged himself as a freelance broadcaster at the British Broadcasting Corporation (BBC) and the ITV. He was also a prolific producer from 1955 to 1962. His assignments took him throughout Europe, including the Soviet Union.

The tall, dashing and handsome bon vivant met, courted and married the lovely Genevieve Turner in 1952. That union produced one son. Tom Adams was called to the Bar at Gray's Inn in 1959. He returned home to Barbados in 1964. The interest in politics was no surprise to his parents or anyone who knew him. He joined the Barbados Labor Party and was elected the assistant general secretary in 1965. That zealous young man was not idle. Not surprisingly, he was influenced by his father and his mother, Grace, who indicated to him, "John, I don't really like politics. Inevitably we are in politics as your father is a politician. If this is what you wish to do, you do have my support unequivocally."

It should be appreciated that although Tom Adams' father was the founder and chairman of the Barbados Labor Party (BLP), it was necessary for him to earn his elevation. And it might have been with less stress had he not been Tom Adams, the boss' son.

Cerebral with a marvelous command of the English language, he was able to convince his constituency of St. Thomas to allow him to represent that district. And he was given the political mandate. He then proceeded to totally reinvent himself to facilitate greater flexibility to his workload in an endeavor to make himself more accessible to his constituents. As leader of the BLP, Tom Adams succeeded his father as leader and prime minister, just like Britain's youngest prime minister, William Pitt, did, as well as Michael Manley of Jamaica.

A scholar who was not unacquainted with the writings of the Chinese philosopher Confucius, Adams nonetheless, as prime minister, disregarded the savant's counsel that "Leaders in their journey up the ladder of success should avoid the society of women." He disregarded that counsel and, fortunately, it did not affect his performance in office. Fact is, he has never pretended to be sacrosanct and has had numerous affairs as Kennedy, Clinton, Burnham, Compton, Manley, Gairy and others did. During the early eighties, he flew in a Cessna plane almost every weekend to St. Lucia to socialize. But this personal activity never distracted him. In fact, he was highly respected and esteemed throughout the Caribbean.

Former Prime Minister Sir James Mitchell of St. Vincent and the Grenadines once stated that his respect and admiration for Adams increased enormously in Canada at a Commonwealth Heads of Government Conference. The host Prime Minister Elliott Pierre Trudeau had called on the Barbados prime minister to give a summary and a sort of 'til-we-meet-again address at this farewell dinner. According to Sir James:

> This was the most eloquent and perfectly articulate off-the-cuff address I had heard. And I have heard many. Tom Adams summarized in detail with an incisive analytical flair that truly amazed and delighted every leader. That made me proud to be Tom Adams' closest neighbor. I have loved him since.

That intriguing Barbados prime minister was also perfectly decisive. In 1979, St. Vincent and the Grenadines had drifted into political chaos—a spate of defiance. The government called to Barbados to send in its security forces. Prime Minister Adams did not hesitate. The forces restored order and this was appreciated as the situation could have developed into anarchy.

However, Tom Adams' political ascendancy began in 1971 when he won the leadership of the Barbados Labor Party (BLP) and became the official leader of the opposition in the Barbados parliament. Articulate, fluent and perceptive, he was a rising star that soared rapidly and brilliantly. With his fascinating oratorical skills, he led a capable team of five: Lionel Craig, Burton Hinds, Henry D. B. Forde, Lindsay Bolden and Elliot Mortley. Later, Billie Antoinette Miller consolidated the firing power. Barbados will long remember how this opposition team dominated to overwhelm the government at almost every presentation. Prime Minister Barrow was no rustic but was unable to contend with this new and powerful wave of politicians.

Tom Adams and his team were enjoying themselves enormously. Barbados noticed and the country's dismal economic performance assisted them. By 1974, inflation in Barbados had reached an alarming forty percent. This was attributed to the Middle East oil crisis that affected the international economy. Barrow failed to find the solution to stabilize the economy. This cost him the general elections in 1976.

Tom Adams and his BLP won the task of wrestling this spiraling inflation that affected every spectrum of the society. As prime minister, it was an almost incredible challenge to redirect a small, open economy that was all but swamped by a then-chaotic world's supra inflationary pressures. He was rigorously tested. His leadership with management expertise was further pushed to its limits when, in 1979, Iran's revolution exacerbated the world condition to send shocks of despair as oil supplies plunged.

Adams rose to the huge challenge at hand. He employed a refreshing discernment and inventiveness by instituting government reforms with some degree of success. For example, he made adjustments to the management of the Barbados international reserves, revamping strategies with lean tailoring to enhance operation of institutions; the creation of the Barbados National Bank, the Barbados National Oil Company and the National Petroleum Corporation; domestication of oil exploration and production and a total reform of the Central Bank of Barbados. These postures impacted favorably and translated into savings of foreign exchange amounting to in excess of forty million dollars by 1983.

The Tom Adams government in 1980 instituted two major landmark pieces of legislation:

1. **The Tenantries Freehold Purchases Act**, considered historic in proportion. It revolutionized land holdings. People who lived on tenantries could now become owners of house spots at nominal cost. Ownership of a home, whatever its size, was vital to Barbadians. The result is reflected in the thousands of lovely homes that now punctuate holdings formerly large-plantation-owned.

2. **The Offshore Financial Services legislation.** It earned Barbados credibility. It was accepted as an efficient and responsible off-shore financial service center. A testimony to this is the range of many large international financial institutions to have been established since. Doubtless the

> impact has been considerable. The manifestation has been a generation of service fees as licensing, rental, residential and vehicles among others; the demand for professional services be they legal, accounting, security, nursing, etc.

One of the sensational political court cases that gave some recognition and prominence to the present prime minister of Barbados, Owen Arthur, was filed by Tom Adams. A by-election was held and the two contesting candidates were Sybil Leacock of the Democratic Labor Party and Owen Arthur of the Adams BLP. When the ballots were counted, the female candidate was declared the winner by one vote. Adams challenged the decision and took it to court, even against the advice of several senior lawyer members of his party. The chief justice of Barbados, then His Lordship the Honorable Randolph Douglas, accepted the arguments put forward by the astute Henry Forde. The result of the one-seat win was disqualified and new elections were ordered. This was held on November 22,1984. What emerged from this political campaign was an opportunity for the entire country of Barbados to experience the political, organizational and oratorical skills of a genius named Adams. He dominated the entire campaign. The result was that Owen Arthur won the election by 238 votes.

Significantly, Tom Adams did not plan to hold on to power indefinitely. He had openly discussed handing over the prime ministership to his deputy, Bernard "Bree" St. John.

According to a close friend and advisor, Claude A. Griffith, Adams was unsure that his party would be given a third term:

> He had, therefore, concluded that the only sure strategy to win a third term and to give Bernard "Bree" St. John a chance at being prime minister was to call a snap election, thereby catching the opposition asleep. He made two decisions at that meeting; planning for a July, 1985 election would start with the selection of candidates after the party conference in January, 1985. He would step down after the snap election and

> give Bree the opportunity he so richly deserved. As he put it, "the people of Barbados would never elect Bernard St. John as prime mnister in spite of his formidable skills."

Griffith, who was general secretary and cabinet minister, felt bewildered by the decision of a leader who enjoyed the office he held as prime minister and who was willing to walk away from it all. He said, "Indeed when I expressed my doubts about this, Tom offhandedly remarked to me, 'one of the legacies which the British ceded to us, was how to hold on to power, but not how to walk away from it' . . ."

To summarize Tom Adams, Griffith expressed the view that, "It is unfortunate that this brilliant and perceptive, yet complex individual did not have the opportunity to write as he had promised me in our fateful 1984 conversation. Any analysis of contemporary Barbados would show that while his father, Sir Grantley Herbert Adams, was a social revolutionary, Errol Barrow was a pioneering builder as an economic revolutionary. Tom Adams was the first manager of modern Barbados. He was effective because he was endowed with the requisite combination of appropriate skills which prepared him for this formidable responsibility—conceptual skills; human skills; technical skills; decision-making skills. He was a complex character—brilliant, personable and charismatic; a flair for the dramatic; unfailingly loyal to friends; frugal, organized mind; mischievous prankster, comedic, jealous, polite and chivalrous; cunning, strategic thinker; meticulous, psychologist and philosopher; loyal and devoted son; caring father."

However, the region and the world will perhaps remember Tom Adams more vividly and fondly on the strength of his leadership performance during the Grenada crisis.

Barbados and the Eastern Caribbean will long remember October, 1983 as one of great significance to the region. Events in Grenada unfolded rapidly after it was announced that Prime

Minister Maurice Bishop was placed under house arrest. The prime minister of Barbados, like the leaders of the Organization of Eastern Caribbean States (OECS), viewed with trepidation for the life of the Grenada prime minister. Plans were put in motion to execute something of an Entebbe type rescue of Bishop from his captors at his residence. Regrettably, Bishop was executed. The result was an invasion of Grenada by American and Caribbean security forces. This military action earned shouts of alarm and anger from the passive prime minister of Trinidad and Tobago, George Chambers, who was the current chairman of CARICOM, and also from President Forbes Burnham of Guyana. Distancing themselves from the popular and majority decision of intervention compelled the Barbados prime minister Tom Adams, a key figure in the scenario, to address his nation Barbados and the rest of the Eastern Caribbean in a radio and television hookup—the aim being to clear the air of misleading statements then pervading the Caribbean.

The *Teller* Magazine then believed that Tom Adams was the most popular prime minister in the Caribbean. Of course, my close friends in Barbados, Arlington and Sesnett and other colleagues did not share this view. Their choice was the "Dipper." That was former Prime Minister Errol Barrow, then the opposition leader. He took Barbados into independence. But then, I do concede that Errol "the Dipper" Barrow was one of that nation's most capable prime ministers. He almost bled to death the sinister prejudicial system of employing only very-fair-of-skin faces within the banking sector. Nonetheless, we spoke to our choice, whom we considered then the most popular leader in the region. We wanted to know how he was able to engineer the economic stability of Barbados compared to Guyana, Jamaica and Trinidad and Tobago, which had all been compelled to devalue their currency. The following was that interview:

The *Teller* Quizzed Tom Adams.

Tom Adams is abundantly endowed. He is sociable, brilliant, handsome, astute, dapper, suave, strong-willed, debonair, perceptive, aristocratic, charismatic, leader of the Barbados Labor Party and the prime minster of Barbados. His capacity elects him the most influential prime minister in the Caribbean today.

Armed with such enviable qualities, it was no coincidence that Barbados has sailed sea-worthily over and through heavy swells of a debilitating world recession with its companion inflation.

Shaken but not battered as Guyana, Jamaica and St. Lucia, in this region, this little nation state Barbados is the prototype of excellent leadership.

As the *Teller* views it, the Guyana leadership overestimated its people. Jamaica's leadership underestimated its people, while St. Lucia's leadership betrayed its people.

The *Teller* spoke to Prime Minister Tom Adams and quizzed him in his office in Bridgetown on how Barbados was able to stay afloat while others with infinitely more resources swamped. Tom Adams is, doubtless, the most popular prime minister in the Caribbean and one of the most capable leaders in the world today.

Teller: Prime Minister, I'll lead off on world recession, since economies in the world have been battered by it. We've had examples of bankruptcies in the United States, bankruptcies in Canada, and West Germany. Amazingly, Barbados seems to have been doing very well. To what extent has the world recession affected the economy of Barbados?

Prime Minister Adams (P.M.): It has affected us chiefly in unemployment. We had some specialized problems in agriculture. It wasn't the world recession so much as very bad weather two years ago which affects not only the crop in that particular year. Rain made it impossible to harvest it. Prevented effectively growing of the cane for the next year and reduced the crop to an acceptable low level for two years. But in the rest of the economy, World recession reduced the demand for our service as tourism, and to some extent for our goods also. There was a lower level of economic activity in the island. Indeed, last year we imported less than we did the year before, a phenomenon that hasn't happened in Barbados for thirty years. And we paid for it in unemployment. As against this, inflation has been way low, 4.5 percent for the twelve months, which ended at the last calculation period, and government finances have improved. But they have improved on the basis on there not being much government activity in capital works, not being a great deal of economic activity generally within society.

Teller: Man being as subjective as he is, would you say that the level of unemployment in Barbados could persuade the man who is not employed to think that government is not performing satisfactorily?

P.M.: No. I say with very little fear of contradiction. Aware of all that is said by opposition commentators, that there is an immense fund of sympathy for the government in the light of what has been happening in the world. I don't know if Barbados is unique in this respect. I think that in Britain, where government policy, far more than the world recession, is responsible for unemployment, it is clear the government catering for now came to no harm. In Barbados, where government is trying to do its best, I think there has been a public response that we are unlucky and "you can't do more than your best" and we can't fully control our own destiny, and that the government should be given a chance.

Teller: Would you agree that like the other states in the region and elsewhere that the movement of the economy with the manner in which it performs is dictated by external influences?

P.M.: Oh, very much so.

Teller: Has the lifestyle of Barbadians changed at all since the recession has punched its way into the life of the country?

P.M.: Well, it's hard to say. People are still buying motor cars. People are still building houses. They're still travelling. People are still educating their children at university, in and out of Barbados. It's hard to say how far there has been a change. I think that sugar workers have not had it so good the last couple of years compared with 1980, when there was a very large crop. A very large pay out. I think that their incomes may have shrunk. I think that workers in the hotel business have not had it so good because we haven't had so many tourists. I think there has been some loss of employment in the retail sector, but I don't think that for those who remained in work that things are bad because inflation has been so very low. Prices of food remained stationary, for over a year.

Teller: Can you state that Barbados, in spite of everything else, has performed very well over the past two years? What percentage of economic growth has registered?

P.M.: I prefer outsiders to say it. We haven't had any economic growth. What had happened is that the last two years have been years of restraint as there was going to be no economic growth. Agriculture falling back. Tourism falling back. We couldn't expect growth and we therefore tried to distribute the hardships very evenly. We followed policies which take into account the fact that it is unwise to try to spend your way out this sort of depression. We found ourselves in because of the effect of the balance of payments and these policies did have the effect of spreading the hardship. There were policies of restraint and so government revenues have improved. We didn't try to waste a great deal of money to gain a little meretricious popularity in the short term. We tried to conserve the government's finances and this is what we've done.

Teller: Yes, but then you were forced to resort to the I.M.F. (International Monetary Fund)?

P.M.: We went to the I.M.F., as much for cash flow as for anything else. A lot of our foreign reserves are tied up in the CARICOM multilateral clearing facilities; some 65 million U.S. dollars and we can't get any money out of that facility. And we constantly have to be getting short-term credits from overseas to meet our day-to-day foreign currency liabilities and we decided to get a substantial sum of money from the International Monetary Fund to avoid a necessity to borrow expensive money in the New York or other money markets.

Teller: At your last meeting in Port of Spain recently, was it not clarified how Barbados would be getting its money from Guyana and elsewhere?

P.M.: Yes, it was clarified but we haven't got it. All we got was the clarification. The promises.

Teller: At this time, what sort of strategy is being employed to further stimulate the Barbados economy? That is apart from promotion for tourism to yield a good season?

P.M.: Well, yes, we've done a lot of tourist promotion, but we are also reopening some construction sites. We are building a very substantial new headquarters for the Central Bank of Barbados and we are giving a thrust in housing. We are encouraging private people to build houses. We are making land available at all levels right up to the fund needed for a modest but complete stone structure. And this is a million dollar shot in the arm, the housing program.

Teller: We are told that all mortgages for home construction were frozen. Is this a fact? What is the reason?

P.M.: What happened was that bridging finance was made very difficult. In other words, the middle class are the better-off people who depend on bridging finance. A loan from the bank while you build the house, leading to a mortgage on the house while the house is building. That is what was frozen, and that made things very difficult for some. It's much easier to get a mortgage on an already constructed house than to get a mortgage on a house to be constructed.

Teller: What prospects do you see for Barbados in the immediate or even distant future—considering that we are yet to be rid of this recession, with the accompanying inflation that still bears down? How do you see Barbados sailing very clear of the economic reefs?

P.M.: We are concentrating on keeping the inflation low. Keeping it at an absolute maximum of 5 to 6 percent in 1983 and 1984, if we can. We see signs of the recession in the United States is virtually over. That people are again spending money and taking trips overseas. And we have concentrated our tourist advertising in the United States so that we are having a great surge of new American visitors. With our balance of payments protected by tourism, with inflation low and with our construction program fueling the economy, we expect that economic growth will resume this year, and will continue next year, and will probably the year after. And out of that economic growth, the government will be in a position to choose to distribute its benefits. Most will probably go into bringing unemployment down again. As I said, most will go into that, the rest may go into welfare benefits for the community. The Health Service is due to come in and it will be a very good time, because it will be coming in at a time when we can more easily afford it.

Teller: You did speak of visitors coming in again because the recession seems to be lifting in the United States. What of new investments from political commentators and social commentators among them? I'm speaking about the two records released recently by your leading calypsonian. It seems to me . . .

P.M.: Who is that leading calypsonian?

Teller: Well I'm referring to the Gabby. The chap who decided to write and sing a piece named "Mr. T." He also produced "Boots." I'd like to record how you react to this. It is said that some politicians or most politicians are ultra sensitive. How do you react to such commentaries?

P.M.: Oh it's a spiteful and ambitious calypso. It has a pleasant enough tune and I see that my supporters are taking it up now and saying that they agree with Mr. T. They are wearing Mr. T. t-shirts, and saying my cup of tea is Mr. T., all of that. I think that's a good humored Barbadian answer to vengeful and unpleasant calypso. Gabby is a politician. He's had connections with Cuba and he's potential candidate for the opposition in the next general election, and I think the words of Mr. T. should be viewed for what they are. They are just crude and unpleasant political propaganda.

Teller: Well, I spoke to him. I interviewed him recently and I did ask him if the campaign had started. Was it an indication that he was going into politics. Moreover, that his name had been mentioned on several occasions; he denied it. He expressed the view that what he was doing, that is singing, was more beneficial to the people than physically entering the political arena.

P.M.: Well, he is perhaps giving a correct answer, that his talents are fundamentally destructive. Don't forget that Gabby had not always been on that side of politics. He wrote a calypso at the time of the last election, about the death of brother DLP. It had a funeral tone in it and it had a refrain: "No more tricks in '76," meaning that the previous government had been guilty of tricks at the elections. So, I suppose that Gabby is a little unstable.

Teller: We are told that you banned the record. Is this true?

P.M.: What, Mr. T? That was never banned.

Teller: No. Boots, Boots?

P.M.: Boots was banned on the Government Broadcasting Station because it suggested that the intervention of the Regiment in St. Vincent in 1979 was not welcomed by the people of St. Vincent, and it also spoke of trigger happy soldiers. It was very derogatory to the Defense Force. And by and large I don't think that in the United States on the top forty that you would expect to hear a song that is critical of the traditions of the American Army. Or in a British Colony you would expect a song quite so unpleasant; again, he has a bitter tongue, or a bitter pen or whoever writes for him. And these are bitter songs. The suggestion that young nineteen- or twenty-year-old boys of the Barbados Defense Force who have never killed anyone in anger, yet were going to St. Vincent to shoot down innocent people, was thought by this station not only to be very likely to affect the government of St. Vincent, but how distasteful to the Defense Force and the traditions we are trying to build.

Teller: We veer on to another subject. Now we know that you probably, because of your father. We know you, probably, are a consummate integrationist. Do you hope to see the integration of even some CARICOM members during your lifetime?

P.M.: Yes. I guess I could say yes. I think there is some basis for a closer integration between Barbados and the OECS and certainly in the areas of functional cooperation between Barbados and St. Vincent and St. Lucia that could go even further than we've gone today. We are all in CARICOM. And we're in a Regional Security Pact. I would think that there is a lot of room for collaboration between the likeminded countries in the Eastern Caribbean. We are moving towards it. However, we would have to see eighties out.

The eighties were out and succeeded by the nineties and on to the twenties. This Caribbean integration came no closer to realization. That absolutely great Barbadian politician and brilliant son of the Caribbean John Michael Geoffrey Manningham Adams suffered heart seizure and passed away in 1984. His loss was shattering. Among the truly brilliant men of the Caribbean the honorable prime minister of Barbados known affectionately as Tom Adams would be placed among the first three. He must be considered irreplaceable.

Chapter 4

Sir Eric Matthew Gairy
Former Chief Minister, Premier and Prime Minister of Grenada

Eric Matthew Gairy sneered and spat in the uncompromising face of small island convention. Grenada, located in the southeast Caribbean, was a British colonial territory. It was the seat of government for the Windward Islands. They comprised Grenada, St. Vincent and the Grenadines, St. Lucia and Dominica.

Upwards to the thirties, forties, fifties and early sixties, skin color determined one's social status. Not unlike Barbados, the white-skinned enjoyed the predominant status, the mulatto or the fair skinned next in line. Blacks were the offspring of Africans forcibly brought out of West Africa to be enslaved on sugar plantations in the Caribbean.

In Grenada especially, again like in Barbados, the only redeeming element that possibly contributed to an improvement of the welfare of Blacks was education. It was out of this social matrix that the boy Eric Gairy was issued forth to leave indelibly an impact on Grenada that resonated throughout the Caribbean and unavoidably the world. He, however, was unlike other brilliant leaders of the Caribbean, most of whom were scholars having attended

prestigious, high institutions of learning. He should be described a natural. They were rare.

From the inception, the Caribbean press tarnished his reputation. Even my distinguished award-winning journalist colleague from Grenada, Alister Hughes, admitted to me in Toronto, "Eric Gairy had some sort of a genius. He was resilient. But I did not like him. I thought he was a fake. I couldn't prove he was."

But, notwithstanding, his supporters cherished him. Born in Dunfermline, St. Andrews, Grenada in 1922 to Douglas Gairy and his wife Theresa née Prince, this child then could not help being affected by his surroundings.

Gairy, as a boy, attended primary schools. Dictated by circumstances beyond his control, he was impelled to private studies. This was understood to mean that he was self-taught from reading and analysis. He was a student of the La Pillette Catholic Junior School and, naturally smart, he excelled at a rapid pace through to the Catholic Senior School. On graduation, his cleverness earned him a teaching job at the Catholic Senior School, his alma mater. Young Gairy was fond of teaching, but recognized that he had to move on. He taught for about two years, then journeyed to Trinidad where he found employment at the American Army base at Chaguaramas. He also became involved with the Uriah "Buzz" Butler Trade Union Movement. It was at this juncture that Gairy quickly understood the utility of trade unionism.

About this time, too, he arrested the opportunity to explore employment elsewhere in the Caribbean to enhance his economic condition. The Dutch islands of Aruba and Curacao, just off the coast of Venezuela, were then the new frontiers of employment opportunities where oil refineries were located. However, it should be recalled that the Dutch were no better than the British, French, Spanish and Portuguese in the early plunder of lands unknown to them, and populated with people with less sophisticated armory for their defense. The Standard Oil Company was in business to exploit the opportunity created to assist the war effort in Europe. The company did not see itself as being a paragon for ideal working conditions for migrants from other West Indian territories. Suffice it to say that conditions under which these young migrants worked desperately needed improvement. The emphasis was on sheer production. It opened an avenue for the Trade Union Movement to insinuate itself. And it did forcefully.

During 1947 and 1948, Gairy had experienced conditions that were inimical to health and good relations between employer and employees. Truly a religious young man, Gairy had established a Roman Catholic youth group in Aruba, and his increasing trade union activities compounded the situation to make him appear to be an effective adversary. His agitation would not be tolerated. He was not a native of Aruba, just a troublesome migrant worker from the British colony of Grenada. The man was deemed a nuisance and an instigator. He was arrested and deported along with two other Grenadians. Gairy, now back home in Grenada, noticed quickly that very little had changed in terms of social development. Materially and psychologically, the people were still oppressed and generally more depressed. Workers throughout the whole spectrum of the society were suffering deplorable conditions like elsewhere in all the colonies in the West Indies. Eric Gairy set about to correct the situation by mobilizing the workers in 1949. He initiated the formation of the Grenada Manual and Mental Workers Union (GMMWU), and not long after, that trade union gave birth to the Grenada United Labor Party (GULP).

The following was an excerpt from a handbook titled *Grenada Silver Jubilee Celebrations.* This was published to commemorate that nation's twenty-fifth independence anniversary.

> Mr. Gairy met great resistance from estate owners. This confrontation resulted in a series of protests by the workers. The then colonial government removed Mr. Gairy from the mainland to Carriacou hoping to control the workers. However,

> this popularity among the workers made it necessary for the authorities to return him to the mainland so he could speak to the workers and have calm restored.
>
> He told them, "Lend me Grenada and I will build you a new Grenada."

Incidentally, Eric Gairy struggled and influenced the introduction of adult suffrage to Grenada in 1957, became chief minister and later premier in 1967. He was the first government leader of the small islands of the Windward and Leeward Islands to take his country into independence on February 7, 1974. Moreover, he had a demonstrated respect and faith in women. He appointed the first female governor general, Dame Hilda Bynoe, and at one juncture his government's cabinet was dominated by females. This was unprecedented in the world.

Panache is a word that should be associated with Eric Gairy's posture. He infuriated the authorities with his eloquent speeches on imperialism and oppression of the working man. Perhaps Gairy was born to be the first chief minister of Grenada—premier and prime minister. He led Grenada ahead of the other eastern West Indian islands, and Grenada was the most literate even at that period.

An effective politician, Gairy of GULP was elected to the Legislative Council in 1951 and proceeded to be exceedingly vocal and combative. Not surprisingly, he was ganged up against in his attempt to change certain patterns of behavior. He was suspended from the council in 1952 for misconduct and his political enemies had increased with time. Nonetheless, he could not be stopped. He was not unlike an onrushing wave that one attempted to stop at one's peril.

Aggressive Gairy had taken leave of absence from the Legislative Council but had exceeded the period councilors were allowed away from office. His seat was forfeited for "over-staying his leave." But the dynamic peoples' Eric Gairy was blessed with resilience. He was re-elected that same year, 1954, to the legislature.

However, the following year, 1955, when events were rapid in succeeding each other, the council voted to suspend him for disruption. The old prejudices with envy had given birth to undisguised enmity.

In retrospect, Gairy had traveled to London as Grenada's representative at the West Indies Federation Conference, and similarly to Jamaica. At that period, he was already accepted as the Caribbean's most dapper politician. Anyone who knew him would conclude that sartorial elegance was high on his enjoyment agenda. He was married with a wife and two daughters. His wife Cynthia was the member in the council for the district of St. David's and a minister of social services. Sometime on his return from attending a conference in Jamaica in 1957, Gairy was disfranchised from public office. The charge was one of disruption. The People's Democratic Party (PDP) political meeting was in progress when Gairy led a steel band through the meeting. This kept him away from active politics for five years. Nonetheless, he was active on the trade union front.

This writer had the good fortune to have made Sir Eric Gairy's acquaintance many years ago in St. George's, the capital city, as well as in Castries, when he was impeccably dressed all in white. St. Lucians, for the first time, were seeing him in person. They considered him fascinating. His political exploits intrigued them, but then to see him in person was an absolute delight. The adulation placed him in the realm of a movie idol. He accepted the attention with grace. Gairy proceeded to influence adult suffrage to Grenada.

Could this people's man allow the power of office to transform him from the compassionate father of the nation to a ruthless dictator? Was this conceivable? What changed Gairy? Circumstances of vicious opposition? Unfortunately he set about to initiate the Public Order Act, 1974. Political parties and individuals were prohibited from using loud speakers without police permission. The next year,

1975, evidently when the New Jewel Movement (NJM)intensified its propaganda against him, he, in an act of desperation, introduced the Newspaper Act. This, in essence, made it impossible to publish a newspaper that was political and opposed to Gairy.

Moreover, again in 1978, when indications were that the NJM had not only infiltrated the unions once controlled by Gairy exclusively, but now influenced their every action, the prime minister brought about the Essential Services Act. It would be unlawful for workers to strike in eleven vital categories.

This was evidence that Gairy had now hardened his resolve to maintain his control that appeared to be eroding; he lost his nerves and direction. This signaled that he was pressured into becoming a dictator. That translated to mean that he had embraced oppression of the people—perhaps inadvertently—violating their human rights in the process. This invited rebellion from both the violent and the passive. Noticeably, the lovable and devoted uncle, Gairy, had changed. He was now unrestrained and intolerant of others. Almost everyone was suspect. He now appeared to assume a Dr. Jekyll and Mr. Hyde personality! Many of his supporters who were not of the fawning nature, but believed in fair play and justice, and who were not really enamored of him, found themselves swiftly drifting away from him as a result of this tyrannical behavior. Many, too, who were incurably judgmental by nature, and occupied themselves searching for flaws, were busy at work fueling the flames of disruption and malice against the prime minister. And was he aware of this situation? Unsavory news always traveled fast. And he reacted with swift reprisals against those whom he presumed had ganged up against him.

But there were other characteristics of Gairy that contributed to the hostility towards him. For instance, he proceeded to acquire estates to bring an end to Grenada's plantocracy. But the distribution was questionable. Lands were not apportioned to the rural folk who really needed holdings, rather, it was claimed; they were offered to party hacks who worked the lands and from which the boss profited.

That once good uncle had procured Progress House, an exclusive meeting place for special invitees and those within his circle. In essence, it was a restaurant and bar where invitees were expected to spend lavishly and charged whether they were disposed to pay or not. It was a business proposition from which Gairy himself benefited. The consensus was that he became inordinately greedy and self-centered and eccentric in the process. He was cofounder of the Grenada Spiritual Baptist Church and his seemingly deep faith in God Almighty was contrary to his ruthless, materialistic posture that was tantamount to being diabolical.

Moreover, his preoccupation with the UFO concept and a passionate belief in it to such a degree that he propounded its existence at international forums whenever the opportunity arose. And one of the negatives of that venerable prime minister was that his numerous, paid informers and private police were a bane to the civility of Grenada. The raping of women with impunity was prevalent and became a way of life. But the pièce de résistance was the function of his hotel.

Parties were given and people invited. Champagne and dinner would be served then Gairy would declare the bill would be paid by persons whom he selected. They were charged and dared not protest. Of course, Eric Gairy possessed appeal as he received a deluge of accolades and honorary degrees from several international institutions of learning. Incidentally, Gairy had made himself president for life of the Grenada Manual and Mental Workers Union (GMMWU) and the Grenada United Labor Party (GULP). All these seeming flaws were identified and highlighted by vindictive Caribbean journalists, as Jeff Hackett who claimed he wrote for the *Express* of Trinidad and Tobago. If one were to read his report titled "Burying Gairyism" on the Internet, one would assume that Gairy was Satan himself. The piece is an exercise in denigration.

He writes,"The Grenada government has indicated that Sir Eric Gairy will be treated in death as a national hero by being accorded a state funeral."

He proceeds to write, "On June 19, High Court Judge Lyle St. Paul gave control of his estate to his two daughters, Jennifer and Marcelle Gairy. . . . On Saturday night, his wasted body was found at his hotel home by an official of his union." That Internet piece attempts to destroy some fifty years of sterling service to Grenada. The contempt the so-called journalist feels for Gairy is reflected in his report even after Gairy's death. It is hateful, rather than objective, reporting.

Following the Grenada debacle, I wrote a piece in the *Teller* Magazine that detailed some vital aspects of his political struggle. The piece is titled "Sir Eric Gairy Confuses Grenada."

> Sir Eric Matthew—an enigma of our time—is still the charismatic, God-fearing and flamboyant trade unionist-politician whom many Grenadians loved and feared and hated.
>
> Beyond the windswept and sea-washed borders of Grenada, Sir Eric Gairy is associated with banditry, with ruthlessness and unorthodox habits that earned him widespread discredit in the Caribbean particularly.
>
> The breathings of political leaders, and writings of journalists in this region, reflect an undisguised contempt for this self-educated and skillful politician.
>
> Ironically, though the abuses never ceased to shower upon him, in the midst of it all, Her Majesty the Queen proceeded to bestow a knighthood upon him. Moreover, he is the recipient of some 31 awards, more than all the CARICOM leaders combined can claim to possess.
>
> In my view, no one man can be so hopelessly putrid of character as Sir Eric is so perfectly imaged. He is up against a gullibility of the ignorant [repeated convincing hear-say or

effective propaganda] envy and a sinister intellectual snobbery, the removal of which perhaps only death can ensure.

Evidently, it has never been considered that the then young black man from the rural east of Grenada had emerged—sans a university degree—to liberate his people from a plantation oppressed and prejudiced society, where the white or fair skin pigmentation was the passport to social acceptance.

It amazes, that it little occurs to the several government leaders and idiotic journalists throughout our region that leaders of Eric Gairy's intrinsic strength, tenacity and capacity have no need to enter the portals of a university or like institution to be educated.

Eric Gairy began his trouble-shooting career as a trade unionist in the Dutch Dependency of Aruba. The early struggles on behalf of the disadvantaged and directionless workers brought him both admiration and contempt.

In Grenada in 1951, plantation workers were earning fifty-four cents per day and he set himself the task to agitate to have their earnings raised to one dollar per day.

Energetic, flashy and courageous, this refreshing trade unionist sporting top hat and tails in the blazing sun, led demonstrations to the delight and satisfaction of the workers whom he chose to represent. His exploits journeyed abroad and sheer dash, flair and style endeared him to the peoples of the Caribbean, if not their leaders.

"Uncle Gairy," as he was affectionately termed, struggled for the masses against colonial administration, the entrenched light skin bourgeoisie, ignorance and illiteracy. He triumphed, and the masses adored him.

Grenadians contributed to the celebrated Uncle Gairy image. They were terribly fond of dashing and flamboyant leaders to the point of adoration. They loved Gairy's style, speech and impeccable dress. Save for Jamaica's Hugh Shearer of that period, Gairy was easily the most stylishly dressed head of government in this region.

Eric Gairy's innate style with class was not easily contained. He was abundantly generous to his people. He improved their welfare. Economic, educational and social development. Employment, better roads, better homes, and better and more school, were some of his achievements. He gave priority to them with zeal.

His struggles never ceased. The British suspended the constitution in 1954 and accused him of squander mania. He was arrested and taken to a warship off shore. Gairy's people supported him. The strikes threatened disorder. He was released and he asked his people to cease their hostilities. They did, and such was the power of his influence.

Eric Gairy dominated the Grenadian political scene for seventeen years and created a new black elitist clique. In former years, black was rated the bottom rank of the social ladder. His severest test as a politician was yet to come. And he had earned some degree of antipathy from quite a few people who were opposed to his flamboyant style of politics. Moreover, there were still many who had never accepted him.

After almost twenty years in and out of the highest office of control on Grenada, it would seem that Gairy's excesses as the cultivation or acceptance of criminal elements around him to defend his cause, his influence in the dismissal of some people from jobs, his acquisition of properties among them, calculated to his disadvantage. His invaluable contribution to Grenada was all but forgotten.

Uncle Eric's triumph over his detractors grew replete with the incidence that all seemed to suggest that he nursed a talent for humbling people. And it is this offensive propensity, more than any of his other habits, that generates fear in those who know and don't trust him.

Perceptive and dynamic, Gairy looked forward to independence for Grenada. He attained it in February 1974, a clear five years before any of the other small islands.

By this time in the early seventies, his problems at home began in earnest. Maurice Bishop, a Grenadian, British-trained barrister was back home to change the status quo. He was already indoctrinated to the Communist ideology, but this he never disclosed to the masses. Apart from being also charismatic and fiery, Maurice Bishop was articulate. His power of language earned him increased popularity. Maurice Bishop, Bernard Coard, Kenrick Radix, Unison Whiteman and Teddy Victor and a few others now formed the nucleus of a new Socialist intellectual elitist group. Disguised Communists.

They had sworn to take Grenada into the Communist camp. They formed the New Jewel Movement and began a systematic propaganda campaign against Gairy and his government. The intensity of it proved infinitely effective. It tarnished Gairy convincingly. Gairy knew they were Communists and warned the nation. Unsuspecting Grenadians did not believe him. This was when his austere measures were introduced.

The hostility unleashed against the New Jewel Movement Communists to counter their struggle to usurp him was counterproductive. He was fighting for survival. He played it rough as he should and most human beings would. And from Barbados came shouts of banditry while from elsewhere, including St. Lucia and Dominica, came disparaging grumblings. The hatred of Gairy was undisguised.

Pitiably, small island regional peoples—irrespective of education—demonstrated an astonishing fund of gullibility that defied comparison. They hastened to believe and condemn with no evidence, asserting a morality and correctness not gifted to man. They are inordinately judgmental. Moreover, they court an irresistible passion for charting the direction of other peoples lives totally, disregarding that each person's distinct individuality is designed to give a color of mosaic pattern of existence that, in turn, brings rewards and satisfaction to represent a multiplicity-of-tastes-order to mankind.

The New Jewel Movement, led by Maurice Bishop, accused Sir Eric Gairy of corruption, rigging of elections, maladministration, murder and other horrendous crimes.

Recently, there was evidence that the burning down of homes and maiming of cattle, the spiriting away of one Ivy Bishop, a policeman, Belmar, and the murder of another police can be attributed to the New Jewel Movement. This revelation broke in prison by the Bishop criminal element, in a confession to some members of Gairy's so called Mongoose Gang. Grenadians now know the truth, but still fear a tarnished Gairy.

It is remarkable that the Bishop Regime's atrocities exceeded Gairy's. People were arrested, held in detention, tortured and murdered by the New Jewel Communists, yet Bishop is celebrated as a martyr.

Hitherto, since the events of October 19, 1983 and the joint intervention in Grenada to re-navigate its course back into democratic waters, and also the return of Gairy to Grenada, no evidence of corruption or murder has yet been found to arraign that former prime minister.

That Gairy's return to Grenada at this time has caused widespread confusion is an understatement. The fear that his party, the Grenada United Labor Party (GULP) may return to power is real. Obviously the fear re-affirms a disenchantment of Gairy.

However, his supporters who were in the majority are not likely to let him down, though he could lose some stragglers and a few aged in death. Positively the greater percentage of the younger folk will not vote for him.

Grenadians at this time are unsure of which party to offer a mandate to control their destiny. Several parties are offering themselves for the contest. The Grenada National Party (GNP) led by the former Chief Minister Herbert Blaize; the Grenada United Labor Party (GULP) under the direction of Sir Eric Gairy; the Grenada Democratic Movement (GDM) controlled by Dr. Francis Alexis, UWI lecturer; the National Democratic Party (NDP) fronted by George Brizan and the United People's Party (UPP) headed by Winston Whyte, a former Parliamentarian are those to the fore.

At this time, mergers were being contemplated to combat the GULP primarily and the New Jewel Movement to a lesser extent.

The average Grenadian was remarkably intelligent; therefore, one need not despair of the decision at the polls. It should be appreciated, however, that on one hand, to conjecture that this intelligence will serve to restrain Grenadians from casting the vote in favor of Gairy, while on the other hand, should the prevailing confusion keep Gairy's detractors away from voting for another party, Gairy's GULP could emerge with a landslide victory as predicted by him.

Gairy was utterly confident and not inactive. And so were some members of the routed New Jewel Movement. They were determined to reassert their Communist grip on Grenada. It was to be hoped that confusion will pale under, as sober thinking returned to the majority of voters on polling day in that island, where spice and nutmeg, "and everything nice" grew more abundantly than anywhere else in this hostile world.

When next I spoke to Sir Eric Matthew Gairy in St. George's for the *Teller* Magazine, after he had been deposed by the Maurice Bishop gang, Gairy had spent a few years living in New York City. He, doubtless, had been maligned to the limits of endurance. And the propaganda took its toll. It was believed and this shattered him. He positively had exhausted his steam. He was in ill health.

The article in the *Teller* Magazine was headed "Gairy's So-Called Mongoose Gang."

Throughout the Caribbean today, and perhaps farther afield, any mention of the word "Mongoose" brings to mind rapidly visions of a Gairy terror on Grenada.

Such was the power and infinite effect of the early seventies Communist public relations or propaganda, unleashed to pervade the Caribbean. It was believable. It was convincing.

The "Mongoose Gang" slogan began in the early seventies, when three notorious street fighters joined the Grenada Manual and Mental General Workers Union, of which Eric Gairy was president. They joined the union so they would enjoy the benefits of employment. At that time, the Pan American Health Organization and the World Health Organization (PAHO-WHO) were undertaking an eradication campaign in Grenada. The street fighters found employment with PAHO-WHO's unit, eradicating Mongooses and Rats. Soon after, the brawlers who do not resist brawls engaged themselves in a sensational brawl.

As is customary, brawls attract crowds. Later, a passerby enquired after the contestants. The reply was, "Those fellows on the Mongoose Gang. You know they killing off Mongooses and Rats."

The opposition New Jewel Movement with imported expert Communist propagandists from North Korea, USA and East Germany began the most vicious denigration of a man in the political history of the Caribbean. Gairy's secret police Mongoose Gang was born.

Up against the influence of the New Jewel Movement's sophisticated aids, Gairy, a tough and fearless politician, was nonetheless pedestrian in this context, to understand the destructive force with which he had to contend.

Gairy fought back with the criminal element that supported him. This writer would and with all the fury I could muster. Anyone would if twenty-five years of struggle on the masses behalf were slipping away. Every Caribbean politician would be encouraged to have the support of strong, fearless and lawless men to keep the peace at public meetings when the law itself appears effete and repeatedly fails to live up to expectations. John Compton's UWP wished they had it in 1979, when they were showered with human excrement.

First, Ivy Bishop, a policeman and a Maurice Bishop supporter, disappeared. Gairy was accused of having wasted him. Recent reports now suggest that the Cubans had spirited him away to Havana. He had, unfortunately, seen them in the process of one of their shipment-of-arms deliveries one evening when he was out fishing. An almost insane series of maiming of cattle and other livestock began and ended in the burning down of homes. Belmar, also a policeman, was killed. Maurice Bishop's father was killed and all other atrocities were attributed to Gairy.

Gairy inadvertently compounded the issue with his government's acquisition of properties. It was a desperate attempt to contain his foes and detractors. He lost the propaganda struggle but won two successive elections. He was then accused of rigging the elections. His horrendous public relations abroad convinced almost every politician and journalist in the region. And they were utterly liberal in their condemnation of him.

All the government leaders: Barrow, Adams, Compton, Bird, Manley, Seaga, and Charles, among others, read the Communist propaganda and ceaselessly unleashed scathing assaults upon Gairy. Propaganda was their evidence. They were sympathetic to Maurice Bishop. He had their blessings in his struggle to liberate Grenada from that "dictator-tyrant Gairy." The campaign was taken by Maurice Bishop himself into the United States to the then influential American

> Ambassador to the United Nations Andrew Young and the Black American Caucus. They too were convinced.
>
> While Gairy is certainly not sacrosanct and is subject to the same abuses and excesses of the Caribbean politician who embraces integrity in public and jettisons it in private, in my view, because of his unswerving belief in the Almighty—for which he is also spurned—he could be less prone to the ills of public office than his counterparts.
>
> Confession by Maurice Bishop's criminal element in prison—since Grenada was liberated from its ill fate—disclosed that they committed all the crimes they had attributed to Gairy's so-called Mongoose Gang. Grenadians are now wiser.
>
> Courageous Sir Eric Gairy is back in Grenada and the many people we spoke with in Grenada confess that Gairy proved to be less criminal and corrupt than the consummate Communist Maurice Bishop. And it was his reluctance to share the revolution's leadership and also the confession of one comrade, Keith Roberts, that Bishop had ordered him to kill his comrade Bernard Coard in Carriacou almost two years ago, when Coard resigned from the central committee; that effectively brought about the destruction of the so-called revolution. In view of the widespread contempt shared by Caribbean government leaders for Sir Eric Gairy, what would be their posture if his GULP won the forthcoming elections?

This writer and an untold number of people in Grenada and the world mourn the passing away of an illustrious Grenadian and Caribbean leader. Incidentally, when Sir Eric Gairy was deposed by Maurice Bishop and his gang, his properties were confiscated by the New Jewel Movement. Since then, Eric Gairy and his heirs had resorted to litigation to have the properties returned to no avail. Succeeding governments resisted the return. Sir Eric passed away in August, 1997. He was seventy-five years old. Nonetheless, his daughters Jennifer and Marcelle persisted and took the case to the Privy Council in London. In June, 2001, the Privy Council ordered the incumbent government to return the confiscated properties to the heirs of Sir Eric immediately and in addition imposed three million Eastern Caribbean dollars in compensation. Even in death, the widely despised dynamic politician Sir Eric triumphed. The Bible says, "When God is on your side, who can be against you!" One year before his death, he was honored by being named the Father of Independence by the prime minister, Dr. Keith Mitchell. He was vindicated.

That he was charismatic is unquestionable. Like Martin Luther King, Jr., Sir Eric Matthew Gairy's design comes perhaps just once in a century.

Chapter 5

Norman Washington Manley
MM; BA; BCL; LLD; MP.
Former Chief Minister and Premier Of Jamaica

If anyone were privileged to have met this sedate gentleman of immense academic abilities, they would not associate Norman Washington Manley with the sport of sprinting. Yet at Jamaica College, he established a world record of ten seconds over a one hundred yards dash. Incredibly, this then unprecedented feat remained unbroken for forty years. He was at the meet when his first son Douglas equaled the feat. Manley the athlete? That's correct. And his ensuing performances were all exemplary, even when he seemingly lost.

Norman Manley, former statesman, legislator, consulting attorney, chief minister, premier of Jamaica, opposition leader in the Jamaica parliament, founder and president of the Peoples' National Party (PNP). This brilliant Jamaican and West Indian son, it seemed, was destined to be a leader of substance. And we had been so fortunate. Born in 1898, Norman Manley impacted the Caribbean with that uncommon skill, as though reserved for those almighty-chosen-few to inherit.

The Caribbean today is a better place as a result of the direct initiative of Norman Manley. Though he failed to realize his vision of a permanent West Indies Federation that would truly integrate the peoples of this Caribbean, his contribution was nonetheless invaluable. His efforts in conjunction with that of the Barbadian stalwart Sir Grantley Adams materialized in an ill-fated federation. The concept did materialize. But it was palpably premature. And this was the condition of most of the Caribbean leaders at that time. These men were undisciplined. And they are no less undisciplined today.

Born in Roxborough, Manchester on July 4, 1893, Manley completed elementary schooling then entered Beckford and Smith High School, Wolmers. From the early age of seven he displayed signals of a very fertile brain. At seventeen he was well entrenched in the Jamaica College academic life. He was also a splendid athlete. At a most memorable sports meet he chalked up a record for the one hundred yards dash. The young, dashing student excelled in all his subjects. He equaled his athletic performance with his academic. On graduation, he accepted a teaching post at Jamaica College for a short stint of two months. Manley won a prestigious Rhodes Scholarship in 1914, and entered Jesus College of Oxford University in Britain that same year. The First World War, however, intervened. The patriotic Manley joined the Army and later won for his bravery a Military Medal. He had enlisted in the Royal Artillery as a gunner. The loss of his brother Roy wounded him terribly but he survived the war as a corporal. On conclusion of the hostilities, the young soldier resumed his studies at Oxford University, where he graduated and earned a Bachelor of Arts Degree.

Manley then proceeded to study for the Bar. He passed his finals with a certificate of Honor. Remarkably, he was also a Lee Essay Prizeman at Gray's Inn. With such an impressive academic record, the qualified Barrister-at-Law was called to the Bar in 1921.

Would such a debonair, attractive and highly intelligent man continue through life alone? Not likely. He was in love with his vivacious cousin, Edna Swithenbank, one of Britain's most celebrated artists. His mother and Edna's mother were sisters. They pledged themselves as one at a quiet wedding considering the incestuous implications. The marriage produced two sons, Douglas, born on May 30, 1922, and Michael on December 10, 1924. Shortly after, on his return to Jamaica in 1922, Attorney Manley was admitted to the Jamaican courts. From this juncture, the brilliant attorney, who adopted the watchword, "Work is the best medicine," proceeded to put this maxim into practice. He allowed his career to fuel him and he was made a Queen's Council (Q.C.). He was so talented an attorney, Manley was engaged to appear in almost every major criminal case of some significance, in addition to circuit actions of importance heard in the thirties and forties in Jamaica. He earned the distinction of having never lost a murder case he defended.

Manley brought much respect to the Caribbean. He was the first Jamaican and West Indian attorney to appear before the Judicial Committee of the Privy Council in London. There he successfully represented his client, an American corporation. The dispute was over a trademark and which company should be allowed to use the trade name "Vicks Vapor Rub." That case was quite celebrated and it enhanced his reputation as a skilled attorney. He also represented a black youth charged for murder during a clash of black and white gangs in England. He won that case and the youth was acquitted. Manley's son Michael once described his father as "the greatest lawyer in the world."

Another celebrated case was the defense of his cousin and political opponent and trade union adversary, Alexander Bustamante, who was accused of a violation of trade union ethics that was tantamount to sedition. Manley won that case in 1938. Two years earlier, in 1936, Norman Manley had founded the Jamaica Welfare, Ltd. He held the chairmanship for ten years. Then, the Jamaica Welfare Ltd assumed a new title, "the Jamaica Social Welfare Commission."

A man of his leadership skill could not avoid being drawn into politics. The opportunity and privilege to contribute more tangibly to the Jamaican society repeatedly presented itself. The people of British colonial Jamaica, like elsewhere in the British West Indies, were oppressed. Some four hundred years of British rule and where hostilities were a way of life, violence was still a feature in Jamaica! He intended to vigorously champion the people's cause. In September, 1938, the most popular attorney in Jamaica founded the People's National Party (PNP). He was elected president, and the constitution was so designed that the president must stand for election every year. His record of integrity made it easy for the executive to elect him every year for thirty-one years until his retirement in 1969. A rationale behind this political move was to champion the advent of adult suffrage in Jamaica. It will be remembered that Britain had for over a century concentrated on Jamaica as a sugar plantation and a base for its ships. Of the notorious seafarers, Captain Morgan was perhaps the best known, and thousands over the years have fought and died in conflict over Jamaica. It is invaluable real estate.

The energetic and now powerful Manley became a persistent advocate of a West Indies Federation and he deserves enormous credit for his indefatigable efforts as he need not have done this. He could have pursued a North American destiny as Cheddi Jagan had intended to "pursue a continental destiny." Jamaica was some 1,150 miles from St. Lucia, the most central of the Eastern Caribbean chain of islands. Moreover, Jamaicans knew very little about these Eastern Caribbean islands. They seemed just as distant from Jamaica as Britain was. Many Jamaicans became acquainted with the East Caribbean islands when the two Maple Leaf ships, *Federal Palm* and *Federal Maple*, commenced a regular trade throughout the region from Guyana in the South to Jamaica in the North. Although another medium-sized, auxiliary ship, the *West Indian*—acquired out of India—had started the route before the federal ships, they should be given credit for the increased awareness of the existence of the Eastern Caribbean states that comprised part of the chain of islands of the West Indies. Jamaicans began visiting the islands and became better acquainted with them.

Nonetheless, Manley was an educated man who had cultivated the propensity to give service to others. He proclaimed that a Federation of the West Indies was imperative for "geographical, economic, educational, social and cultural development of the region."

Similarly, he campaigned for internal self-government for Jamaica. Unfortunately his PNP was unsuccessful in the first general elections, called under the new Constitution in 1944. And it should be noted that this new Constitution was allowed as a direct result of an intense collaborative effort by Manley and his cousin Bustamante. As boys, they had lived at the Manley's family home in Kingston until Bustamante was adopted by a Spaniard and taken to Spain. Ubiquitous, Manley seemed inexhaustible. He traveled up the chain of the British West Indies as a relentless advocate of Federation of the grouping. He held meetings and gave numerous eloquent speeches explaining the benefits of Federation. In each member territory, the campaign for representatives to be elected was being intensified. Norman Manley, perhaps more than any other politician, save Grantley Adams of Barbados, Dr. Carl La Corbiniere of St. Lucia and Robert Bradshaw of St. Kitts-Nevis-Anguilla, exerted himself to hasten the process. Finally, the West Indies Federation was realized in 1958 to endless jubilation.

It will be recalled that in Jamaica, Manley and his PNP contested the general elections in 1949. The PNP failed again to capture the legislature but Manley was elected. He was the official leader of the opposition. And his contribution could be described as immeasurable. He kept the ruling administration alert with his incisive debates that invariably were no less caustic than stimulating. In 1953, an event unprecedented in the West Indies occurred. The Constitution of the People's Progressive Party (PPP) led by Dr. Cheddi Jagan in British Guiana was suspended. It was claimed by Sir Alfred Savage, the then governor of that colony, that the prevailing posture of the government ministers indicated that the government was heading into communism. The Winston Churchill government in London suspended the Constitution. It was a difficult period for British Guiana as all the colonial leaders had agreed with Britain on the suspension. As the opposition in the Jamaica legislature, Manley dispatched a cable to the British government, "It was a betrayal of the cause of colonial peoples the world over and a reckless and stupid betrayal of those who voted for them."

Why he was so driven to condemn a Caribbean counterpart was still unclear, save that he feared a radical application of the Communist ideology, which was alien and thought to be considered a betrayal of the region's traditional heritage. So what? But then, experience had testified that he was a man of strong views either for or against.

Manley was confident that people would understand the necessity for federation. The region had been suffering a political fragmentation that placed it at a disadvantage. The period of micro-nation states was now passé. Survival depended on larger groupings of human resources that contributed to the supply and demand capacity of the nation state. Moreover, the larger the size, the more effective and forceful the idea being conveyed to influence a result with some sort of efficacy. Manley was a vocal advocate of an egalitarian society. He advanced that a society where there was a dearth of opportunity for almost everyone could not claim to be pursuing the true philosophy of adequate national development. Political prejudices were too rampant. And he pointed out that true socialism was the avenue to pursue. This thought, however, conflicted with his condemnation of Cheddi Jagan earlier. Jagan propounded socialism. In one of his very many speeches, Manley declared, "What is the essence of socialism? It was never put any better than by Professor Arthur Lewis when he said with stark simplicity, 'Socialism is about equality.' Equality," Manley continued, "only exists when the exploitation implicit in the class system is abandoned."

This seemingly persistent Norman Manley and his PNP won the general elections in 1955 and he became the chief minister. Again in 1959 he and his party were returned to office and the British government granted full internal self-government. He was now the premier of Jamaica and the minister of development. Manley's aspiration was to, as rapidly as possible, initiate the introduction of the sort of institutions that must enhance the socioeconomic, educational and cultural development of the Jamaican people, particularly the masses. He played a significant role in the establishment of the Bank of Jamaica, the Social Welfare Commission, the Cooperative Movement, and the Jamaica National Trust, among others. He performed phenomenally to create a better and more just and comfortable Jamaica.

The premier's political opponent was his cousin Bustamante, who also was the president of the Bustamante Industrial Trade Union and controlled thousands of workers who believed in him. Bustamante was an integrationist. He had indicated that on several occasions, speaking on platforms in the Eastern Caribbean. But political expediency impelled him to oppose the premier relative to Jamaica and the West Indies Federation. General elections were some fourteen months away. But Manley opted to take the issue to the people in a referendum on the secession of Jamaica from an infant federation. Bustamante encouraged this referendum. This was a classic example of intellectual immorality, but it was amply documented that when crafty politicians assumed a momentum in the quest for the power of office that stood within reach, they gave absolutely no quarter. Bustamante convinced Jamaicans that he wanted to take Jamaica out of that relationship called federation. He had tested the thinking of his Union membership and, evidently, it was consistent with the mood of the rest of the nation. They did not comprehend the benefits of federation. At one point, he told Jamaicans that the Eastern Caribbean islands were suffering abject poverty and the British wanted to get rid of them.

"In the circumstances Jamaica would be forced to carry the burden of support of these poor islands." Jamaicans believed him. They wanted out.

A powerful intellectual who trusted the sincerity and probity of people, Norman Manley, however, miscalculated. Doubtless, he was also naïve. He was too clean a character of integrity—a rare politician—to presume that birds of one feather would hesitate or resent flocking together.

Manley perceived an English-speaking Caribbean nation being led by Jamaica, the largest island unit. But sadly, Jamaicans courted other ideas planted in their thinking by Bustamante. This occurred in life. Your story was true, but the person who listened thought the other side of the story was more credible. You lost and the bad guy won. This was the case of the beautiful gentleman Manley. He lost the referendum. And he, a brilliant and proud man, could not accept that the majority of the peoples of this world do almost invariably behave senselessly. Why? Simply that they pursue their own agenda—sane or insane! And perhaps this accounts for Manley's frustration that led to his retirement, again perhaps prematurely. He was determined to see the realization of one West Indian or Caribbean nation. Unity in the Caribbean then was only an exquisite Manley vision. At this moment of writing, attempts are repeating themselves.

In a booklet titled *East Caribbean Unity*, a compilation of two significant speeches on Caribbean unification, the former prime minister of St. Vincent and the Grenadines, James Mitchell, said, "At this point in time in our history, I feel a strong sense of worry about the twentieth century closing and leaving us all stranded. As I travel around the world, I get even more worried. I worry when I see and study the rate of progress in the Far East, worry when I witness the impact of the battles between the old giants of the West and the new giants of the East. I worry when I see the strong uniting to increase their strength, and I worry about the indecisiveness of the weak and their and our disunity." Mitchell was targeting a verity.

In the year 2001, the Caribbean leaders are still shamelessly straggling in a torpor of self-indulgence. For instance, India is a sub-continent with over one billion people. It is headed by one governor general and politically led by one prime minister. This English-speaking Caribbean, one of the smallest regions in the world with miniscule population of 6.1 million, placed itself on display with eleven governors general and eleven prime ministers! This is ludicrous!

These leaders would veer off course as they failed to grasp both the concept and precept of a Caribbean nation of one people, and the oppressive society from which they were jettisoned psychologically affected their psyche. British colonial color prejudice had propelled these casualties to shelter themselves within and under the umbrella of education. This acquisition of education is only one step. To discipline oneself was another. The discipline primarily shaped the determination to travel along the difficult route of life with integrity. Education free of discipline was meaningless. It was merely a leverage that proved untenable as it yielded to temptation at the slightest provocation.

Discipline conducts behavior. Education offers immense benefits, but very many people, as in the case of wealth, cannot handle its possession. Education, in many cases, allowed some people to display their cunning prowess. They perceived situations subjectively rather than objectively. And they stayed immovably obstinate. The crux of the problem was the fact that most of them had not had the opportunity to practice and cultivate decency and integrity.

Shot out of being penury stricken, they aimed at education as a conduit to transport them from the environment of their youth. At this new juncture or milestone of their lives, they were in a state of confusion, being unable to perform adequately. These educated morons sought to become representatives of the people, though unable to regulate their lives. At meetings they proceeded to put their education on display. Most of their decisions were invariably less representative of the sensible views of the people, but rather more of their own. They were motivated by their own uncultivated agenda. They became self indulgently protective of their position. Their upbringing was less than civil—education rescued them and they were not prepared to abandon their holding for the good of the majority. As they saw it, education was designed to be acquired to one's advantage in life. This was the dilemma that cultivated gentlemen and statesmen from Jamaica faced with the West Indies Federation. He inadvertently got involved with rascals as politicians and he learned that too late. The young Norman Manley could not conceive of being betrayed by his own people, to whom he had introduced adult suffrage. Obviously, he was unacquainted with the East African proverb that, "If you save my life and one second after, I have occasion to oppose you—I will."

Moreover, Manley's well-intentioned visions of federation were dashed. Jamaicans had opted to reject federation. While to him, this eventuality was inconceivable, he proceeded to arrange for Jamaica's smooth and prudent withdrawal from the West Indies Federation. Moreover, with remarkable discipline, he formed a joint committee to work and produce a constitution to facilitate an independent Jamaica. Still undaunted, he elected himself to be chairman of the committee. This service was vital and had to be done properly with close scrutiny on all the connecting elements. Reports suggested that he chaired the sessions with "rare distinction" and free of the irritating bitterness of a loser he led the team to negotiate Jamaica's independence from Britain.

The independence hurdle was complete. Now Manley concentrated on going to the people to re-elect him to office. After all, there was no one more brilliant in Jamaica and he had given some thirty-one years of dedicated public service to Jamaica. His campaign was nothing short of splendid. He was at the zenith of his oratorical distillations as he proceeded to flay the opposition whom he claimed "employed lies, subterfuge and hypocrisy." Jamaicans listened and voted for the opposition. Bustamante and his Jamaica Labor Party (JLP) won the elections to become that country's new prime minister. This was a traumatic experience for Manley. He accepted his rejection as "man's prerogative to choose his course in life—the clear road or the obstacle-cluttered uncertain short-cut."

In spite of these setbacks to his political career, Manley accepted his role as opposition leader and perhaps more than any other politician in Jamaica before him, initiated the definitive action role expected of the opposition in parliament of undeveloped or developing nations universally. His superior standard of parliamentary opposition is now a legacy too often found, hard put to follow.

But like any exquisite melody that fails to play on indefinitely, Norman Manley opted to end his public career. He retired in 1969, and at what was considered his last public expressions to his PNP's annual conference he summarized the mission of his political career: "I say that the mission of my generation was to win self-government for Jamaica. To win political power, which is the final power for the black masses of my country from which I spring. I am proud to stand here today and say to you who fought that fight with me, say it with gladness and pride. Mission accomplished for my generation."

He opted for retirement and handed over the leadership of the party to his capable son Michael in 1969. Later, his passing away on September 2 of that same year was mourned throughout the Caribbean that he attempted to integrate to no avail. As this writer saw it, Caribbean leaders were diseased by the salt of the sea that separated them. Fragmentation evidently kept them sheltered like potentates within their own domain. Seemingly this will not be traded in our lifetime. That enormously talented Jamaican and Caribbean attorney-politician-statesman will ever be cemented in this region's history.

Chapter 6

Dr. Cheddi Jagan

Former Chief Minister, Premier, Prime Minister and President of the Co-operative Republic Of Guyana

Perhaps Dr. Cheddi Jagan, a truly affable human being, deserved a posthumous medal for the strength of his Marxist conviction that both intrigued and fascinated the Caribbean. Unfortunately, though Dr. Jagan has yet to be accused of being corrupt or of suffering from cupidity as several of his Caribbean counterparts, he was despised for his honesty and holding on tenaciously to his ideological conviction. He was distinctly different from most of the leaders of his time, including his former intellectual colleague, the tyrant Forbes Burnham. In fact, he was free from the numerous ills of his political colleagues. Anthony Mark Jones in his *Caribbean Men* booklet identified that a "combination of specific reasons" could have fashioned Dr. Jagan into the unorthodox leader that he turned out to be. That, in my view, was a reasonably acceptable analysis of Jagan's persona. Yet Jones failed to point out that Jagan was infinitely more intelligent and perceptive than most of the Caribbean leaders in office during his era. I am rather fortunate that I knew Dr. Jagan in my lifetime. I was a young reporter and feature writer at the *Evening Post* in Georgetown. He was the premier of British Guiana. After forty-three years, on reflection, he had been my most stimulating interviewee (both print and radio). He had never failed to be gentle, courteous, articulate, considerate, perceptive and humble.

Many of our leaders were admittedly quite knowledgeable, but Cheddi Jagan possessed wisdom and discernment. He marshaled far greater powers of understanding of the intricacies of international politics, and the growth and development of states, than any of his colleagues without exception. Born on March 22, 1918 at Port Mourant on the East Coast of Georgetown, Cheddi Jagan grew up as a child in abject poverty. His father was an indentured laborer from India who struggled exhaustively with no seeming signs that some modicum of economic progress was in the offing.

A child was not responsible for his condition, whether penury stricken or not. But he never forgot the condition of seeming hopelessness in the brutal struggle for survival in the twenties and thirties. How could he forget the boyhood home and inhuman conditions? He begged the question why poverty seemed chained to so many people, while others clearly enjoyed the thrill of regimenting workers as though they were inanimate objects of contempt? Cheddi Jagan witnessed the pain of being a child of the underprivileged class, and the failure of his parents to realize their goal to provide adequately for the family. The youthful experiences were traumatic such as would affect his adolescence on into adulthood. Was it of necessity that people were colonized, then oppressed and suppressed?

Young Jagan from elementary school entered Queen's College, the principal secondary school in the capital city of Georgetown. He was an above average student who worked hard. His supplementary education took him on to Howard University and Northwestern University in the USA. There he was amply prepared for the social and political studies with which he was deluged. Later he persevered and qualified as a dentist at the University of Chicago. While attending the University of Chicago, he met the alluring American-born, Socialist-oriented Janet Rosenberg. Not long after, they decided to pool their resources in marriage.

Cheddi Jagan and his wife returned to British Guiana and, almost inevitably, they sailed into politics. As compared with others, their views were considered absolutely radical. British Guiana was a British colony and repressive. It had pursued a life of dependency. Now the Jagans struggled to bring about a change in British Guiana generally. Janet had evolved from a family well known for the expression of strong Communist sympathies. Invariably sound and articulate, Dr. Jagan was able to impress his listeners. To politically motivate the people, Dr. Jagan began the drive from the grass roots level. He organized a group called the Political Affairs Committee. This soon emerged into a full-fledged political entity named the Peoples Progressive Party (PPP) in 1947. Jagan was elected leader and Forbes Burnham, chairman.

Universally, every political party published its cherished philosophy and it was termed a manifesto. The PPP was no exception. It found enormous appeal with supporters. At that period of British Guiana's history of neglect, and when Guianese were not even allowed to vote, they welcomed the local initiative to bring about the introduction of adult suffrage. There was preponderance on the immediate end to colonialism, and the sub-continent of India's independence was used as an example.

At this early point of their struggle, Jagan and his PPP had registered a considerable following and this represented some 90 percent of the Guianese population. Following an intensely emotional campaign, general elections were called in April 1953. The PPP won eighteen of the twenty-four seats in the House of Assembly. The ensuing months found Dr. Jagan's views increasingly more candid and refreshing, but potentially dangerous. They were considered alien and totally anti-Anglo-American. He termed it "paternalistic and repressive." Understandably, the British authorities feared the threat of the Communist ideology. The British themselves were obnoxious Imperialists with their Capitalist system. It was their way of life and did not pay supine inattention to the possibility of disruption.

Cheddi Jagan and Janet Jagan, the secretary of the PPP, did not disguise their political persuasion. It was anti-Capitalist, but British Guiana was still a colony! The British took note of the provocative pronouncements that they considered subversive. The then governor, Sir Alfred Savage, recommended a suspension of the Constitution, and the portfolios of cabinet ministers were taken away from them. The British colonial office sent in British troops to restore—they claimed—some semblance of order.

Cheddi Jagan and Forbes Burnham journeyed to the British capital to articulate their case. They were met with widespread sympathies throughout Britain, Europe, Africa and India. On their return home, a restriction was imposed on their movements. Jagan and some of his ministers disregarded a travel restriction order. They were arrested and imprisoned for six months. Relative to that period of unrest, Dr. Jagan writes in his booklet, *A West Indian State*—pro-Imperialist or anti-Imperialist:

> Practically all the West Indian leaders praised the British government for destroying the Constitution and forcefully removing the People's Progressive Party from government in 1953. Guiana's PPP, Joshua's People's Political Party in St. Vincent and the Grenadines, and the West Indies Independence Party of Trinidad and Tobago were the only political organizations, which had not joined the Cold War. Grantley Adams had sent a telegram congratulating the British government.
>
> Our experience of Jagan and his sympathizers leads us to feel certain that social and economic progress in the British West Indies is much more likely to be harmed by that sort of person than by the most reactionary. However much we must regret suspension of the Constitution, we should deplore far

> more the continuance of a government that put Communist ideology before the good of the people.

Alexander Bustamante, the chief minister of Jamaica, had dispatched:

> If British Guiana were fighting for complete self-government within the democratic nations, I would have stood behind British Guiana, but British Guiana today can get no sympathy from me—can get no sympathy from the free thinking world. I am sorry for the people there. I am not sorry for the leaders. They are not leaders at all. They do not know what they are doing.

Other Caribbean leaders had dispatched similar messages. Elsewhere, however, the British faced strong and relentless criticism. The action was described as "immoral and unjustifiable" within Britain. The opposition in the House of Commons flayed the government of Winston Churchill and the British press enjoyed a field day chiding the government.

The frontline Caribbean leaders are indicative of the most prominent who are totally involved in the political struggle for leadership. The result was they contacted the British government to congratulate them on the suspension of the constitution in British Guiana. Grantley Adams especially was steeped in the British tradition of paternalism. He was less likely to yield to radical change than Manley, and Manley less than Eric Williams. These men were primarily scholars. They saw the need to control the lives of the masses, in the old and familiar tradition though the original intention was to bring about a change for the people. They were trained as attorneys and at professorship, not as leaders of governments. They resorted to almost unending rhetoric as keen administrative abilities were wanting. They were in that context speaking for themselves rather than for the masses. In the circumstances such as what existed, these leaders never sought the views of the people; they simply and arbitrarily expressed their sentiments in behalf of the individual states. In reality, these leaders were tantamount to being long fed on sardines; consequently, it was difficult to have them accede to the unfamiliar fare of caviar.

Grantley Adams, a prominent attorney, could take his English wife and drop her off at the Aquatic Club but he could not enter. He accepted it that he was black. That was the sort of social aberration Cheddi Jagan would not condone, nor would his wife Janet. The British perpetuated this unacceptable behavior. It was considered "private club exclusivity."

I wrote a piece many years ago in the *Teller* that related to the debacle that concerned Dr. Jagan. It was headed "Slaves in Freedom." Here is an excerpt:

> And the democratic system under which we live permits the more clever, industrious and ruthless to control the destiny of the entire working class to the latter's disadvantage. Injustice and inequality prevail after 150 years under the façade of liberty.
>
> Leaders of the Caribbean—and this was not singular to St. Lucians—may be likened to neo-Colonists. They are masters of greed and exploitation. It is an accomplishment practiced as integral elements of their survival philosophy. Everyone agrees that the society is unjust and corrupt, yet the system prevails.
>
> After 150 years, unemployment, degradation, sweatshop labor, deplorable housing, sickening health facilities, ignorance, illiteracy and squalor are permanent features of the human condition in the Caribbean. Pride, decency, integrity and respect are irreparably scuttled.

Dr. Jagan was not unaware of the Caribbean mentality. The leaders would not be empathetic. His Socialist ideology was the alien rival of capitalism on which these leaders were nurtured. To them, all the prejudices and disadvantages of an abrasive capitalism were oppressive, but nonetheless served to strengthen them. They would sooner perish with capitalism rather than experiment with what the Anglo-Americans proclaimed evil communism, though it had made enormous strides internationally. The Anglo-American propaganda machinery broadcast that socialism was sinister. It was a strategy to inject fear and rejection in people within the Capitalist system.

Dr. Jagan and his PPP had incurred the displeasure of most of the sycophantic Caribbean leaders. His seemingly bad behavior earned him enemies. On his return to British Guiana and serving his six months in prison, he intensified his political campaigns. At that juncture, his popularity increased considerably within the East Indian population in British Guiana.

The British government, on removal of the PPP government, then proceeded to install an interim government. But there was no end of political activities though the British military troops were in attendance in Guiana. By this time, Dr. Jagan had lost the post as party leader to Forbes Burnham. Moreover, these two major players in this volatile political scenario did not harmonize their expressions. There was dissention between Dr. Jagan and the chairman of the party, Forbes Burnham. It was ludicrous. The PPP had two leaders. Cheddi Jagan had the support of one faction, and the Party Chairman Burnham, the other faction. Jagan controlled the support of most of those of Eastern Indian heritage, and the next elections would be a bitterly contested racial race. Burnham had been the favorite of Guianese of African descent. The other racial elements in British Guiana were Chinese, Portuguese, Whites, and Amerindians. These were up to grab. The slogan *Apan Jhaat*—that translates to mean "Vote for your Own," a seemingly innocuous statement, penetrated the interior of Guiana, and the country was never the same again. This gave birth to a nasty, violent racial revolution that damaged, perhaps irreparably, the once sweet harmony and tranquility that existed among the races, but especially between the two factions born of the African and East Indian heritages.

Inevitably, this vicious racial campaign was efficacious. The 55 percent representation of East Indians of the total population of British Guiana gave a distinct advantage to Cheddi Jagan and his PPP. He and Forbes Burnham had inevitably fractured to destroy their association and cooperation, but anyone who followed their relationship closely must have concluded that it would be only a matter of time before a severance would occur. Forbes Burnham was immensely talented to lead, not to follow. A man of his intellectual capacity would not hesitate to usurp a leader whom he presumed possessed fewer abilities than he had. Now there existed a dilemma of two leaders of two PPPs. The obvious bitterness and discontent that pervaded the land of British Guiana had intensified. There was open undisguised racial conflict. Hatred was widespread.

The British called elections for August 1957. Undoubtedly, as was expected, the votes polled were race inspired. Dr. Jagan's PPP won nine of the fourteen seats in the legislature. Statistics suggested that many were disillusioned with the trend politics had followed. Former friends who enjoyed a warm relationship were now suspicious of one another. Politics had divided them into reprehensible racial factions. And the effects were negative. Unemployment had soared by some 24 percent, which indicated a marked decline in an economy that otherwise should have prospered with a Guianese government in control of the country.

A crucial meeting of the Burnham faction was held to determine their identification. Burnham suggested a new name for their party—People's National Congress (PNC). This was adopted. Now officially, there was a new party on the political scene. This succeeded the faction of PPP that Burnham had led. The PNC also introduced a newspaper to the electorate. The paper to rival the PPP newspaper *Thunder* was named the *New Nation*. Working from their own methodical timetable as usual, the British considered and held a constitutional conference in London during 1960. This conference would decide on a change of the electoral system. The opposition leader, Burnham, had argued for a system of Proportional Representation (PR). That a voter should be free of the restriction of voting within a district constituency, the machinery should accommodate one single constituency and the citizen is allowed to vote for the party in which he chooses to place his trust. Dr. Jagan had vociferously opposed this Proportional Representation. In the circumstances, his PPP would be placed at a distinct disadvantage. The arguments were advanced, and on conclusion the British disregarded them. Rather, the conservative government of Winston Churchill offered them what they described as an advanced constitution that allowed a status of internal self-government. Britain would retain responsibility for foreign or external affairs, which included defense. Incidentally, it will be recalled that at the last election held in 1957 there existed fourteen constituencies, each represented by a single candidate.

The demarcation of the new constituencies was effected by an electoral commission appointed by the British government. Now in place were new boundaries with thirty-five constituencies with one representative each. This determination, Jagan discerned, would affect him and his PPP. He termed the boundaries rearrangement "gerrymandering by the British." His persistent argument against Proportional Representation, which was being advocated by the opposition leader Burnham, was an Anglo-American collaboration. Nonetheless, he won the elections by a percentage of votes numerically, but the combined votes of the parties excluded him from office, which would have been a third term in office.

It should be remembered that the 1959 elections were one racially divisive proposition; some 40 percent of the electorate had kept away from the polls. Since then, British Guiana's premiere business entrepreneur, Peter D'Aguair, saw the need to make a difference on the political landscape. He and others of similar capitalist persuasion decided to pool their resources. Substantial votes were of the minority races such as Portuguese, Chinese, mixed races, Amerindians and whites. They could reject the two major parties, the PPP and PNC, whose supporters were evidently emotional.

The new political organization was called the United Force (UF). This group of business interests was bent on winning political power. The UF candidates campaigned throughout British Guiana on a totally pro-capitalist and anti-communism ticket. The intention was to attract and recruit those who feared the PPP's socialism or communism and dubious about the PNC riding on too comfortably between the two galloping steeds of capitalism and socialism. Cheddi Jagan's PPP support was primarily rural with smatterings in the urban areas. Burnham's PNC support came from the urban areas with black concentrations. The professions and intellectuals were also a percentage of his support base.

In 1960, the British held a constitutional conference in London. Cheddi Jagan argued for independence from Britain and Burnham spoke of elections on the basis of Proportional Representation. Not long after, independence should follow. General elections were held in 1961 with three political parties vying to control the majority seats in the thirty-five-member National Assembly.

At this juncture, talk was rife of a probable merger between the PNC and the UF. Later, however, this was dismissed through innuendoes that a demand of leadership in exchange for collaboration was resisted and rejected by Burnham. Nonetheless, general elections were held in 1961 and the People's Progressive Party triumphed again. PPP won twenty seats. This represented 42.6 percent of total votes. The PNC came in next with eleven seats, representing 41 percent of the votes. The United Force was next with four seats, a total of 16.3 percent.

Mathematically, Jagan and his PPP had lost much from its power base. Either PPP had lost 7.94 percent to the PNC or that percentage was withheld in storage for the next elections. Parties after many years of struggle should increase vote percentages. Not lose them.

Several months later, the Cheddi Jagan government ran into difficulty. A budget was introduced, it was claimed by those who opposed it, that it was designed to further tax the underprivileged especially. Within days it was evident that chaos was in the offing. Jagan was a people's man. It was inconceivable that he would be afflicted with insensitivity to a degree such as would lend to a calculated imposition on the poor. Nonetheless, it should be recalled that the leader of the opposition, then Forbes Burnham, was also the president of the Guiana Trade Union Council. He agitated and led demonstrations in Georgetown. He recruited artisans, clerks, and students, housewives, even professionals to join forces with strikers. They were impressive in their expressions of disapproval of the budget.

One of the favorite target areas for demonstrations was the National Assembly building. The two parties in opposition collaborated to march peacefully around that building. While permission was allowed to demonstrate, it would seem that the parliament area was declared restricted. This was met with defiance. Premier Jagan ordered the riot squad to rain tear gas to disperse the crowds. This was an error of judgment. The peaceful protests exploded into lawlessness and the rampage of Georgetown. When men were determined, they risked death for their conviction. The situation was now one of anarchy. Premier Jagan appealed to the British government and troops were brought in to quell the disorder.

Jagan made the sensible decision to withdraw the budget. He also requested a Commonwealth Commission of Inquiry. The view was to save face. He had contended that the disorder was intended to overthrow his legitimate government. The PPP leader did get the Commission of Inquiry. The result was found not to be any attempt to overthrow his government but rather "a situation comparable to an act of spontaneous combustion when some highly fermented substance is subjected to long pressure."

Cheddi Jagan was an astute politician and the experiences of disorder from the fifties served to solidify his discernment. He was not unaware of the deviousness of man. In politics, most practitioners were invariably driven to abandon integrity to win office. He was told of the alliance between Burnham and D'Aguiar. This did not unduly disturb him. His wife Janet assured him that they would find a way "to circumvent these nefarious forces that were ganging up."

The British government extended an invitation to the three political leaders to travel to London in October 1962 for a Constitutional Conference. This would be a prelude to the granting of independence. The conference in London was largely confrontational. Jagan, as customary, advanced that Proportional Representation was unacceptable as it seemed a deliberate attempt to make it easier for the opposition forces to expel him from office. He reiterated that he already had the mandate from supporters, the majority racial group and others to seek independence. Burnham, like Jagan, asked for independence, but he emphasized as he did at previous conferences that Proportional Representation was a prerequisite to precede independence. The will of the people should be reflected in general elections then followed by independence.

D'Auguiar was visibly lukewarm on the independence issue, as though he tried to maintain a stance to the far right and a short distance from Burnham. The British Secretary of State for the Colonies Duncan Sandys could not get an agreement and, after weeks of repetitive arguments, he was disillusioned by the uncooperative behavior of the Guianese politicians. He adjourned the conference and sent them back home.

Another constitutional conference was convened for October, 1963. Unfortunately, the postures of the three politicians were unchanged. The secretary of state was determined that a solution would be arrived at. He fortified himself with a letter that allowed him freedom to choose an equitable solution that should accommodate the independence aspirations of British Guiana. He dropped a shattering statement—if they failed to sign the document, he would adjourn the conference and postpone that desirable independence date indefinitely. Sandys got their attention. The document was signed. It stated that:

1. New elections would be held under British supervision before the end of 1964.
2. The electoral system would be changed to that of Proportional Representation to elect a fifty-three-member unicameral House of Assembly.
3. A new voters list would be prepared under British supervision.
4. A constitutional conference to set the date for independence would be convened as soon as possible after the election.

Cheddi Jagan had signed that letter, and after he had read it. But he was opposed to Proportional Representation. Yet he signed the document. Why? Following the conference, Jagan stated at a press conference, "I do not feel bound to accept Sandys decision." Jagan was palpably unhappy. Distressed, he said, "The solution Sandys had in mind is likely to put the PPP out of office."

Tension had re-instated itself in British Guiana and, not long after, violence recommenced throughout the country. The campaign for general elections was at full throttle. Jagan attributed the chaos in Guiana to the British imposition of Proportional Representation. He gave to understand that the violence would cease only when Sandys withdrew the plan.

The disorder was widespread in British Guiana. The British government stepped in and amended the Constitution to allow the governor to effect a state of emergency if necessary. Governor Sir Richard Luyt had replaced Sir Alfred Savage, who had suspended the Constitution in 1953, and jailed Cheddi Jagan and Forbes Burnham and other government ministers. Now, Governor Luyt proceeded to incarcerate frontline members of the PPP. Deputy premier Brindley Benn (of African heritage) was one of them. Some members of the opposition PNC were also arrested and imprisoned. Governor Richard Luyt brought in the British troops again. This was September 1964. Order was restored, though tension was still alive and would take some time to diffuse. Registration for election, set for December 7, 1966, had been in progress for some time. Never had British Guiana witnessed such a deluge of publicity materials. It was estimated that millions of booklets, posters, fliers, banners, pamphlets and other printed material and tokens to induce voters were in circulation from the opposition camp. Au passant two other parties entered the political fray. The leaders were both of the East Indian heritages. They were, some claim, "opportunists." Anti-communism was their message; the hope being to win the faint-hearted, the skeptics, the ambivalent, or undecided away from the PPP.

Remarkably, the two main opposition parties, PNC and UF, had devised some kind of diabolical alliance to resist any temptation to assault each other. On the surface there was only one issue evident that they had in common—to remove Cheddi Jagan and the PPP from the government, to wrest political power away from him. And they succeeded decisively. The result of this crucial election was almost similar to that of 1961, but as Dr. Jagan had feared, the change to Proportional Representation tipped the balance against him. As Forbes Burnham anticipated, the scale would tip in his favor. It was questionable that he registered—and at every election since then—5 percent, 10 percent, and 20 percent more than the registered African vote. Burnham was cunning. And he found a device to usher him into office and to keep him there indefinitely.

Peter D'Aguiar's United Force carried 12.5 percent of the vote. This was some 4 percent less than the official registration for the combined races (e.g. Portuguese, English, Amerindians, mixed races, and Chinese). Cheddi Jagan's PPP registered almost the same 45 percent of his East Indian registered vote. Though, in essence, his PPP was the majority party, the opposition parties pooled their votes to overwhelm him. They won the elections and British Guiana. Doubtless, there was considerable intrigue in politics, though this knowledge was esoteric. But the Anglo-American machinery had influenced many election results all over the world, particularly in undeveloped and developing societies or regions as the Caribbean. Mendicancy was the root cause of the problem. The effect was we were brutally manipulated in a manner that proved propitious to the metropolitan interests.

In his book *A West Indian State: Pro-Imperialist or Anti-Imperialist*, Cheddi Jagan quoted a passage in Arthur Schlessinger, Jr.'s bestseller, *A Thousand Days: John F. Kennedy in the White House.* It established how the Anglo-American cooperation and influence had been effectively one of dictation rather than cooperation from 1776. Reading historian Schlessinger's 858-page book was totally enlightening.

It will be recalled that Forbes Burnham had requested a change in constituency system. He advocated one of the Proportional Representation (PR), which the British disregarded until the President Kennedy administration suggested that PR should be introduced in British Guiana to remove the PPP government of Cheddi Jagan.

Reading Jagan's book, one was left with the impression that "the British described Burnham as an opportunist, racist and demagogue intent on personal power." This piqued my interest, as I do have Schlessinger's book on my library shelf. I bought the book seven years ago in Toronto, Canada but never took the time to read it.

Jagan was correct about the British opinion of Burnham, but he omitted the American opinion of him, that:

> . . . his party, the PPP, lived by the clichés of an impassioned, quasi-Marxist, anti-colonialist socialism. Events had convinced us that Jagan, though perhaps not a disciplined communist, had that kind of deep pro-communist emotion which only sustained experience with communism could cure.

This was saying that Cheddi Jagan's facts were only half-truths. That the United States assisted Burnham into office was not mentioned at all. This suggests that if this were the case, Schlessinger would not fail to make mention of it. That is, unless it was covertly CIA, as usual free of presidential directive. Forbes Burnham's entry into office locked Cheddi Jagan out and confined him to the political wilderness for almost two decades.

The accusation that the Burnham government rigged every election since he assumed office in 1994 has been confirmed by Neville John, a friend and former editor of the *Daily Chronicle* in Georgetown. Neville and I were in Toronto in 1974. He had just arrived in Toronto from Essex, England. We spoke of former times in Georgetown when, as a practicing attorney, Forbes Burnham was paid $700 to represent Neville. He warned Neville that if he failed to bring the balance of $100 to his office, he would not appear to defend him in court. Three hundred dollars of the $700 had come from my wallet.

"By the way, I rigged the elections for Forbes in England," Neville stated.

"You did? How could you? And why did you? If I recall correctly, in 1958, in Georgetown, you paid Forbes Burnham $700, short of $100, to represent you. He failed to appear because you were $100 short of $800. I was there. Three hundred of that seven were mine. Have you forgotten?"

"Oh how could I? Well, I did recover my $700. I charged the embassy £700, plus another £700 for his discourtesy and greed. I was paid £1,400 to rig the overseas vote in London. Forbes has devised this method to stay in office in perpetuity. Cheddi may as well give it up. He doesn't stand a chance."

Then, in Toronto, it seemed that Neville John was correct. But he was wrong. Forbes Burnham expired, but could not rig his turn to pass on. Having been anchored in the political wilderness for almost twenty years, the indomitable Cheddi Jagan and his PPP contested the elections on October 5, 1990 and this time triumphed.

Seemingly, the evil entity that repeatedly kept him out of office retreated from service. Now fair and free elections had been restored. Jagan still retained his intellectual vitality, but now seventy-four years old, the embattled years had slowed his steps.

The struggle to resurrect Guyana's economy that had been almost comatose with Burnham's compliments was intensified, and his lifting of some repressive measures did not prove a proposition of ease. Cheddi Jagan's life journey was almost at its end. He had fought one relentless but fascinating battle. Four years in office as president of Guyana, and his wife Janet prime minister, he fell ill on February 14, 1996. He was flown to the USA for treatment, but this was to no avail. He died in March and was returned to Guyana for burial. The foremost vociferous advocate of Marxism in this region—doubtless proud of his contribution to human development—passed on.

Positively, Dr. Cheddi Barret Jagan was one of the most charismatic of Caribbean leaders of our epoch, and a place for him had inevitably been etched on the pages for confrontational politics of Caribbean history. The name Cheddi Jagan is now synonymous with Guyana and the wider Caribbean.

CHAPTER 7

Michael Norman Manley
B.SC. Econ. London
Former Prime Minister Jamaica

When the illustrious sons of Jamaica and the Caribbean will have been numbered, there is no doubt the chronicle will include the debonair, handsome, gregarious trade unionist, journalist, economist, leader of the People's National Party (PNP), and former prime minister, Michael Norman Manley.

The celebrated English and Jamaican sculptor Edna Manley, wife of Rhodes Scholar, barrister-at-law, politician, trade unionist, and former premier of Jamaica, Norman Washington Manley, gave birth to a son on December 10, 1924. He was named Michael Norman Manley. No one gave it a thought then, but this newborn was destined to bring about changes for the better in the lives of an untold number of people throughout his native Jamaica and elsewhere in the world.

Being the son of celebrities, Michael could be described by many then as privileged. He and his older brother Douglas enjoyed what they later termed "a normal and satisfactory upbringing. Mother was always there when we needed her." In an interview on the Canadian Broadcasting Corporation (CBC) television in Toronto in 1988, Michael Manley explained that he and his brother knew "it would not be easy for us as both our parents were accomplished." I had listened to the then prime minister of Jamaica whenever he visited Toronto. The then prime minister of Canada, Pierre Elliott Trudeau, and Mr. Manley were close friends. CBC television was made available to him to articulate issues that affected him and Jamaica. Thousands of Jamaicans were then residing in Toronto and elsewhere in Canada.

The American administration banned American citizens from visiting Jamaica, which was a major tourist destination in the Caribbean. "We will not be dictated to by the U.S. government. Their behavior is wicked; it's reprehensible." Canada's prime minister understood the American behavior. As next-door neighbors, it was Trudeau who curbed the American domination and expansion in Canada. It was in Toronto, Canada that I wrote a piece on Michael Manley and the other leaders of the Caribbean. They were indecisive and feckless as it related to integrating the region. The piece was titled "Will CARICOM States Shack-up together?" It is summarized in one paragraph:

> To speculate on events that affect the Caribbean was but one of the frequent exercises of nationalistic West Indians who, for economic or other reasons, were transplanted into Canada. The big event of the past month was the Caribbean assistance of $200 million to Jamaica. This was discussed at length at the Castries Barber Salon on Bathurst Street, Toronto. The consensus was that the commonwealth Caribbean states were destined to shack up together as one integrated unit. But perhaps only a series of crises could bring about this realization.

In retrospect, Michael Manley, like his father Norman before him, attended in his adolescence the Jamaica College in Kingston. Perhaps not a Rhodes Scholar like his father, Michael Manley nonetheless was studious and bright. He was admitted to the University of London in 1944. Britain was then at war with Germany. Manpower was needed. Soldiers were being conscripted from all the British

Colonies and commonwealth states were also sending assistance. Michael Manley enlisted in the Royal Canadian Air Force in 1943. Later, he was demobilized at the rank of pilot officer. He resumed civilian life and his studies at the University of London in 1945. This war pilot went on to graduate with a B.S. in Economics. It was during that period that he met that dashing French Canadian bon vivant from Montreal, Pierre Elliott Trudeau. They remained life-long friends.

On graduation, Manley was employed as a freelance journalist with the British Broadcasting Corporation (BBC) until 1950 to 1951. As most students do following graduation and a stint of working experience, he headed home to Jamaica in December, 1951. Michael Manley loved the journalism profession. He joined the news publication, *Public Opinion* as associate editor. Following his father Norman, he joined the People's National Party (PNP) and was elected to the executive, a member of cabinets, in 1952.

Brilliant and dynamic Michael Manley resigned from the *Public Opinion* and joined the staff of the National Workers Union. As a full-time staff member of the NWU, he began his trade union activities to improve the welfare of sugar workers. He initiated the drive to wrench away the firm grip held by the Bustamante Industrial Trade Union (BITU) on the sugar industry. The president of BITU, W. A. Bustamante was his cousin. Jamaica was not unknown for violence. His task was enormous: to train, guide and direct effectively. The confrontations with rival groups were not irregular. Michael Manley was elected island-wide supervisor of the union and its vice president in 1955. The struggles were not being made any easier and he discovered that in life few people were gifted with sincerity and probity. Most people were prone to take from you rather than give. The situation in Jamaica was volatile. He organized a strike in the sugar industry in 1959. This led to the establishment of the Goldenburg Commission of Inquiry. Amazingly, this resulted in a record settlement in 1950 of £1,200,000 to workers.

It was superb representation that earned confidence in the leadership. With this success engineered by way of agitation, Michael Manley's popularity increased immensely. He was deemed the labor savior of Jamaica. From then onwards, he was associated with every major change that increased wages and improved working conditions in Jamaica. This tenure of office revolutionizing colonial working conditions embraced the period from 1953 to 1960.

Unavoidably, Michael Manley's administrative abilities were in demand. In 1961, he was elected president of the Caribbean Bauxite and Mineworkers Federation and, in the following year, he was appointed to the Jamaica Senate. If one were to describe Michael Manley then as being busy, that characterization would have been an understatement. Yet he found the time and energy to distribute himself, serving, in addition, on a number of statutory boards and joint industrial councils.

Significantly, Manley was the principal negotiator for the NWU, which then boasted over 101,000 members who were organized in 200 branches throughout Jamaica. One of the outstandingly remarkable events of Michael Manley's life that allowed insight into the genuine character of the man was that of his second marriage. It was at a period when the fair skin color qualified a person for social acceptance throughout the Caribbean with a notorious slavery orientation. Then, the darker you were, the more stigmatized the persona. That was until the Black American entertainer James Brown's philosophy, "Say it loud—I'm black and I'm proud" swept the world. This had an infinitely positive effect on black people. It gave them a psychological leverage to accept themselves as being of a unique creation. As ludicrous as this sounded, this was the norm of total ignorance.

The six-foot two-inch, debonair, handsome, affable, aristocratic and socially well positioned Michael Manley never failed to demonstrate his passion for women. And he admitted that two of his favorite dissipations were the society of women and smoking cigarettes. His poet daughter Rachel in her book *Drumblair* (published by Vintage Canada, a division of Random House, Canada) declared:

> His own world was happiest for him when it included women. He had few male friends and they were even if lifelong merely occasional.

Evidently he was an accomplished romantic, the ultimate loverman, and marriage held no dread for him. Following his graduation from London University, and a brief stay employed with the BBC as a journalist in London, he had made the acquaintance of the white, chic and intelligent Jacqueline. He was in love and consumed with her. Marriage is a serious proposition a person did not venture into with haste. The decision was to share his life with her. The poet daughter Rachel Manley is a product of that marriage. Frequent differences that led to conflicts gave birth to disillusionment. Jacqueline returned to London and they later agreed to a divorce.

The dashing Manley was not inactive, and as though unavoidably, love raised its delicious head again; sensual and powerful. Thelma was an irresistible, gorgeous, exotic dancer of a mixed sort of Indian-Hispanic. He had to possess her exclusively, and would not settle for a mere affair. They sprinted with ease into marriage and given some time, the union was shattered. The marriage ended.

Then entered Barbara, a public relations writer of an advertising agency. She was a stunningly beautiful Ethiopian, princess-like with a noticeable dash of the Asiatic. He loved her enormously. It was believed that she brought some luster to his life and his career, and his parents loved her. Just when it appeared their life together was nothing short of wonderful, tragedy insinuated itself. She was diagnosed with cancer. Family, relatives, friends, acquaintances were all grievously wounded by this sad turn. She later died as her husband held her to him protectively.

The fourth wife was Beverly, a classic ebony beauty and a broadcaster attached to the Jamaican Broadcasting Corporation (JBC). On the surface, the relationship seemed to be ideally harmonious and it shocked Jamaica when it was announced that the marriage was dissolved. It is not unreasonable to presume that the average man having experienced four trials that could be totaled as traumatic failures would be reluctant and dissuaded from any further attempts at matrimony! Fact is, Manley was not an average man but an extraordinary character with an incredibly undaunting perspective on life that held no qualms for him. He was relentlessly fearless. He was irrepressible and confident and this combination propelled him to journey back into marriage as though of necessity. This political stalwart, this trade unionist, this stimulating orator, this writer, this bon vivant extraordinaire, this prime minister of Jamaica was filled to capacity with love and it was vital to share it, not with just any woman, but a special woman who had to be his wife.

Obviously, Manley treasured that state termed marriage. He proposed to the white, vivacious and affable Glynne. It was his last display of his enjoyment of marital bliss. His wife Glynne survived him.

Notwithstanding an utterly packed agenda of activities, Michael Manley was a member of the Caribbean Labor Congress, the Sugar Industry Labor Welfare Board, the Scientific Research Council, the Pensions Authority, Labor Advisory Council. This incredible agenda was all consistent with his watchword, "There are no substitutes for honesty and hard work."

Anyone may assume that Michael Manley's life was filled to capacity such as would not allow him free time to write. He was a regular columnist with an articulateness that touched the senses. But he was also a politician and an active vice president of the

People's National Party (PNP). Eventually, in 1969, he inherited the leadership from his distinguished father, Norman. He contested the general elections in 1972 and won his seat. His PNP also gained the majority seats in the Jamaica House of Assembly. Being leader of the PNP and the prime minister of Jamaica could not be described as positions of ease. Rather, they were charged with complexities and represented stresses.

At that period of the middle to late seventies, the Caribbean, not unlike elsewhere, was affected by the Communist ideology all dressed up as socialism. Prime Minister Manley, like his father, was attracted to socialism, as when cultivated and applied justly everyone benefited, not just a few, while the masses remained indigent as prevailed with capitalism. Britain courted socialism during the years Aneurin Bevan and Harold Wilson were prime minister. And so did most of Africa. Manley then was hugely respected and considered one of the esteemed frontline leaders. As Jamaica's prime minister, he embarked on what political analysts described as a "radical" socialist economic program that was intended to catapult Jamaica out of its stagnation. Fearlessly, he advocated the philosophy of the Non-Aligned Movement—rejected any semblance of support for the then senseless Cold War battle being waged between the then Union of Soviet Socialist Republics (USSR) and the United States of America. He was an eloquent speaker and was frequently in Africa expounding his perceptions on the injustices endemic in the Capitalist strategies as they related to economic planning and development in the under-developed and developing economies of the world, particularly in Africa, the Caribbean, South America and Asia. He was acknowledged as a major third world leader, a stalwart of the Non-Aligned Movement and Socialist International. Quite likely it was perceived by observers and detractors that Manley was promoting communism. This incurred the displeasure of one of his neighbors, considered the most powerful country in the world.

It is not unknown that the United States of America, because of its huge size, human resource, wealth and power of arms, imposed itself as the owner, ruler and controller of this western hemisphere. Moreover, it insinuated itself all over the world, save in the eastern block of Europe, where Russia predominated policing to its interests. This attitude has been universally accepted as a blatant nationalistic malaise termed hegemony.

But then, the USA saw the posture as security or self-preservation. However, what astonished every nation in the world—save Britain, which was the other ruthless Anglo half of the inordinately ambitious Anglo-American predomination from 1776 into this prevailing twenty-first century—was that America nursed an entirely different conception of its role as bully of the world. The USA's right was its might. And this it intended to preserve at any cost. Even mosquitoes will be swatted when necessary. There is the forty-year-old animosity of Cuba and Castro, and as was mentioned earlier, the USA obviously adhered to the philosophy that "if you're a friend of my adversary you are not my friend." This, doubtless, was the dilemma that Michael Manley faced when he assumed the government of Jamaica in 1972. One of the major problems of regions like the Caribbean was its legacy of slavery and poverty the imperialist nations as Britain, France, Holland, Spain and Portugal left behind. These islands were virtually discarded as sugar plantations from such long distances away, then had become unprofitable to maintain. The inhabitants of this region and elsewhere were treated in a manner less than humane. They were considered natives, and not in any way associated with civility. Remember the concept! They were far away lost nations discovered by advanced civilizations.

However, during his tenure of office, Manley proceeded to introduce numerous vital social projects that impacted on the underprivileged generally. He followed the pattern of his father before him. But significantly, he initiated the vigorous effort that earned Jamaica the majority shares in that country's bauxite industry.

It took the civilized British in the Caribbean just as long as it took the American whites to understand that black Americans were no less human than they were. And what astonished all the more was the knowledge that these white Americans had failed to bear it in mind that we were all made of dust with the same red blood flowing through our veins, and we were all sustained by the oxygen that we breathed. The brutality to humans over the centuries by succeeding governments of the British can't possibly escape divine punishment.

The Americans themselves were at this juncture of the crossroads of their nefarious history that was reminiscent of Rome when it predominated the world. The United States of America was in its decline. And no other country in the world suffered repeated tragedies of fires, snowstorms, hurricanes, earthquakes, daily murders, and military tragedies as the USA. According to the Bible, "No one escapes being accountable"—from Babylonia's Nebuchadnezzar in 607 BCE to our common era, and beyond.

Consequently, it was this legacy of poverty left by the British that propelled the need to solicit and accept the charity and goodwill of the USA in this region. But it should be understood that if any state failed to serve the U.S. interests, be it economic expansion or the dubious security reasons, that state will be swatted.

Michael Manley had assumed office at a time when the USA was obtusely intensifying its isolation of Castro and Cuba. That island nation was next to Jamaica. One of Jamaica's principal revenue earning industries was tourism. The economic viability largely depended on this tourism, and the substantial percentage of that business originated out of the USA. There was a noticeable slump in the Jamaica economy and the prevailing political tensions further exacerbated the situation.

Notwithstanding Jamaica's economic struggles at that juncture, the majority of Jamaicans appeared to empathize with their prime minister. He was genuinely a hardworking, considerate and competent prime minister. His woes were led by continuing rising unemployment. Where such a condition existed, one could hazard that danger lurked close by. The idlers were too many and they appeared to increase daily. Regular eruptions of violence followed. In spite of all these negatives, Michael Manley was re-elected to office for another term in 1976.

Having been allowed a lease on his efforts to resuscitate his nation's economy, he proceeded apace with a few adjustments to his socialist economic plan that could not work successfully free of substantial injections of financing. The decline in the tourism industry was the fatal blow to the economy. Manley's political safaris to Africa continued and he consolidated himself as the best known Caribbean leader and of the third world.

Unfortunately, the economic decline in Jamaica persisted. It took a downward spiraling plunge and it never recovered. It had been alleged that the defiant Prime Minister Manley would not disavow Fidel Castro. In fact, Kingston, the capital, was punctuated with Cuban doctors contributing to the health services in Jamaica. Washington resented the Manley administration's relationship with Castro and his presence in Jamaica. It should be remembered that Cuba is an American disease. Manley refused to discontinue his relationship with Castro. Then it was to his detriment. The Central Intelligence Agency—it was alleged—commenced its destabilization. They cultivated the acquaintance of the Jamaica Labor Party and doubtless helped them into office. The months rapidly succeeded each other to another election day in 1980. He and his PNP were soundly defeated. Manley's attempts to restore the health of the economy was admirable. It failed to translate into investments and earnings. Manley lost again to Prime Minister Edward Seaga in 1983, when he called snap elections two years earlier than constitutionally due. The following piece was excerpted from the *Teller* Magazine in 1986:

> Doubtless, Michael Manley, the present opposition leader, had over-asserted himself in office carrying Jamaica into the Socialist camp close up to communism. Positively astute and obstinate, he could not accept being told to end his attachment with Fidel Castro of Cuba. Being next-door neighbors, economic assistance from Havana was readily available to Kingston. Cuban doctors were then a permanent feature in the life of Jamaica and it appeared then that CARICOM was about to lose a senior member.
>
> The Jamaica government's repeated pronouncements of American imperialism had further angered the USA government and a schism had developed and widened. Over a period of three years, two not insignificant features emerged and worsened, namely unemployment and violence. These scampered out of control and Jamaica was totally destabilized. This was the situation that ushered in Edward Seaga and his party into power.

It will be recalled that snap general elections were held in 1983 and Edward Seaga's Jamaica Labor Party (JLP) won, as expected, the majority vote in parliament to form the next government. The next five years in the opposition could not have been the best for Michael Manley's political life, as even that was threatened. Bodyguards were assigned to him. It was not easy to concede, but Jamaica then was one of the most violent countries in the world, close behind the USA. About that time, the Jamaica dollar was already devalued. It never recovered. At this time, it is about the second lowest currency in the Caribbean behind the Guyana dollar.

Here is another excerpt from the *Teller* Magazine on the Jamaica situation:

> This country now appears permanently married to the International Monetary Fund (IMF) and has, among other problems, earned widespread disaffection for the government.
>
> The popularity polls taken in Jamaica have fluctuated and although the most recent reflected some gain to the incumbent, Seaga is aware that the seeming specter of losing the next elections to Michael Manley looms menacingly real.
>
> As it stands, the problems of Jamaica cannot be easily solved in one or two terms; therefore, now or later Seaga must reluctantly give way to Michael Manley. This, as we understand it, represents democracy at work.

Interestingly, there ensued a violent spate of political factional clashes between supporters of Seaga's JLP and supporters of Michael Manley's PNP. Several killings were reported. Jamaica experienced something of a déjà vu. The British bandit Captain Henry Morgan had terrorized the Spanish and French in Jamaica within its territorial waters. Subsequently, he became governor of Jamaica.

Michael Manley won the next election in 1989 and, as a result, served three separate periods as prime minister of Jamaica. During his struggles for nine years in the opposition, Manley took a positive degree of re-orientation. He was a sensitive and flexible leader who was imperfect. In his earlier determination, he had taken a wrong turn away from the viable economic highway. He reviewed it and recognized his folly. Now he was revitalized. He abandoned both his trademark bush jacket and the polemics that he perfected in his castigation of capitalism. Reality pointed to the fact that his very existence was inundated with supply and demand, free market enterprise engineered by private investment and, in particular, foreign investments, the propeller of capitalism. Manley stood up, conceded his error. He took a U-turn and propounded the benefits to be derived from capitalism in our Western society.

Interestingly, he resolved his anti-Imperialist difficulty with the USA government while he still considered Castro of Cuba a valued friend and neighbor. This most agreeable and rehabilitated Manley overwhelmed his rival Seaga at the 1989 general elections. He was again the prime minister of Jamaica for a third time. According to an Associated Press report, Manley claimed that he had learned from his mistakes: "I think there are two types of people. Those who won't learn and those who try to," he said. "I try to learn." This identifies him as a politician of class.

Doubtless, the many years of multiple stresses took their toll on this wonderful human being. The spells of illness repeated themselves to such a degree that he agreed to retire. He handed over the prime ministership and the leadership of the PNP to the competent Percival James Patterson in 1992. Manley had been suffering from prostate cancer. He died in 1997. He was survived by his wife Glynne, three daughters and two sons.

When it was announced that this brilliant and charismatic son of Jamaica—who had contributed so immeasurably to enhancing the welfare of most of his people—had passed away, a dark cloud seemed to hover over Jamaica. It was a colossal loss, not only to Jamaica, but the entire Caribbean, Africa, and the world in general. Michael Norman Manley unquestionably will be registered in the pages of history as one of the beloved illustrious sons of Jamaica, Africa and the Caribbean.

CHAPTER 8

The Right Honorable
Dr. Eric Eustace Williams, Ph.D.
Former Chief Minister, Premier and Prime Minister of Trinidad and Tobago

Eric Eustace Williams emerged into this world of conflict on September 25, 1911. He was the son of humble parents, his father being a middle salaried government employee, and his mother the typical stay-at-home housewife. The colonial island of Trinidad at that period was not unlike any other British West Indies territory. They were all overseas, residential, slave-sustained, sugar estate utilities of imperial Britain.

How could anyone at that time have discerned that the mathematical equation, "One from ten leaves nought," or "I will break Chaguaramas or Chaguaramas will break me!" or "Money is no problem," "When I talk, let no damn dog bark", or "If you're not with me, dust be your destiny," would be attributed to little Williams later in life. These are all illuminating breathings which gave birth to postures that affected the lives of tens of thousands in Trinidad and Tobago, the wider Caribbean and beyond.

Attending elementary school, the little boy Eric displayed the potential to be an exceptional student. He was utterly receptive. At the Tranquility Boys' Intermediate at the age of ten, he won one of eight scholarships and entered the Queen's Royal College (QRC). That was in 1922. From there onwards, his education was state financed. Diminutive in stature and fond of cricket and football, Eric Williams was skilled in passing examinations with ease. Repeatedly he proved to be a prodigious learner and went on to win the QRC's coveted prize. This was a consensus of votes by both teachers and students that reflected the best example of academic excellence.

Like most scholars, study was a pastime he enjoyed. In fact, acquiring intellect was presumed the felicity of this young man's life. Eric Williams accelerated his scholastic pace and, in 1931, he won the Trinidad Island scholarship to Oxford University in Britain. Obviously being a noted scholar was a privilege that tended to imbue in one an especial celebrity-like status. The young intellectual star worked a stint as acting master at his alma mater, Queens Royal College, and at the Government Teachers' Training Institution.

Doubtless erudite, the little Williams entered St. Catherine's Society Oxford in 1932 and, not unexpectedly, excelled. At that elitist institution, where for centuries the young from varying economic backgrounds intermixed as students with one purpose in mind—to graduate—Williams experienced the unkind visits of racial and other social ills. These were less battering than slight bruising. He was from the colonial Caribbean island of Trinidad. It was a cosmopolitan society where many were afflicted with false values beyond limits. He was constrained to concede it, but this was one of life's factors. Eric Williams did not allow these mundane irritations to distract him. He had resolved that there were specific people-related follies or foibles that it would prove impossible to remedy. A person obviated being swamped by them, or rather, one deflected them by the disregard route but remembered them as experiences that were stored away in the fund of knowledge for perhaps later retrieval.

Scholar Eric Williams was fiercely competitive. He studied and performed from seemingly unending zeal. The result was sterling academic performance. He attained his Bachelor of Arts in reading for history; the study stimulated his interest to embrace teaching as his profession. This positively was a departure from the long held tendency of colonial students to read for law, medicine or engineering. However, the pièce de résistance was that at this elitist institution, punctuated with the rich and aristocratic from Britain and all over the world, Williams triumphed. That was in 1935. He complained of being discriminated against at classes at Oxford. He was often placed at the far rear where it was difficult to hear the instruction with facility. Often he was forced to strain his organ. He charged that his hearing problem developed at that institution. He placed first at St. Catherine's Society, Oxford and he attained First Class of the History Honors School. Notably, it had been many years since the school had taken this distinction in history. His reward was the House Scholarship of St. Catherine's Society.

The encomiums were numerous, and he intensified his academic zeal. In 1936, consistent with his scholarship winning habit, he was awarded the Leathersellers Exhibition Scholarship. But Williams was just heating up. This was followed by taking Oxford University's Senior Student Scholarship during the academic period of 1936 to 1938. To crown his efforts, he was offered the Beit Fund Grant for research in colonial history.

Trinidadian author Anthony Mark Jones writes in his book, *Eric Eustace Williams—His Publics,* that at that time in London, C. L. R. James, Trinidadian author of *The Black Jacobins*, and who had taught Eric Williams at the Queen's Royal College in Trinidad, influenced the decision to tackle colonial slavery in the West Indies. Williams had visited him for the weekend and suggested that he would be pursuing his doctorate, but as any historian, he was unsure which angle he ought to embrace. C. L. R. James suggested to him that he should seriously consider Abolition and Emancipation of Slavery in the British West Indies. He pointed out to him that during his own research in France to write *The Black Jacobins*—and he had taken Williams with him to Paris more than once—he had seen the need for this sort of revelation. This gave birth to a celebrated and marvelous dissertation titled "Economic Aspects of Abolition and Emancipation of Slavery in the British West Indies." He commenced it in 1936, completed the thesis and received his doctorate in philosophy in 1938.

Oxford was proud of this brilliant Caribbean scholar and graduate, a result of that institution's education. Later in 1964, Dr. Williams was awarded the Fellowship of St. Catherine College and a year later, in 1965, an honorary Doctor of Civil Laws degree.

By this time, it was not just all studies and no romance. The young Williams had met his first wife, Elsie Ruberio, presumably while he was acting master at his alma mater, Queen's Royal College in Port of Spain. She was the attractive daughter of J. Ruberio, a wine merchant from South Quay. Her mother originated from St. Vincent and the Grenadines. Evidently, this wife was an educated woman, as she also journeyed to London and engaged herself in studies. She and her scholar boyfriend, Eric Williams, got married in London. That first marriage produced one son, Alistair, and one daughter, Pamela. The young couple, following the completion of his doctorate and its subsequent publication in book form, moved to Washington DC, USA. He assumed an appointment as assistant professor of social and political science at Howard University. Later, he was appointed to the full professorship, and he lectured until 1942. The marriage ended in divorce a few years later.

Dr. Williams' second marriage was to his rather pretty secretary, Joyce Moyou. She was the mother of the enchanting Erica who, when grown, was her father's constant traveling companion. This wife Joyce, according to the Anthony Mark Jones report in his book *Eric Eustace Williams—His Publics*, gave him invaluable assistance, typing all his manuscripts and bringing some order to his academic agenda. Unfortunately, she passed away before his transition to being the powerful, money-is-no-problem leader of Trinidad and Tobago.

Dr. Williams' third marriage was veiled in some dubious elements. This wife was a Guyanese doctor named Mayleen Mook Sang. She apparently was unable to stabilize the relationship. At that time, it will be recalled the press had reported her claims of abuse and violence by her husband, Dr. Williams. Upwards to today, an intriguing mystery surrounds that marriage. Perhaps it may not have been consummated. There was talk of a marriage annulment.

Recognized as being refreshingly cerebral and doubtless destined to make a contribution to education and history in particular, Dr. Williams was given a Julius Rosenwold Fellowship for travel and study in Cuba, Haiti, the Dominican Republic and Puerto Rico. This sojourn was hugely successful and covered the years 1940 through 1942.

The now popular, respected and eminent scholar was contracted as a consultant for the Anglo-American Commission in Washington, DC in 1943. By then, he had written another book, *The Negro in the Caribbean*, in 1942. This was being consistent with the discipline of being an historian. Any historian of substance must have this capacity not just imparting knowledge in classrooms, but should codify in writing for the preservation of the knowledge acquired. This then was history being held in store for posterity. That publication was followed by several books, *Capitalism and Slavery* (1944), *Education in the British West Indies* (1946), *Inward Hunger: The Education of a Prime Minister*, *History of the People of Trinidad and Tobago* (1948), *Documents of West Indian History*, and *From Columbus to Castro* (1979).

As fate directed it, Dr. Williams was returned to his homeland Trinidad in 1948 where he assumed the position of research secretary of the Caribbean Commission. Distressingly by this time, perhaps the peculiar pressures associated with the academic profession had victimized the marriage relationship of Dr. Williams. He and his wife had separated and irreconcilable differences further wedged them apart and kept them there. A divorce followed. It must be concluded that either an exceedingly busy working schedule, which was a frivolous excuse, or increasingly avenging defiance compounded that problem. Dr. Williams failed to meet his support payments, as many men did, and it was not because of inadequate earnings. Neither was it because of any contribution of his support to his parents and his eleven siblings back in Port of Spain, Trinidad. He was the second of thirteen children; a sister, the first, had died many years earlier prior to any thought of his academic odyssey being conceived. It could be reasoned also that, even as the eldest of twelve surviving siblings, with a Christian obligation to contribute to their welfare, which included their education, he had his limits. That even a respected philosopher and historian must have knowledge that a person was constrained to extend his expense beyond his income. Assisting his parents and siblings would not in any way place his immediate family—his wife and children—at a disadvantage. Was the professor a noted womanizer? It was the Chinese philosopher Confucius who cautioned centuries ago that a man who has a family and is expected to lead and succeed in public office "should avoid the society of women." This still holds true today.

Another theory concerning his indebtedness was a speculation that secretly he may have been a gambler, or nursed a proclivity to the stock exchange. Upwards to today, these had not been proven and perhaps only a cherished reticent few may know the precise details of the celebrated professor's domestic debacle. The courts in the USA considered the professor's persistent reluctance to meet support for his family an odious disregard and violation of the family law. They warned that if he failed to meet payments by an ordered deadline, he would be arrested and incarcerated.

Professor Williams was not noted for any inordinate dissipation. True his indulgence in drinking was above that of the average beer drinker. But he did not consume beer or any other liquor to such a degree, as would upset his equilibrium. He perhaps reluctantly made some payments to obviate an arrest, but he further avoided such a possibility by ensconcing himself in his homeland Trinidad.

It was presumed that the support debt owed, which he had fatuously allowed to accumulate, threatened the professor's freedom. This motivated the acceptance of the position of research secretary of the Caribbean Commission in Port of Spain. Not long after he was promoted to deputy chairman of the Caribbean Research Council of the Caribbean Commission. This office anchored him in the Caribbean from 1948 to 1955. On reflection, given Dr. Williams' international reputation as a brilliant academic, it pointed to a practicality that he could have best served the wider world in the United States of America, Canada or Europe, but judiciously chose, however reluctantly, to serve in the Caribbean. Ultimately, it proved propitious to Trinidad and Tobago and the wider Caribbean.

At this juncture, one cannot help but wonder in what course Trinidad and Tobago and the Federation of the West Indies would have taken if Dr. Eric Williams had not made the decision to remain in his hometown! He, philosopher and historian who was in demand in the wider world, was now forced by circumstances into politics. But as we, au passant, mentioned relative to the academic demand for proficient historians, C. L. R. James' observation in the *Black Jacobins* (published by W. H. Allen and Company, the Sekforde House, London) should be inserted here: C. L. R. James points out:

> Today by a natural reaction we tend to be personification of the social forces, great men being merely or nearly instruments in the hands of economic destiny. As so often the truth does not lie in between. Great men make history, but only such history as it is possible for them to make. Their freedom

> of achievement is limited by the necessities of their environment. To portray the limits of those necessities and realization, complete or partial of all possibilities, that is the true business of the historian.

Does the preceding statement vary in any manner in content or form to a representation of Dr. Eric Williams, the historian who now chose a new career in politics? How could the two entities merge free of conflict? Could they and would they complement each other? Why would a reputable historian and philosopher abandon these disciplines to be a politician?

The philosopher and the historian unswervingly pursue truth. Politics is inevitably one of calculated expediency. The shifts of position must be geared to circumstances irrespective of truth—this contradicts and is a variance with philosophy and history. Would it be fair to assume that Dr. Williams, a great historian and philosopher, was an instrument in the hands of destiny? Did his family-support indebtedness force him to abscond to Trinidad?

Dr. Williams' working relationship with his colleagues at the Caribbean Commission was not free of conflicts. As he later explained to huge crowds in Woodford Square in the heart of Port of Spain, "The Commission's function was intended to investigate situations with a view to improving conditions for the Caribbean states. Competent Caribbean professionals were available, but expatriates who are unfamiliar with the Caribbean were still being brought in to work."

This sentiment was probably expressed in no uncertain a manner and probably repeated. This led to the decision not to renew his contract. In essence, Dr. Williams was dismissed from his position with the Commission. He served both in Puerto Rico and in Port of Spain and was privileged to visit and attend meetings in almost every Caribbean territory.

Unknowingly, that Trinidadian philosopher and historian's dismissal was perhaps fortuitously a catalyst for the ensuing phenomenal changes in Trinidad and Tobago politics.

The erudite Trinidadian proceeded to embark on a series of political lectures to the citizens of Trinidad and Tobago. The other Caribbean islands were also in political transition. The venue for these illuminating lectures was Woodford Square. They were eloquent, incisive and provocative. It was tantamount to a distinct lesson in Caribbeanization; it was indoctrination and the populace responded enthusiastically. They were proud of this world-famed Trinidadian professor, who was now back home to educate them. However, the crucial moment that gave an appearance that Dr. Williams would enter the arena of politics was the moment of his public debate with Fr. Basil Matthews, a Dominican priest. The learned Dr. Williams triumphed, as he was abundantly skilled in his profession, where a strong command of language was a prerequisite for success. This notable event gave birth to the conception for the formation of the People's National Movement (PNM) in 1956.

While Trinidad and Tobago was doubtless the most cosmopolitan of all the Caribbean states, enormous credit had been attributed to Dr. Williams for influencing the veering away from a similar Black-East Indian racial tragedy, as prevails in Guyana today. In Guyana the situation was somewhat reversed. The East Indians are numerically superior in total population percentage. In Trinidad, it would be naïve to believe there are no prejudices. Later, another prominent religious figure, Anglican Archbishop Abdullah, had challenged Dr. Williams to a debate on Woodford Square. Dr. Williams had made himself available, but the Archbishop failed to appear. He, however, challenged Dr. Williams to take some form of punitive measure against the Jehovah Witness religious group in Trinidad and Tobago. He charged that they did not vote! Eric Williams responded that Abdullah should go to the prisons, then check the thousands of criminals incarcerated, identify their religion and, if he found a Jehovah Witness among them, let him know. His information was that all criminals were Anglicans, Roman Catholics, Methodists, Seventh Day Adventists and people of other religious persuasions. He pointed out Jehovah Witnesses paid their taxes. The prejudices were multiple. These existed in every province within which homosapiens co-exist. But it was a more acceptable appreciation of life's realities from a sophisticated perspective than the ensuing senseless posture that obtained in Guyana.

An acknowledged authority on Caribbean history, the question arose of what ideological stand this new political leader will embrace when his new PNM is launched. He had read Marx, Lenin and Trotsky while at Oxford. But since he had crossed the Atlantic to settle in North America, and while he engaged in journeys through the Americas, the doctor seemed to have courted some degree of ambivalence. While his breathings reflected empathy with both pragmatism and capitalism, his early Socialist beliefs appeared to be wavering and leaning to the side of economic cupidity so endemic in capitalism. He appeared to discount that socialism, if and when practiced in its true form, served the people infinitely better than the "might is right" of capitalism philosophy, along with concomitant ills and weaknesses cultivated by greed and corruption. This capitalism bred haves and have-nots. Socialism failed when those who were privileged, administratively abused this privilege, indulging the behavior of Capitalists. This ambivalent posture by Williams, the political leader of PNM, opened him to the charge of being considered mercurial.

Notwithstanding, Dr. Williams did redirect the political perspective of his fellow Trinidadians. Political speeches laced with harangues were totally informative and educational, and Anglo American imperialism was constantly being bombarded. The University of Woodford Square became a most popular venue for the PNM. Beyond doubt, the following was considerable; at one of his most memorable addresses to the masses, he articulated emotionally:

> I was born here and here I stay, with the people of Trinidad and Tobago, who educated me free of charge for nine years at Oxford, who have made me what I am or who I have been or might be at any time; the victims of the very pressures which I have been fighting against for twelve years. I am going to let down my bucket where I am right here with you in the British West Indies.

From there on, Dr. Williams took control of the nation of Trinidad and Tobago.

Dr. Williams launched his People's National Movement (PNM) party on January 24, 1956. He faced the polls later, on September 24, 1956, and emerged victorious. He became chief minister. From then, he worked assiduously to wrench Trinidad and Tobago from a totally dependent Crown Colony to the freedom status of independence on August 31, 1962. Dr. Williams and his PNM intended to bring about as swift a change as possible in the twin island nation, but they were constrained by constitutional implications. They were now working towards internal self-government. They requested constitutional reform. On this issue, as chief minister, he addressed the nation. Here is an excerpt from that address:

> The whole history of the African population of the West Indies inevitably drives them towards representative institutions fashioned after the British model. We shall be wise if we avoid the mistake of endeavoring to withhold a concession ultimately inevitable until it has been robbed by delay of most of its usefulness and of all its grace.

Then, Dr. Williams attempted to distinguish between the extant single legislative council chamber and what he proposed to introduce, a bicameral legislature:

> The abolition of the single chamber legislative council and the substitution of a bicameral legislature. That is automatic. No defense of this is needed. The single chamber is colonialism in conception, in form and in operation. If you want to get out of the rut of colonialism, you can do so only by abolishing the single chamber legislature. If you want to get out into the stream of democracy, you can do so only by substituting a legislature of two houses. There is no argument whatsoever. We have had our period of transition. You can't run with the hare and hunt with the hounds. The single chamber legislature must go or it must stay. If it stays, you must stop talking about ending colonialism. If you wish to have self-government, it must go.

As may be imagined, the problems of leading a government of a developing nation were numerous, and discussions were also being held on the launching of the Federation of the West Indies. Member states were unable to arrive at a suitable location for its headquarters. There was a tentative consensus that it should be located in one of the less developed islands like Grenada, and Trinidad and Tobago especially could not agree with certain proposals being advanced. The discussions were heated and emotional.

The territories of Jamaica and Barbados were discounted as sites for the federation's headquarters of government until it was eventually agreed to locate it in Port of Spain, the Trinidad and Tobago capital. A suitable building and modern amenities were a major consideration and Port of Spain qualified free of any struggle to compete. The Federation of the British West Indies was celebrated in 1958. About this period, the anti-American sentiment had intensified. It was believed that since "The Doctor" was threatened with imprisonment for the nonpayment of family support sums, he owed in the USA. He courted a vicious antipathy to the USA, matched in the Caribbean region only by Cheddi Jagan and Fidel Castro. In the circumstances, the issue against the Americans was their occupation of Chaguaramas as an Army base.

An excerpt from Dr. Williams' book, *History of the People of Trinidad and Tobago* states:

> Without any agreement at all, and without the approval of the government of Trinidad and Tobago, the American Military Command had virtually made Piarco Airport in Trinidad a United States military airport. The entire situation was embittered by the public knowledge that officials of the United States Naval station in Chaguaramas were intervening in local politics.

Evidently, public feeling was one of agitation; the ill will of 1941 was resuscitated. The feeling was reflected in this unique sonorous monotone of the premier of Trinidad and Tobago at a speech at Arima in July, 1959. He declared:

> The whole West Indian movement is moving towards control of its own affairs. I, too, would like to know the clause in Adams' will which denies the West Indian people a share of the world, especially a share of the world that rightly belongs to them. And what progress have we made if, instead of the fortress in the sixteenth century, you could see in St. Kitts a tremendous fortress built by slave labor; Brimstone Hill symbolizes the time when that tiny island of St. Kitts was divided in half to the French and half to the British with a constant warfare until the British took over the whole island. What progress have we made, if we have substituted Chaguaramas, the naval base of the twentieth century, for Brimstone Hill, the military base of the eighteenth century, and Morro Castle, the military base of the sixteenth century? Are there still to be bases defending Spain's treasure fleet on one hand, British sugar lifeline on the other, and in this case, the lifeline of the United States of America? Historically speaking, where are we going? We come to the population and we say Cabinet Government as a step towards full internal self-government. If you don't have control over a part of your territory, if people are allowed to land a plane here without permission, if they could claim

> all sorts of economic privileges that you cannot guarantee to your own population? It is the Americans who have to answer the question; it is we in Trinidad who ask the question; what is their answer: are they for colonialism or are they against it? This is British colonialism, this is Spanish colonialism; this is French colonialism; if the Americans do the same thing, it can only be defined as American colonialism. All over the West Indies, this movement is breaking out. Venezuela, Cuba. And Cuba has a base, Guantanamo Bay, imposed in 1906 by a permanent treaty with the United States. Ours is ninety-nine years like the Philippines. Theirs is permanent. What sort of thing is this? What is sacred about ninety-nine years? One of the Kings of England, King Charles, I believe, gave a contract to a company which he dignified by permitting it to use the title "Royal," gave the Royal African Company a contract for the monopoly of supplying slaves to the West Indies for 1,000 years. We should still be slaves today. The contract should come to an end in the year 2,663 [laughter]. And look at us here in 1959 enjoying some sort of Cabinet Day. That we have to decide. The ninety-nine years don't mean a thing, really, because as you know, I think we have said it before. Let's say it again for the record tonight—they are not committed to the development of the areas.

The premier of Trinidad and Tobago was fighting on some four fronts. He was talking constitutional conference for independence with the British. His quarrel was with the West Indies Federation government, accelerating the pace for economic development domestically, and the problematical issue of Chaguaramas. His breathings were totally anti-American. If he had the power, they would have been expelled not only from his country but the entire Caribbean. Relative to that nation's domination of the region, he wrote in his book, *From Columbus to Castro*:

> United States supremacy in the Caribbean was further underlined when, in 1917, the United States purchased the Virgin

> Islands from Denmark for the sum of $25 million in order to get possession of the harbor of St. Thomas. World War II provided the same thing for yet a further advance this time in the British West Indies. In 1940 the United States received from Britain 99-year leases of naval bases in Trinidad, Guyana, Antigua, St. Lucia, Jamaica, the Bahamas as well as Newfoundland and in Bermuda. The difference was that no dollars were involved, only fifty over-aged destroyers for Britain with its back to the wall against submarines. It was a dirty deal that the United States boasted about.

In his book, *History of the People of Trinidad and Tobago,* Williams drew attention to how the British were ridiculed by the American ambassador in London, John Winant. He considered how they were effectively humbled for accepting such a rotten deal of fifty almost unserviceable destroyers in exchange for ninety-nine-year leases of areas in lands they had plundered, and then colonized their peoples. Now these people's lands were being bartered without their permission. Ambassador Winant declared, "It was a struggle for them to break habits of 300 years." This suggests a mere *necessitas non habet legem.* Necessity knows no bounds.

Events moved swiftly in a now-booming Trinidad. The Caroni oil fields were yielding unprecedented profits and so was the Pitch Lake industry, being the sole supplier to the entire English-speaking Caribbean. Remarkably at this time, most of them were enjoying internal self-government and heading towards independence.

Now that they were no longer lending unwilling acquiescence to decisions that affected their welfare less propitiously than that of the colonial office, they were forging ahead rapidly with their infrastructural development. After registering too many years of neglect, most of the states were concentrating on the industries of tourism and agriculture. This suggests that roads had to be repaired, reconstructed and in many cases new highways, main roads and feeder roads were being of necessity, prioritized. In this respect,

Dr. Williams' Trinidad was enjoying unprecedented economic development and independence was imminent. This was in 1962.

Jamaica, a senior member of the West Indies Federation, opted for general elections, which were tantamount to a referendum. A negative response would give Jamaica the license to secede from the West Indies Federation.

Without hesitation, the premier of Trinidad and Tobago, Dr. Williams, made his immortal statement that, "One from ten leaves nought." He took Trinidad and Tobago out of the Federation. That same year, two events occurred. Premier Norman Manley's Peoples National Party (PNP) faced the polls at general elections and lost and Jamaica, led by William Alexander Bustamante, attained independence. That same year, on August 31, 1962, Trinidad and Tobago also attained independence. The philosopher, historian, and politician became the nation's first prime minister.

It should be noted that from observation, the English Caribbean's major flaw was this inability of its leaders to initiate an "ingenious" and novel economic development strategy to propel the states out of any semblance of inflationary or deflationary or recessional or stagnation phase. Everything appeared to depend on chance—that a movement would come about totally discounting the fact that the economy of any country was meant to be controlled and not allowed arbitrary shifts of direction. It had that invisible rein that should be tugged at or eased, but never to be allowed total freedom. It begged for periodic adjustments. Most seemed to be rather loquacious, mouthing some sort of political science clichés unrelated to the prevailing economic debacle that proved them more proficient in absurdity. Their most vicious and effective adversary was evidently an inadvertent inferiority complex and an ignorance of economics.

If only Caribbean leaders could learn this philosophy. Most enter politics with little knowledge of its shifting dynamics with concomitant elements and the tenable route to pursue. Most study law and experience trade unionism, uncertain of the ephemeral nature of a political adventure that is influenced by sheer socio-economic developmental vagaries made rampant by the absence of a supportive, vibrant industrial machinery. Few ever study how to jump-start a nation's economy that has slowed down then stalled from inactivity or, to put it bluntly, stagnation!

Trinidad and Tobago progressed under the leadership of Dr. Eric Williams. He achieved his aspiration to get the Americans out of Chaguaramas. In fact, it was an American government decision that the maintenance of these bases in the region would be too costly holding on to them. No, Eric Williams could have forced them out if they wanted to stay. They were closing military bases even in the USA itself. The infrastructural development throughout was admirable. Doubtless, Dr. Williams was assisted by his good fortune of oil and Pitch Lake deposits in Trinidad, and the Middle East oil crisis benefited his nation considerably. Visually, the capital Port of Spain was the New York of the Caribbean.

Trinidad and Tobago, embracing the period from the late sixties to the late seventies, was the richest nation in the Caribbean. With a population then of some one million, a construction boom of daringly modernistic proportions began and rivaled Hollywood, California in beauty and artistic intensity. The nation of Trinidad and Tobago was awash with petro-dollars. With billions in reserve, Trinidadians then enjoyed a lifestyle that paralleled that of Saudi Arabia. The poverty syndrome of these islands impelled the Trinidad and Tobago prime minister to zip open his amazing fund of generosity. Dr. Williams had on various occasions emitted breathings of Caribbean cooperation and interregional assistance. He invited the leaders and they trekked to see him at Whitehall, the prime minister's office. He loaned millions of dollars to every CARICOM member territory. At one juncture, only St. Lucia's premier, John Compton, had passed up his offer of a loan of petro-dollars. This writer recalled this as a fact. A St. Lucia government delegation was invited on a state visit to Port of Spain. As the director of the then Government Public Relations and Information Services, I was a member of that delegation in 1978. The other members were Premier John Compton, J. M. D. Bousquet, the minister of communications and works, and Winville King, cabinet secretary.

On arrival at Piarco International Airport, we were met by a Trinidad and Tobago welcome delegation led by, if I recall correctly, Minister of Education George Chambers. We were ushered into the VIP lounge to meet the press. Premier John Compton was bombarded with questions relating to the expulsion of Dr. Walter Rodney of Guyana from the University of the West Indies, Mona, Jamaica.

Free of hesitation, Premier Compton said: "Jamaica is presumptuous and imprudent to take a unilateral decision to declare Dr. Rodney persona non grata. This should have been a Caribbean decision. Not a Jamaican decision. The University of the West Indies is a Caribbean institution with the site being located at Mona, Jamaica. It is a privilege Jamaica enjoys and Jamaica has abused that privilege."

"Are you saying that other Caribbean leaders including Prime Minister Dr. Williams were not told of the decision to expel Dr. Rodney?" I questioned.

"If I were consulted, I would have opposed the decision," he responded.

"Was Prime Minister Williams aware of this decision to expel Dr. Rodney?" I asked.

"You should put that question to Dr. Williams," he replied.

"Will this be part of your discussions, Premier Compton?" I asked.

"Talk to me after our discussions," he responded.

Compton was sharp, candid and provocative. The fact was, Premier Compton then was the only Caribbean leader who spoke out with disapproval to chide the government of Jamaica.

Dr. Walter Rodney was of a Socialist persuasion and anticapitalist. A noted historian, he had authored the book, *How Europe Underdeveloped Africa.* It had enlightened misconceptions, stirred up debate and incurred some displeasures.

During this state visit to Trinidad, it was at a time when the distinguished doctor was at war with the local press; as a result, he avoided the press as he would AIDS. The perception was that the abundance of respect, affection and adulation with which he was being constantly deluged, perhaps even inadvertently, formed an image not unlike that of an untouchable deity. And the former president of Russia, Boris Yeltsin, in his biography, *Against the Grain*, explained that bad attitude. He conceded:

> I will never get used to it. Every time I am slandered, every time someone purposefully sets out to provoke me, I am terribly disturbed and I suffer, although it is high time I learned to react calmly and dispassionately. I can't.

This sentiment was symptomatic of Dr. Williams. At some periods, he appeared to forget to concede that he was a human being made of mere dust. Of course, Dr. Williams, being a philosopher and historian, should defy and deny such inflexibility of the sort; in practice this amounts to want of discipline. He suffered from an inordinate sense of a superiority complex, as though he couldn't suffer the kind of people who made him their leader. He was elevated way beyond them. The major problem was his inability to accept criticism. Williams deluded himself that everyone else failed to understand that he was an intellectual of no mean proportions. He was on a pedestal all by himself.

At Whitehall I was ushered into his office. He pushed his chair backward, stood and shook my hand in greeting. Dr. Williams possessed a low, monotone sound for a voice. It was unique and ideal for the skilled parodist as it boasted strength of an unwavering character that was totally free of any sort of inflections. You heard it once and it won't be easy ever to forget it. And you will never ever mistake another voice for it.

"Mr. James, welcome to Trinidad. Is it your first visit? We are so pleased to have the St. Lucia delegation visit us. And we are impressed with Premier John Compton's efforts in St. Lucia. Now what can I do for you? How may I help you?"said he, all in one tone—forty-six words.

I drew up a chair to the left side of his huge desk and positioned my mini tape recorder at a clearing on his desk that was surprisingly orderly. My knowledge of the venerable doctor was that he was an orator—a man of words. As a result, I did not trouble myself to prepare a questionnaire. I was taught at Radio and Television Arts (RTA) Class at Ryerson any sensible interview demands a questionnaire unless it is an impromptu meeting. I was positive that I would begin with a provocative question and proceed on the basis of his responses. I began:

"Dr. Williams, we are rather pleased to be here. We hold great admiration for how Trinidad has progressed under your leadership. It has been widely circulated that Trinidad and Tobago proposes to assume the role of big brother to your neighbor Grenada."

"That is incorrect," he said.

"But before we left St. Lucia, I heard that being broadcast on Radio St. Lucia. And on arrival here, I heard it on 610 radio this morning being repeated," I pointed out.

"That is incorrect," he insisted. He was motionless and his staring penetratingly searing. Not a smile in the offing.

"Everyone has been so thrilled by this report of Grenada's adoption."

"That is incorrect," he was adamant. He sat there motionless and continued his stare unwaveringly. I felt uneasy. Intimidation seized me for what seemed like an interminable period. I was unprepared to interview the awesome, erudite, philosopher, historian, prime minister of Trinidad and Tobago. What a disaster. I was devastated. The silence, too, was conspicuous. Then, I remembered that three weeks earlier I had visited Uncle Charles, former politician and father of George Charles, St. Lucia's first chief minister at Mon Repos. He had a copy of Dr. Williams' new book, *From Columbus to Castro.* I had run through a couple chapters. I did hear from some source that Dr. Williams had written that voluminous book all in six months without revision. Books such as that involved research, writing, then first, second and third drafts. Normally a historical dissertation such as *From Columbus to Castro* would consume five to ten years.

"May I ask how was it possible that a busy prime minister as you are, with such a packed agenda, could find the time and energy to write such a voluminous book, *From Columbus to Castro,* in only six months? Such a writing feat is associated with celebrated writers as Ian Fleming of the James Bond fame and Somerset Maughan?"

Obviously, the flattering remark touched his ego. It thawed him out. Instantly there was a remarkable transformation. Dr. Williams eased back in his high-back executive chair, released a semi-smile and declared pleasantly, "Well, I'll have you know that from a young boy at school at Tranquility Boys' Intermediate to Queen's Royal College, English and Latin were my favorite subjects. Even at Oxford I excelled at Latin. Yes, Mr. James, that book was written in six months. And there is no need for me to revise. I know what I wish to say. I just express it. English is a subject you must know its elements or you are unable to command it. Even the majority of the English people themselves are unable to speak and write English properly."

Upwards today, of the many personalities whom I had interviewed, my four favorites were Chief Minister Ebenezer T. Joshua of St. Vincent and the Grenadines; Dr. Cheddi Jagan, president of Guyana; Prime Minister Tom Adams of Barbados and Dr. Eric Williams, prime minister of Trinidad and Tobago.

Of necessity, there may be two of the many events in the political career of Dr. Eric Eustace Williams that will have left an indentation on his psyche. His protégé from Tobago, A. N. R. Robinson, who later became prime minister of a coalition government in Trinidad and Tobago and later president of the Republic of Trinidad and Tobago, was arrested but later released for lack of evidence that he intended to overthrow the Williams administration. A. N. R. Robinson was connected to Geddes Granger and his Black Power revolution that had been foiled by that nation's Coast Guard in 1970.

A. N. R. Robinson held the powerful portfolio of the minister of finance. He and his wife, who were both Economists, created a budget package that was exciting in theory, but when translated into practicality, it was horrendous. The private sector resented it and erupted. They planned to shut down business throughout Trinidad and Tobago. Eric Williams considered the gravity of the situation. He withdrew the offensive budget and replaced it. In fact, he assumed control of the finance portfolio. A. N. R. Robinson was tantamount to being dismissed. He was idle and free of any governmental or ministerial responsibilities. Understandably, he sulked and talked to the extent of being loquacious. The prime minister heard. News, particularly adverse, never failed to be transmitted and with haste.

About that time, the Black Power movement had gained support. Some elements of the Army had defected and thousands were tramping on Port of Spain when the Navy with its guns created a landslide blockage. This allowed the police and other military units to reorganize themselves and reassert control. It was during that crucial period that A. N. R. Robinson was arrested and incarcerated with a charge of sedition. The Black Power leadership had proposed to make him the new regime's prime minister. There was no evidence that A. N. R. Robinson was culpable. He was released.

This Black Power unrest in 1970, and the oil and sugar workers strikes, had almost toppled the Williams administration. As a result of this momentous event, a state of emergency was declared by Prime Minister Williams on which the journalist Owen Baptiste wrote the book *Crisis*. The following is an interview with John Humphrey, an architect, trade union and political activist. He also gave Owen Baptiste his version of why Dr. Eric Williams had placed his mentor, C. L. R. James, under house arrest.

> And to get a clear perspective of the present situation, we'll have to go back to 1965 when C. L. R. James was holding meetings in London with nationals. I know about it. In those days, I did not have special contacts but knew about it. James came down to report on a Test Match, but that was a front. While he was here, he was meeting with the oil union and sugar workers. At that time, they were well represented. Bhadase was head of the union. James was trying to get Weekes into sugar. That's the move he was making. Williams was so scared of it that he established a state of emergency and actually put James under house arrest. Now, if you refer to Inward Hunger, you will see where Williams boasts that his greatest achievement was to pass legislation preventing oil and sugar from uniting. So, you see how important he considered that. Now he knows that whoever controls the economy, controls the country. Oil and sugar united controls the economy.

And relative to the Black Power Movement in 1970, Humphrey opined:

> In 1970, we had the Black Power Movement. That was a movement of depressed urban population, youth, unemployed Africans, and a few intellectuals. In other words, no economic power. So, Williams was able to put it down. In 1970, when the street demonstrations nearly overthrew the PNM government—that's all they were, but they almost overthrew them—Williams called first to the United Kingdom and was told that in a domestic affair they would not intervene. He

> then called on Venezuela asking for 2,000 troops, air and sea support. I understand he got anti-riot equipment. When he called on the United States, they immediately obliged by selling him all the arms he requested and they dispatched a flotilla of ships from Puerto Rico, purporting to be prepared to evacuate U.S. citizens. But it was an invasion force to be deployed in the event that Williams was overthrown. It included an assault carrier with large helicopters and combat troops—the 2,000 Williams was asking for. I understand that when the Venezuelan military realized that there was a possibility of U.S. military occupation of Trinidad, they prepared for a mass mobilization of forces to deal with it. Because of our government's incompetence we almost lost our country.

Now, just where did Eric Williams go wrong? The problem with these heads of government was they were as imperfect as any human being, but they never conceded to making an error. They understandably concealed their vulnerability. Most of them proved to be egomaniacs. They enter politics to liberate, to enhance the welfare of the people, but somewhere along the way, midstream, they commandeer the country as though it were their personal property. They veered away to fight the people they were to represent, and as Owen Baptiste, in his book *Crisis,* pointed out:

> One is reminded of an observation made by the United States Secretary of State Henry Kissinger in the *New York Times Magazine* in 1971, the year that democratic elections were reduced to sham in Trinidad and Tobago.
>
> I believe in the tragic element of history. I believe there is a tragedy of a man who works very hard and never gets what he wants. And then I believe there is the even more bitter tragedy of man who finally gets what he wants and doesn't want it.

That little Williams was truly representative of the vast potentiality endemic in the child irrespective of familial status can neither be disputed nor refuted. He methodically developed into an eminent philosopher, historian and statesman with an illuminating intellect that was not commonplace. But this exceptional human was supremely egotistical. He forgot that he was a mere human. Those associated with him, to him, were not up to his level and expectations. He became most intolerant and his assumed superiority proved a positive detriment to him. The professor had long established that he had few uses and little affection for the kind of people whom he encountered. They revered him, potentate-like; he preferred to keep at a comfortable distance away. And he had indicated that in the event that he passed away, he did wish to be put on display as was the custom for heads of state. The citizens of Trinidad and Tobago never saw the corpse. Even his death was brought on by his reluctance and defiance to be told what to do. He had become furious with his doctor and ordered him away.

Williams suffered from diabetes. The doctor asked him to take his medication at specific periods. When he was found, his housekeeper had summoned the doctor, who was reluctant to respond as he was arrogantly dismissed sometime earlier. However, on arrival, it was too late. Williams himself hastened his death. The man became delusional and this affected his equilibrium as a mere mortal. An extraordinary man with a consistent and fascinating history, he died on March 29, 1981.

Trinidad and Tobago, the Caribbean, the wider world, and the twentieth century will have benefited from Dr. Eric Eustace Williams' fleeting passage. His impact was considerable and will not be easily duplicated in our lifetime.

Could one speculate that his was an especial mission to educate the repressed people of the Caribbean? His was a brilliance that never dulled. How could such a tiny region born out of slavery produce such an exceptional intellect as Eric Eustace Williams? This must be a paradox.

CHAPTER 9

Right Honorable
Sir William Alexander Clarke Bustamante
P.c., Ll.d, Mp
Prime Minister Of Jamaica

The name William Alexander Clarke Bustamante was synonymous with the Trade Union Movement in Jamaica and throughout the Caribbean. One imaged too, a determined and dedicated trade unionist of average height, leading strikes in the blazing sun with windswept, flowing white tresses. He had not been unacquainted with being arrested for instigating disorder. Though the dynamic Bustamante could not be accused of being an orator, he had a way with words that he employed effectively. For instance, while he did not have as impressive an academic background as his cousin, Norman Washington Manley, his capacity to sway a crowd was phenomenal, and he was able to convince Jamaicans to trust and place their confidence in him. They did, and he took Jamaica and Jamaicans out of the Federation of the West Indies in 1962. That same year, he took Jamaica into independence and became its first prime minister.

The embattled son of Constantine Clarke and an Irish planter was born in Blenhein, Hanover, Jamaica on February 24, 1884. Her half-sisters were the mothers of Norman Manley and Edna

Manley. This son was destined to revolutionize the system of the matrix of the working-man's landscape in Jamaica. William Alexander Clarke Bustamante began his early education at a primary school and later accepted private studies arranged by his mother. Later, he saw the need to supplement his education at the La Salle Extension University, Chicago. He graduated with a diploma in Commercial Spanish and Italian and Portuguese at the Royal Academy in Madrid, Spain. It will be noted here that Clarke was adopted by a Spanish seaman named Bustamante at the age of 15. Now Bustamante, in 1905, he left Jamaica and proceeded to travel extensively. This was a component of his educational development. He was by then a trained dietitian and he accepted a post at the Hospital for Joint Diseases in New York, USA. Consistent with the character of patriots who must return to home base, Bustamante returned to Jamaica in 1922. Not long after, he questioned that decision to return and he departed from Jamaica again.

One of the realities of island life was that if one from his youth traveled and worked abroad, nostalgia forced him to return home. When he did, he came face-to-face with the reality that there were two distinct approaches to survival in the same century. In the developed countries, life was rapid with not inconstant mobility. A major factor also was that the populations were not mere thousands, but millions. The machinery of production never stopped, hence the seemingly unending lifeline. It is obtuse to try to compare the economies that dictated the difference in lifestyles for the lower income bracket masses especially. In the huge economies, some people held down two or three jobs. In the puny economies, there was a dearth of employment opportunities. Very many people were unemployed and were chained to this status only to consider themselves causalities of social injustice.

Moreover, the overwhelming pace did not lend to the endemic insularity found in the cozy island environment. When faced with it, one wished to hurry out again in haste. This was the scenario within which Bustamante was webbed. He departed from Jamaica one more time. This sojourn extended into twelve years. He returned to Jamaica, as if with a vengeance, to attempt to correct a multiple of ills in a colonial Jamaica. The British expatriates did not seem to have any form of humanity. They maintained an opulent life style within a penury stricken environment. Their purpose, as had been traditional, was simply to facilitate their interests and not necessarily that of the colonials. This was saying there was no obligation of commitment to enhance the socioeconomic and educational development of Jamaicans. In fact, this was the policy of the British throughout the West Indies, essentially to control in a manner that kept the erstwhile system intact, dictated by the colonial office.

But changes were inevitable, and many unseen factors in the British capital would suffer repercussions in the colonies. As an example, though the statistics indicated that the Jamaican population had increased appreciably, the economic performance in London would not lend to the increase of subvention or grants to maintain the costs of living and other services, including education for Jamaica. The legislative council in Kingston would have to employ its initiative to produce earnings by way of taxes. This was considered a self-help initiative. Water, for instance, was a precious commodity that was being consumed free of cost. This would end. The population shift from rural to urban areas had imposed a strain on the water supply. Moreover, the sanitation and health services were determined to eradicate the malaria fever that was quite prevalent at that time. Malaria was being spread by mosquitoes in the tropics; consequently, drinking water in catchments had to be treated. While treatment was seen as imperative, the distribution through conduits to residences was vital and it would be costly. The alternative was that the services had to be sold. At first, this was difficult to comprehend. Water was free. It fell from the rain clouds in the sky. The air being inhaled was also free. Why one would have to pay for water was not easy to appreciate. This was the situation in Jamaica, like elsewhere in the West Indies, when Bustamante returned to his homeland in 1934. He also, like the largest percentage of the people, had failed to fully grasp the significance of the payments being imposed through water meters. The perception was that poor people should not be paying for water. They were already paying their dues by being poor. They did not understand, and could not understand, and would not understand the basic hidden principle of a seeming free democratic society. Nothing was free. And the minority rich was sustained by the largest percentage of the poor masses. If they failed to expend on services to them, the clever, thrifty rich would be unable to separate themselves from these masses.

Bustamante then was in his prime, and filled to capacity with vitality. He saw an issue to champion and he seized it. He began a vigorous campaign, opposing the rent on the installation and use of the water meters in the business areas. That was in 1935, and this haranguing waged on for several months into 1936. Emotional issues that affected the lives of the poor and uneducated never failed to harvest recruits. This, in essence, began an utterly productive career for William Alexander Clarke Bustamante as a trade unionist.

In November 1937, he joined the Trade Union Movement. He was employed as the treasurer of the Jamaica Workers and Tradesmen Union. Bustamante called upon his many years of experience residing in foreign countries, where he had learned from the successes and failures of others. He harnessed this wealth of knowledge and excelled as a vibrant leader. Only perhaps very few doubted his capacity to lead, and this he did by organizing strikes throughout 1938.

Though not unaccustomed to strikes in the United Kingdom, the British authorities, during the month of May 1938, arrested Bustamante on sedition charges. Not insignificantly, the authorities declined at first to allow bail. They were so determined to lose him away in jail for a cooling off period. And this, as a violation of his civil and human rights, was totally discounted. With skilled legal representation by his political rival and cousin, Attorney Norman Manley, he trashed and shredded the complaint against him, and the charges were later reluctantly dropped.

As in most areas of endeavor where many people were competing for elevation to the summit of the persuasion, Bustamante found himself in conflict with those who questioned his approach. They expressed the view that he was too brash and daring. They favored the more conservative approach rather than his, which was considered crudely confrontational. He resigned from the Jamaican Workers and Tradesmen Union (JWTU) and founded the Bustamante Industrial Trade Union (BITU) in the latter part of 1938.

Plodding relentlessly along in the movement, Bustamante accelerated his pace. His BITU made its debut. It called a nationwide strike in February of 1939. Here it should be recalled that Adolph Hitler, the clever chancellor of Germany, had invaded Poland and was rampaging through Europe. Britain was at war with Germany. This translated to mean that the British colonies and commonwealth were also at war with Germany. The BITU then was the most influential and proficient in the movement. Any disruption to services would not be tolerated. Bustamante was again arrested for questioning. He was accused of creating a situation that would militate against Britain's war efforts. He responded, "Britain's war efforts were not my business. My business was the Jamaica workers' war here against the British colonial influenced injustice." They failed in their efforts to silence him; rather he stepped up his pace of labor agitation for his workers. Again he was arrested and incarcerated under the defense regulations. This most flamboyant of trade unionists was released from prison in 1942. Without hesitation, he set about the reorganization of the BITU, but while imprisoned, he had a vision that should propel Jamaica and Jamaicans out of British colonization. But they needed machinery. This machinery was found in all the metropolitan states. That was, a political party. This party would consolidate its forces of people to struggle on to attain self-government.

The BITU then proceeded in 1943 to found the Jamaica Labor Party (JLP). Not unexpectedly, Bustamante was elected the first president. His political efforts with rewards began when, a year later, he was elected Member of the House of Representatives (MHR) for West Kingston in December, 1944 in the first general elections to be held under adult suffrage. Triumphantly, the Jamaica Labor Party won the elections capturing twenty-two of the thirty-two seats, and Bustamante held the portfolio of minister of communications.

Bustamante was moving along politically. As MHR for Kingston, he was in reality the ex officio member of Kingston and St. Andrew Corporation Council. He held the mayoralty from 1947 to 1948. This fearless and vigorous leader unavoidably suffered the same fate as many leaders before and after him of his persuasion. Situations did not always work out according to plans. Moreover, it was understandable that when conditions were flowing smoothly, a mound or a crater will appear sometime to impede mobility.

The BITU, as a member of the Trade Union Council, had organized a major strike at the mental hospital. This escalated into rioting during which someone died. Bustamante was arrested on charges of manslaughter. It was a celebrated case and, remarkably, he was defended with ingenious skill and acquitted in 1948. The next year, 1949, was a good year for the JLP and Bustamante. It was the second straight victory at the general elections. Bustamante was elected MHR for South Clarendon, and his influence extended overseas as his reputation grew. In 1950, he was invited to be a member of the Caribbean Commission. He served there until 1955, when the JLP was defeated by Norman Manley's PLP.

William Alexander Bustamante was a vigorous leader of the opposition. This was saying that he performed creditably, as he did when the leader of government. This consummate trade unionist and politician could be likened ideally to Russian politician Khrushchev. Opined author Edward Crankshaw in his book, referring to Khrushchev, said:

> His mind was a politician's mind, the sort of mind found in all men who rise to power by persuasion and intrigue and who repose their power on the consent of the persuaded.

I remembered Bustamante speaking at political meetings both in Kingston, Jamaica in 1955 and in St. Lucia about one year later. My view of him had always been that he reflected the image of a dashing showman with flamboyant white hair who impressed, but was no sedate Norman Manley, nor the oratorical Michael Manley.

Nonetheless, Bustamante was knighted by Her Majesty Queen Elizabeth II in 1955, and later chosen to be the president of the West Indies Democratic Labor Party. His tenure of office began in 1957, and he served until 1960 when he resigned to concentrate his efforts on seceding Jamaica from the Federation West Indies Federation. His professed love for the West Indies was weaker than his love to control Jamaica.

Bustamante employed all the cunning stored within his arsenal. He was that astute politician who seized every opportunity that presented itself to arrest power of office. And one of these rare opportunities was made possible by Barbadian Grantley Adams, prime minister of the two-year-old West Indies Federation. He announced that retroactive tax legislation would be introduced. This, doubtless, would affect Jamaica. Bustamante grabbed this and employed it as a ruse. Skilled superbly in painful duplicity, he deployed this characteristic at will, free of any apology, and it found immense appeal with very many of his followers. They perceived it as uncommon, political psychology. He told Jamaicans, "Those West Indian islands in the east were all islands, small and poor. We in Jamaica would have to carry the burden of supporting them. Jamaica can only take care of Jamaica." He was infinitely persuasive.

The premier of Jamaica, then Norman Manley, did not have to go to the polls. General elections were not constitutionally due before the next year, 1962. But he had placed undue faith in the human element and its need to reason rationally. He explained the history and the cultural dynamics that irrevocably linked Jamaica to the West Indian islands in the east. Moreover, they were sure markets for Jamaican exports by virtue of the family relationship.

Rhodes Scholar, brilliant attorney, conscientious trade unionist Premier Norman Manley underestimated. He was so positive that Jamaicans would respond in the affirmative that he yielded to a referendum. Jamaicans to stay in the Federation or pull out of it. He lost and he was devastated. In his view, Jamaicans had chosen senselessly, but the die was cast!

Fact was, Bustamante knew Jamaicans more intimately than his cousin and political rival, Manley. At that time in 1961, the majority of Jamaicans knew very little about the islands to the east. They were acquainted with Puerto Rico, Cuba, Haiti, all units of the Greater Antilles. They vacationed in the USA, only some 150 miles away, and in Canada, Mexico, the Bahamas, and even Bermuda. They traveled to Europe, but the distance of 1,200 miles to the then obscure East evidently made travel to the region seem prohibitive. Jamaicans became acquainted with the Eastern West Indies when two maple leaf ships were presented to the West Indies Federation as an independence gift. Only then did a percentage of Jamaicans find the time to get to know the islands. Bustamante was an absolutely cunning politician. He closely observed the pattern of behavior of Jamaicans generally from every strata of society. He employed the strategy of perhaps the most effective of Greek philosophers, Socrates. Questions were significant in his quest to arrive at conclusions. He allowed his students to find their own answers. Bustamante made a study of his people and grew to understand and know them and their behavior more intuitively than his cousin and opponent Manley, who believed he knew them.

Elections were about a year away. Bustamante and his JLP caucus agreed that they should nudge Manley into a referendum. They assumed that he would agree to it, lest he was accused of being devious and unwilling to appreciate that Jamaicans did not want to stay in the federation. His scores of discussions had convinced him that Jamaicans were agreeable to the union. Later, he would discover that he was mistaken. They loved and admired him, but misled him. He allowed the people to decide, and they did to his utter disappointment. This compelled the Manley administration to take Jamaica out of the Federation. That memorable event took place in 1961. The next year, Manley called the general elections and, again to his disappointment, Bustamante's PLP won decisively and took Jamaica into independence on August 6, 1962. This William Alexander Clarke Bustamante, the bon vivante, embattled trade unionist—arrested and jailed more than any other trade unionist in the Caribbean—the consummate politician became the first prime minister of Jamaica. He had left his imprint on Jamaica and the Caribbean. He was easily the most flamboyant of them all. His watchword was, "Always to serve the people of Jamaica to the limit of my strength."

Sir William Alexander Clarke Bustamante retired from politics in February, 1967 when he passed on the leadership of the JLP to Donald Burns Sangster. No one would dare accuse him of not extending himself to full capacity. When he died in 1977, Jamaica and the Caribbean mourned the loss of a genuinely outstanding Jamaican and West Indian leader.

CHAPTER 10

Right Honorable George Cadle Price
Former Chief Minister
Premier and Prime Minister of Belize

Many considered George Cadle Price the accomplished politician of British Honduras. He was the mayor of Belize City in 1961, when a ferocious tropical hurricane demolished the capital. Belize City was a short distance away from the Caribbean Sea. It was vulnerable. It had been slapped on numerous occasions. George Price was mayor from 1956. He was shattered by the devastation. The dead casualty toll had exceeded three hundred, while thousands were made homeless.

The full measure of the man, George Price was then extended and put on display. The true mettle of man was sometimes revealed in the most difficult of circumstances. Latent talents then emerge both to test and discover an unlimited strength of character to motivate either victims or casualties of despair and offer redirection. His strength of leadership was formidable and exemplary. He possessed the dynamic energy that fueled the initiative to build nations. But there was need to peer into George Price's beginnings.

William Cadle Price and his wife Irene were thrilled that a son was born to them on January 5, 1919. Like most parents, they attempted to exceed their best in providing for him, first by raining endless love upon him with such values as respect and honesty. He graduated from the elementary school phase on to the St. John's College in Belize City, then on to St. Augustine Seminary, Mississippi, USA. This education was to prepare him for the multiple stresses that awaited him.

On his return home, he sifted through his options and chose public service as a career. He was elected to the Belize City Council in 1947. But a man of his dynamism was not adequately challenged by being a mere councilor. He was elected president of the General Workers Union that same year, and he held this position until 1952. Moreover, he was elected a member of the British Honduras Legislative Council. In 1950, he tackled the responsible role of being founder-member of the People's United Party (PUP). As elsewhere throughout the Caribbean, huge servings of anti-imperialistic domination platitudes were a regular fare at meetings. PUP was being taken seriously. It would be the forceful political proposition to effect change in that British colony of Honduras. Many perceived PUP to be somewhat more left, straining the center to its side. That the grouping was positively militant was unchallenged. Fact was, it had evolved out of an earlier effort, the People's Committee, agitating for independence for British Honduras.

Unlike the French—who would not release any of its stolen territories or properties until French citizens were massacred both in and out of France—Britain had set a constitutional timetable to free her colonies. They were not moved by intimidation. It was simply expedient for them to rid the colonial office of the financial burden of supporting alien cultures that offered no tangible benefits to the British people. Their methodical approach to independence was impressive and civilized. George Price was elected party secretary in 1950 and gravitated to become leader in 1956. Appointed a member of the Executive Council in 1954 to 1957, he was returned to serve again in 1961 until 1965.

It was during his mayoralty in 1961 that the Belize tragedy that destroyed most of that capital city occurred. Can one conceive of the huge responsibility to issue rescue directives, hospitalizing the injured, re-housing the homeless, offering relief assistance, cleaning-up operations, ensuring some semblance of order was restored in the wake of the tragedy? While multiple teams worked diligently to bring some degree of comfort to those severely affected, George Price, of necessity, had a formidable task ahead of him to reconstruct Belize City. Additionally, the dawn of 1963 found Price leading a delegation to London for constitutional talks that would usher in the status of internal self-government.

In 1965, he led his People's United Party to an election victory to control the House of Representatives and became the premier of British Honduras. That Central American country was enjoying internal self-rule. This was allowed the previous year, January 1, 1964 and that was accompanied by a brand new Constitution.

Not unlike the other Caribbean colonies that progressed on to independence, this form of constitution allowed for a cabinet led by a premier and ministers. There would also be a national assembly that consisted of a Senate and a House of Representatives. It also allowed for a governor who would be the British Queen's Representative. The electorate would elect eighteen members to represent them for five years, as prevailed elsewhere in the Caribbean.

George Price's British Honduras boasted a geography of some 8,867 square miles, with more than several offshore islands, not unlike the Bahamas. The population comprised descendants of African slaves who commanded 42 percent of the approximately 200,000 people. Other races were East Indians, Maya and Carib Amerindians and Europeans.

In retrospect, just as the former British Guiana was Britain's sole stolen property in South America, British Honduras was Britain's sole real estate in Central America. And this possession-thing all came about in 1638, when British log-cutters adventured into that area of the world. The British man then seemed ubiquitous. There was a fortune to be made in that rich resource logwood and mahogany. Not long after, as in gold-rush times, the British settlers followed.

Then, the two neighboring lands were occupied by Spain. Today they are known as independent states of Mexico and Guatemala. Spain then attempted to expel the erstwhile adversary, the British, but failed in the process. The Spanish assault was repulsed in 1798. Interestingly, with a powerful garrison or warring machines based in Jamaica, the British considered it convenient to make British Honduras a part of Jamaica in 1862. However, some twenty-two years later, in 1884, Britain reversed that decision and made British Honduras a separate colony.

When Guatemala attained its independence in 1821, it audaciously claimed British Honduras. Britain, a world power, deemed it necessary to negotiate a treaty with Guatemala. The boundaries were delineated between Guatemala and British Honduras in 1859. Nonetheless, the boundary contention still rages. Unfortunately, again, like the Venezuela claim on Guyana, Guatemala persists relentlessly that the land mass Belize occupies is Guatemalan territory.

It was a momentous occasion for George Price when, in 1973, his PUP government returned to the name Belize and abandoned British Honduras. Moreover, a new capital city had to be built to replace the demolished Belize City. The construction for this new capital began in the late 1960's and proceeded apace. It was named Belmopan, which is a derivation of Belize and Mopan, the river.

Belmopan was inland and well away from the direct path of the tropical hurricanes. Substantially financed by the British, it was completed in 1970 and occupied. Again in 1980, as premier of Belize, George Price, headed a delegation to London to confer on the attainment of independence. He returned home triumphant.

The next year, 1981, he took Belize into independence and became that new nation's first prime minister.

Prime Minister George Price was not flawless. But he must have pursued a brilliant political strategy as he was repeatedly re-elected to power. He boasted an almost impeccable record of consistency as Sir John Compton of St. Lucia, Vere Bird of Antigua and Barbuda and Sir Lynden Pindling of the Bahamas.

Perhaps in recognition of his sterling public service to Belize, George Price received the Outstanding Alumnus Award from St. John's College in 1971, and he was made a member of the Queen's Privy Council in 1982. However, the human behavior allowed for agitation when short of satisfaction. Perhaps George Price had exhausted himself into complacency. Or it was not likely that he nursed periods of political invincibility as man, given power, deluded himself into a state of immortality. This is not an uncommon occurrence as they spiraled down into an offensive dictatorship.

In 1984, the perennial Price was unseated by Manuel Esquivel of the United Democratic Party (UDP). But he proved to be a one-term prime minister. Belizeans remembered perhaps Price's devotion to the nation. They missed him and perhaps suffered from remorse of conscience for having rejected him. They appreciated that as a human being he was susceptible to mistakes and these were venial.

Esquivel was expelled from office at the next general elections. Price was returned to power in 1989. Apart from being the head of the government of Belize for three tumultuous decades, he held crucial ministries such as finance, economic planning and foreign affairs. He was also the chairman of the Reconstruction and Development Corporation. On reflection, of the old school of Caribbean leaders, only two had survived to the year 2001—Sir John G. M. Compton, former prime minster of St. Lucia and the venerable George Cadle Price himself.

The vital question was how much service can one individual give to his country? The seemingly insuperable Price, comparatively, had contributed infinitely more than his share of love, affection, loyalty and dedication to Belize. Now in his eighties, he can rest assured that his intensive political career was unlikely to be replicated in Belize and the wider Caribbean. He was of the breed of man who had set so thoroughly rapid a pace that ordinary men were unable to follow.

CHAPTER 11

Maurice Rupert Bishop
Self-appointed Former Prime Minister of Grenada and Carriacou

The charismatic and cerebral Maurice Rupert Bishop chiselled his name into political history of the English-speaking Caribbean. He, as the leader of a revolutionary gang of militants, contrived to overthrow the legitimately elected government of Grenada in 1979. He was only thirty-five years old.

Bishop detained and incarcerated people at will if he perceived they did not agree with his so-called revolution.

"Consider how people get detained in this country. We don't go and call for no votes. You get detained when I sign an order after discussing it with the National Security Committee of the party or with a higher party body. Once I sign it, like it or don't like it, it's up the hill for them," he boasted. And this was later revealed in a confidential report released by U.S. Department of State and Department of Defense, September 1984 in Washington, DC.

Maurice R. Bishop was born in the Dutch island of Aruba of Grenadian parents in 1944. Was it then written in the wind that this infant babe would effect a coup d'etat at thirty-five in 1979? Would that have changed the course of history? This rested as intriguing speculation.

Young Bishop probably helped to pack his suitcase when his parents decided to return home to Grenada in 1950. Then he was a mere six-year-old. He had already attended kindergarten and elementary school in Aruba, and he was extraordinarily bright for his age. He entered the Wesley Hall Junior Primary School and the St. George's Roman Catholic Primary School in St. Georges, the capital. The boy from Aruba excelled. With academic prowess, young Bishop jostled his fellow students aside and left them behind in the wash of his educational thrust. He won a scholarship to the Presentation Brothers College and he had just served notice that he would be a powerful intellect with whom they must reckon.

Bishop's academic route was not unlike that of the intellectually gifted before, during and after his life span. They won scholarships with ease. It was a pastime in which they luxuriated, to effectively beat others at study and examinations. It placed one apart and elevated one on an academic pedestal not easily obtained. Depending on one's genetic quality of discernment that embraced a particular area of interest, one would proceed to overwhelm it to one's satisfaction, be it for the improvement of the immediate society, the world at large or not. Distressingly, too many men have become casualties of their insipid misperception of their purpose in life. Very many labor unendingly under the misconception—influenced perhaps by abrasive environment—that their role was to take control and command the lives of others.

Remarkably, the soi-disant luminaries of our epoch had not deviated, but rather followed similar patterns of approach to gain control of the lives of others—they exploited poverty to its limits. And the world was fertile with poverty. Men, for years immemorial, had yielded to persuasions that would lend to some form of relief from oppressive poverty. Eric Matthew Gairy began splendidly by assisting the oppressed and suppressed. He wrenched them out of the morass of sixty-five cents an hour to $1.25 and it progressively increased.

The stimulating book *The New Politics of Poverty*, authored by Lawrence M. Mead, (published by Basic Book, a division of Harper Collins Publishers, Inc.) pointed out that materialism was the strategy now employed to win recruits for this poverty syndrome.

> Workfare is only the most developed instance of a trend: Government is moving away from freedom and toward authority as its basic tool in social policy. Opportunity is no longer enough to overcome low income, given the dysfunctional character of serious poverty today. The ghetto has become to a great extent self-perpetuating, and for many residents, there remains no alternative to society attempting to redirect behavior. A tutelary regime is emerging in which dependents receive support of several kinds on condition of restrictions on their lives.

Gairy had introduced this to Grenada but Maurice Bishop considered it a justifiable leverage for control in a different form. He considered Gairy an oppressor and himself the liberator. Gairy had freed his people from British colonialism and neglect. Perhaps he went astray at some point to such a degree as to have invited a revolution!

Maurice Bishop followed up the scholarship to the Presentation College by winning the Principal's Gold Medal Award for "outstanding academic and all round ability." In addition, he was made president of the Students' Union, foundation member and president of the Historical Society, president of the Debating Society, editor of the college newspaper and cofounder of the Grenada Assembly of Youth After Truth (GAUT). This organization was purported to be aimed at stimulating the consciousness of young people in Grenada.

With such a packed agenda of responsible offices, one was liable to assume an inordinate sense of importance. Perhaps one could lose one's equilibrium, or one could almost irresistibly hasten to court narcissism rather than humility. Following young

Bishop's graduation from Presentation, he found employment at the Registry where he worked for a brief period in Grenada, before leaving for Britain.

On arrival in London, Bishop entered the University of London, Holborn College of Law. He also attended Gray's Inn, but later suspended his schooling at this institution for a period. Driven to advance, Bishop started postgraduate work at King's College. Here the studies embraced the constitutional development of Grenada. This, too, he suspended in favor of employment to earn extra cash. He worked as a surtax examiner in the British Civil Service. However, it will be recalled that his purpose in London was to qualify as an attorney. Evidently, he understood that, but this circuitous route only served to hurry his return to Gray's Inn. He returned to the Inn of Court and successfully passed his Bar finals examination.

Interestingly, like former president of the Co-operative Republic of Guyana, Linden Forbes Sampson Burnham, who was a president of the West Indian Students' Union, Bishop made that presidency. He was also a very vocal member of the pressure group campaigning against racial discrimination. Buoyant with this energy and quality to lead, the intention being to bring about a change in circumstances, Maurice Bishop cofounded a clinic for legal aid. As had been claimed, time must move on, and so did the ebullient Bishop, as he said au revoir to Britain in 1970 and he returned to Grenada. Inevitably, he was soon active in local politics. Observation taught that people with as sharp an intellect as the recently qualified attorney would not be satisfied to just concentrate on building his law practice.

Somewhere in 1973, the young, articulate attorney, after several discussions with like-minded people formed a political group named Movement for Assemblies of the People. There, however, existed another similar group called Joint Action for Education Welfare and Liberation. If we were to analyze the names of these groups, we could immediately interpret that a man affectionately called, Uncle Gairy, who brought some enlightenment to Grenada in the late fifties, sixties and early seventies, was now considered an oppressor of the people. How could this have happened?

Consolidating their strengths, the Movement for Assemblies for the People and the Joint Action for Education Welfare and Liberation pooled their resources. They merged with one purpose in mind: to unseat Eric Gairy's government. The merger became the New Jewel Movement (NJM).

The New Jewel Movement commenced a scathing campaign for the general elections three years away. They organized huge demonstrations. Ironically, the protest was intended to discourage the granting of independence under the Grenada United Labor Party (GULP) government. Businesses were closed down and during one of these violent clashes, Rupert Bishop, Maurice's father, was killed. Obviously, Gairy was blamed. Amidst all this unrest, Grenada was granted independence in 1974. Incidentally, it was later revealed in top secret and confidential documents that the NJM had cleverly set out to enlist affiliations with international socialist organizations in an endeavor to solicit their assistance in preparation for the violent overthrow of Grenada's government. Observers had been to meetings of the Socialist International (SI) many months before the revolution. Bishop, in late 1979, had applied for membership in the Socialist International. This application was accepted in November, 1980 in Madrid, Spain.

The battle for the election was fierce. The NJM fielded bright university graduates fortified with the evils of capitalism and all the virtues of equality endemic in socialism. The NJM made some ground, but only with the younger people and some privileged older folk, who never accepted this "black boy from the East," as Gairy was described, and who was now the head of government. The 1976 general elections were absolutely vicious with an all out war against Gairy and his government. They gave no quarter; in fact, political turmoil was the order of the day. But again, Eric Gairy triumphed. Maurice Bishop won one of the three seats the NJM captured. He became then the official opposition leader in the House of Representatives. His refreshingly illuminating mind became what could be described as clouded in chaos.

The events that followed were fast and furious. Prime Minister Gairy had just left the country for the United States of America in March 1979. Frustrated, opposition leader Bishop led an armed revolution and assumed control of the government. They called themselves the People's Revolutionary Government (PRG). Bishop promised that he would legitimize his government by holding general elections. But after three years, he had failed to keep that promise. The *New York Times* reported that "Bishop had slowly spiralled down to the sphere of normalizing his political activities," which was at variance with the concept of the revolution. Evidently, his PRG colleagues disagreed with his changing posture. They debated it, but Bishop claimed the accusation a figment of "their too active imagination." It was remarkable that through a report claimed in The *New York Times* that Bishop had gradually modified his posture, the U.S. Department of State document showed that top secret papers seized stated that the New Jewel Movement was fundamentally opposed to the democratic ideals of the Socialist International. Bishop had convinced the legitimate Caribbean governments that he would call elections.

The seized papers contradicted such an idea. In fact, on February 13, 1982, Benny Langaigne, the permanent secretary in Maurice Bishop's office, showed the prime minister a draft letter addressed to the official magazine of the SI socialist affairs. "The letter protested a story in the magazine stating that Grenada would have elections in the near future. In fact, the NJM had no such intention."

During this period, the other leaders of Caribbean governments were in constant discussion about this military state situation in Grenada. Most were not sympathetic to Bishop, as they appeared to openly loathe Eric Gairy.

The church in Grenada was considered a threat to Bishop's revolution. Understandably, the priests preached God as a vocation, and the PRG propounded atheism. This placed the two sides at variance. The pulpit pronouncements were regular. They questioned the detention of over 400 citizens at Richmond Hill, and the reluctance to hold elections, the violations of human rights and the abuse of power generally. The church solidified its belligerence when Methodist Minister Ledson refused to officiate at the burial of comrade Demo Grant. Bishop responded by deporting Ledson from Grenada. The church saw this as persecution and intensified their campaign of sermons of opposition to the so-called revolution. The church then was put under close surveillance, as it was considered a "potential source of major internal counter revolution." Whatever might be said about the church, it failed to yield in subservience to the PRG. In fact, the church—led by the Roman Catholic Bishop—did make it difficult for Bishop and his PRG up to the very last, and should be commended for their resistance to dictatorship.

Bishop, his wife Angela, Bernard Coard and the rest of the PRG unleashed a vicious propaganda campaign against Gairy and his GULP government that proved efficacious. Even crimes perpetrated by them and their fanatical supporters were attributed to Gairy and his Mongoose Gang, as they were termed. The Caribbean beyond Grenada believed totally. Even that celebrated American ambassador Andrew Young of the United Nations was convinced that Gairy was truly the bandit politician and discouraged any assistance to him.

The Barbados prime minister, Tom Adams, had attempted to reach out to Bishop, but this communication was deprecated. Bishop responded with venom. He claimed that the Barbados prime minister was an Anglo-American Imperialist "Sambo-yard-foul."

It would be unfair to omit to mention here that the PRG enjoyed the support of Dr. Fidel Castro, Cuba and Libya's Gadaffi to some degree.

The Point Salines airport was being reconstructed by Cuba, and it was alleged that the multiple arms found to be widespread in Grenada were all imported from Cuba. It was no secret that Cuba supported revolutions in Africa and Latin America and our Caribbean was no exception. One conclusion attributed to Socialist International (SI) declared that Bishop and his colleagues not only wished to establish communism in Grenada, they wanted to be active members of the Soviet Empire. "To this end, they sought ways to curry favor with the Soviet and other block countries, and loyally followed the instructions that came to them through Cubans. This, on both the domestic and international levels, the Grenadians emulated the USSR and tied their destiny to the Kremlin." This was found in a U.S. State Department and Department of Defense document published in Washington.

Ironically, the absolute distaste for Maurice Bishop that should have prevailed during this crucial period in Grenada and the East Caribbean was absent; any lingering bitterness was against Gairy influenced by PRG's effective propaganda. Two periods of the latter part of the twentieth century, I recall when the entity propaganda was used most effectively was by Gobbels during World War II and Bernard Coard of the PRG from 1972 to 1983. The result was that the liberator-father-of-the-nation image of Eric Matthew Gairy was almost totally decimated.

Accounts in detail of what transpired and what culminated in the execution of Maurice Rupert Bishop were already mentioned by Prime Minister Tom Adams of Barbados and Prime Minister Sir John Compton of St. Lucia. Suffice it to say that during the period when Bishop was first placed under house arrest for his seemingly "wavering attitude," I met the Barbados Prime Minister Tom Adams in his office on Bay Street, St. Michael. He indicated to me then that, despite the heated political exchanges across the Caribbean Sea between himself and Bishop, he really was fond of him. That at the time of the interview—a mere three days before Bishop was—he intimated to me that the OECS, Jamaica and Barbados governments were in the throes of effecting an Entebbe-like rescue of Bishop. The states of the Caribbean grouping were excluded from this arrangement—Trinidad and Tobago, led then by Prime Minister George Chambers and the tyrant from the South American continent, Guyana, President Forbes Burnham.

Of necessity, it should be mentioned here that 1972 through 1983 was a period of intense volatility for the Eastern Caribbean. Socialism was the candy being dangled as the easiest and quickest way out of our multiple economic woes. It was alleged there was a nefarious design already approved just waiting to be effected. This was supported by funds and arms from two sources, Havana and Tripoli. The target considered the most vulnerable was the OECS. A subsequent confidential document seized by the Americans disclosed a candid statement made by Socialist International. It advanced:

> Nonetheless and despite considerable assistance from the USSR and its proxies, the People's Revolutionary Government was a failure and the failure led to intense internal conflict and eventually to the overthrow and murder of Bishop.

Comrades Bishop and Coard had taken Grenada. The next in line to follow would be Dominica, where the thrust was being led by the Douglas brothers, Michael and Rosie. Arms were already in place in Dominica. Then next to follow would be St. Lucia, where George Odlum and Peter Josie were heating up the atmosphere. George Odlum had already seized Radio St. Lucia, but his plans were thwarted by his SLP's overwhelming victory at the polls the next day. When this takeover was realized, neighboring St. Vincent would be next.

And by the way, the faith of the Socialist fort in Kingstown, St. Vincent was being propounded and held by Dr. Ralph Gonsalzes, (recently elected prime minister). Long term plans included Antigua, where the articulate Tim Hector was keeping the flaming fervor of socialism burning with similar performance by Bobby Clarke in Barbados. It was interesting to note here that Bishop, many years before usurping the Eric Gairy's regime, had chosen to be someone extraordinary, a Communist. In the Caribbean that was a fearsome ideology. It was a sinister entity. On Monday, September 13 1982, Bishop delivered a "Line of March" speech for the party to the Central Committee of the General Meeting of the party. As chairman, among the many vital points he advanced, were the paucity of the revolution's inheritance and then examined some possibilities or models for the economic development of Grenada. He said:

> We believe that there are four main possibilities for economic development of Grenada and countries like Grenada. The first of these is a total private sector free enterprise system of economic development, your Seaga of Jamaica or your Puerto Rico model of development, where free enterprise is given full rein where the private sector is able to rule uncontrolled. The second model is a total state sector approach where just about anything important is owned by the state, where the state owns virtually everything that matters. The third type is a mixed economy, but with a private sector dominant, and of course, that is the model that we have chosen in Grenada.

Emphasizing that the objective was a deliberate concentration on the development of a Marxist-Leninist approach, it must be in the first instance to construct this socialism as rapidly, but as scientifically possible. That being so, Bishop declared, clearly they could not adopt the path of total private sector, free enterprise model because that would be inconsistent with what they believed in and for what they had been struggling.

Pragmatically Bishop explained that they could not opt for the total state sector model, as the state did not have the necessary material of financial resources, management and skills resources, access to markets, international contacts, and so on. He pointed out that all of this should be obvious, but reflected on the tremendous difficulties that they encountered in finding the dollars necessary to pay the down payment to the British company that would be installing the radar, communications and navigational equipment for their new international airport, or reflect on how difficult it had been to find guaranteed markets for their primary products and their agro-industrial products, or how difficult it was to find engineers or architects or science teachers or managers; and he noted that he did not even stress on good managers, he just said managers.

"No," he emphasized, "it would be impossible at this time for the state on its own to build Grenada. That, of course, means that an alliance is necessary, an alliance in the first place between the working class and the bourgeoisie in particular, the rural peasantry, and in the second place an alliance with those elements of the upper petty bourgeoisie and the national bourgeoisie who for different reasons, are willing to be involved in building the economy and the country at this time."

This address to the Central Committee of the NJM could be described as the prototype of a Communist manifesto, the essence of which being the development of almost resourceless and primitive Grenada by a revolutionary government whose function demanded the introduction of a strategy that would embrace a dual private sector and state with a private sector domination. It was a deceptive plan within which the masses would be effectively exploited to achieve the Communist objective of PRG. Bishop had stratified the people as bourgeoisie, middle bourgeoisie and petty bourgeoisie and the proletariat. He contended that the first and second category of people who were part of PRG would doubtless lend some degree of credibility to PRG, as nice people were a part of their structure. Bishop compared what he presumed to be a winning strategy to that of the recently failed revolution in Gambia. It failed because the comrades proceeded to eliminate the bourgeoisie. "That was a mistake, that same day they overthrew them," he said.

Evidently, the usurper Bishop was committed but his colleagues did not have absolute faith in his sole leadership, hence suggested that it be shared with Bernard Coard, with the latter being chairman of the Central Committee. The distrust fomented and became pervasive. The rest had been recorded and repeated ad nauseam. He concluded by reassuring the gathering that, "We believe that as a party, individually and collectively, we must now develop ourselves into becoming a more professional, more disciplined, more Leninist so that we would be able to meet the demands of this period. We also believe firmly that the path we have chosen is the right one."

The unstable scenario in the Eastern Caribbean was brought to an end, when with the approval of the leaders of the OECS, Prime Minister Eugenia Charles of Dominica traveled to Washington, DC, USA. She appeared with President Ronald Reagan on U.S. network television to give assurance and justification that the American invasion of Grenada was solicited, that the situation was not Panama repeating itself. The American invasion restored Grenada to democracy and the experience was now enshrined in Caribbean history. But this Grenada debacle, little did we know, registered international implications. The British were severely embarrassed that Grenada, being a member of the commonwealth of nations, was invaded by the Americans, though the British had expressed disapproval. This was what Margaret Thatcher, the then British prime minister, wrote in her book *The Downing Street Years* (Harper Collins Publishers, Inc.) American interests had outweighed other Anglo-American concerns. According to Thatcher:

> At best the British government had been made to seem impotent: at worst we looked deceitful.
>
> At this point my attention was abruptly diverted by events on the other side of the world undoubtedly influenced its reaction to the events which were taking place on the island of Grenada in the Eastern Caribbean.

However, on Wednesday, October 19, 1983, according to Thatcher, a pro-Soviet military coup had overthrown the government of Grenada.

> Our understanding was the Soviet Union had nothing to do with the developing Grenada scenario.

She expressed the view that it was a pernicious regime.

> The new regime was certainly a vicious and unstable bunch. With the exception of General Austin who led the coup they were all in their twenties and a number of them had a record of violence and torture. Maurice Bishop, the overthrown prime minister, and five of his close supporters were shot dead. There was outrage at what had happened in most of the other Caribbean countries. Jamaica and Barbados wanted military intervention in which they would have liked the Americans and us to take part. My immediate reaction was that it would be most unwise of the Americans, let alone us, to accede to this suggestion. I was afraid that it would put foreign communities in Grenada at severe risk. There were some 200 British civilians there and many more Americans. The main organization of Caribbean States, CARICOM, was not prepared to agree to military intervention in Grenada. However, the Organization of Eastern Caribbean States (OECS) decided unanimously to put together a force and called on other governments to help in restoring peace and order in the island. Clearly, an American reaction would be crucial.
>
> It should not be forgotten that the USA dominated the entire continent of North and South America. The Caribbean

> was located within North America, Thatcher claimed, It was easy to see why the United States might be tempted to go in and deal with the thugs who had taken over in Grenada. But as I always pointed out to the Americans afterwards though apparently to little effect, Grenada was not transformed from a democratic island paradise into a Soviet surrogate overnight in October, 1983. The Marxist Maurice Bishop had already come to power there through an earlier coup in March, 1979; he had suspended the Constitution and put many of his opponents in goal. He was indeed, a personal friend of Fidel Castro. The Americans had had hostile relations with his government for years. Bishop was, admittedly, something of a pragmatist and had even made a visit to the United States at the end of May, 1983. It seems that it was, in part, a dispute about the Grenada government's attitude to private enterprise which brought about the clash with his colleagues in the Marxist New Jewel Movement that ultimately led to his fall.

This view about the reason for the collapse of the leadership was incorrect and sheer speculation. Again, a top secret document showed and detailed that:

> The internal crisis that led to the fall and murder of Bishop in the autumn of 1983 did not indicate any strong divergence of views between Bishop and those who replaced him. Rather, the struggle appears to have been almost exclusively personal. The complaint against Bishop involved inefficiency, insufficient ideological coherence and lack of strong leadership and guidance, not political deviation or betrayal of goals of the revolution.

Thatcher claimed that there was strongly adverse international reaction to the American intervention and in the circumstances gave a boost to any Soviet propaganda of East versus West. Fact was, Russia was not terribly interested in Grenada. Cuba and Libya had responded to a call for assistance. She wrote:

> In its early reports, Soviet television news apparently thought that Grenada was a province of southern Spain. But soon their propaganda machine began firing on all cylinders. The Cubans were portrayed as having played a heroic role in resisting the invasion. When I went to the Commonwealth Heads of Government meeting in New Delhi the following month it was still Grenada which was still the most controversial topic of discussion. President Mugabe claimed that American action in Grenada would provide a precedent for South Africa in dealing with her neighbors. My own public criticism of America and refusal to become involved in it also led to temporary bad relations with some of Britain's long-standing friends in the Caribbean. It was an unhappy time.
>
> I told my colleagues that our advice against U.S. intervention had, I believed, been sound. But the U.S. for its part, had taken a different view on an issue which directly touched its national interests.

This was the British Prime Minister Margaret Thatcher's account of the Grenada crisis, and her egoistic conclusion was divinely inspired: "Britain's friendship with the United States must on no account be jeopardized." This was but one confirmation that the sinister Anglo-American world domination will quite likely persist until the end of this system of things. But it should be recalled that in this self-indulgent world, self-interest was given priority. It will be recalled that while the American government had in earlier years imposed trade sanctions on apartheid South Africa, Margaret Thatcher acted on the premise that economic factors outweighed moral and humane concerns. Any concerns for the oppressed Blacks in South Africa were superficial. She was Imperialist to the core. Nonetheless her strength was admirable. She was the "iron lady."

Self-appointed Prime Minister Bishop, the tall, handsome, charismatic, articulate Communist could be likened to a meteor. He emerged, soared, glittered brilliantly, and then plunged into evanescence; evidently he took along with him the thrill of communism, as at this point in time, little is heard of it as they propounded it then in this Eastern Caribbean region. They had characterized it as socialism.

As was mentioned earlier, Maurice Rupert Bishop had probably either ingested too little or too much of the Communist ideology. It worked for Castro, of necessity in Cuba, and we continue to applaud him. We understood also that "necessity knows no bounds." Castro was never any consummate Communist. The U.S. government pushed him into making a choice for survival. He made it and pleased himself as others did, given the circumstances. Suffice it to say that Bishop, a young and dashing man, proceeded through ideological over-indulgence to inflict multiple stab wounds of delusions upon his person and fell a casualty of his reckless miscalculations.

CHAPTER 12

The Right Honorable
Vere Cornwall Bird
Former Prime Minister of Antigua and Barbuda

The "Big, Old Bird." That was how many Antiguans referred to their former Prime Minister Vere Bird, affectionately. Physically, he was the biggest of the Caribbean government leaders, and one of the most successful. He had served as leader of his country the longest in the Caribbean a little ahead of former Prime Minister George Price of Belize, Sir Lynden Oscar Pindling, former prime minister of the Bahamas, and Sir John Compton, former prime minister of St. Lucia. He was successful in the context of retaining the confidence of the people and being voted repeatedly back into office. Over the many years, the four leaders in question prospered. This was success in any language that understood the power of the American dollar. Vere Bird towered over his twin island state and he was loved and revered by very many. How else could he have survived so many years facing the polls? And we are told his victories were not of a Forbes Burnham style or model of the Co-operative Republic of Guyana!

Prime Minister Bird was perhaps the first and only Caribbean government leader to have had a Salvation Army orientation. When one looked at the Bird, he quite likely compelled thinkers to reflect on the probability that he could have emerged from the lineage of the early inhabitants of Barbuda, located some eighty-six miles from Antigua. Barbuda was the primary breeding factory for big, strong, healthy and black slaves.

Vere Bird is one of the principal harbingers of local politics. Not unusually, he came through the practical route of the Trade Union Movement. He was soldiered to the idea of forming the Antigua Trades and Labor Union, and he became one of its founders and vice president.

But his formative years saw him being big for his age and making it through primary school. Beyond that tutoring, it was all private study; ambition and self-discipline were excellent co-partners that ushered one on to success in life. According to Napoleon, "Ambition is of little account without opportunity." He learned that from keen observation. Big Bird found employment as a clerk at a store in St. John's, the capital. At this source, it gave him the opportunity to serve a multiplicity of tastes. He observed silently the behavior of people, and how meticulous and sometimes inordinately selfish and obstinate some can be to achieve their own ends. Vere Bird observed that man was creative, but was ceaselessly in need and would stretch to any lengths to satisfy this need. He concluded that man was intrinsically selfish and greedy. But then, the Bible had already established that fact. It was no theory.

Often pensive, at times he found himself sailing away in an extraneous dimension where man did not exist. He was searching and exploring until it dawned on him that he had a Christian calling that was totally overwhelming. Unavoidably, he succumbed to it. He enlisted himself in the Salvation Army. True to his faith, the Big Bird worked diligently and rose to the rank of captain. Captain Bird was born Vere Cornwall Bird in1909 and began his early education at the St. John's Boys School and the Salvation Army School in Trinidad, and was later dispatched on assignment to serve in Grenada in 1939. How much his religion impacted his becoming involved in the Trade Union Movement was difficult to determine, but the Big Bird agreed to be one of the founding members of the Antigua Trades and Labor Union. Later, he was invited to be a member of the Trade Union Executive Committee.

His work for people did not go floating into oblivion. Bird was elected a member of the Legislative Council of Antigua in 1945. That same year, the now quite active trade unionist and politician traveled to Trinidad to attend a conference of the Caribbean Union. In 1946, the Caribbean Union Conference was held in the neighboring island of St. Kitts, which he attended.

The next year, 1947, Bird journeyed to Jamaica to attend the now annual Caribbean Union Conference and he was appointed the vice president of the Caribbean Congress of Labor. In 1951, he was made a member of the Executive Council and later, in 1953, invited to be a participant at the West Indian Government Conference in London. By this time, Vere Bird had become a noted Caribbean trade unionist and, in 1956, appointed a member of the Caribbean Commission. He was also made minister of trade and production, Antigua, an office he held from 1956 to 1960. In 1960, he assumed the role of chief minister of Antigua. This was rather impressive for a product of Booth's Salvation Army. In 1967, he became the leader of the Antigua Labor Party (ALP).

The period of 1965 to 1971 may be described as quite eventful for Vere Bird politically. As Antigua's chief minister in 1965, he became a founder of a new Caribbean economic trade initiative with representatives from Barbados and Guyana. It was named the Caribbean Free Trade Association (CARIFTA). The following year, 1966, he led Antigua to the United Kingdom to negotiate a sort of quasi-independence status termed Associated Statehood with Britain. The following year, 1967, he became the premier of Antigua, but lost the next elections in 1971. There were multiple allegations of corruption. He also held a stranglehold on the electronic media in his small nation. Vere Bird and his sons owned the private Radio ZDK while the Antigua Broadcasting Service (ABS) was controlled by his Antigua Labor Party government.

In fact, Antigua, it had been alleged, was the most corrupt of all the Caribbean territories, but almost all the Antigua government supporters enjoyed a slice of this corrupt cake. The Old Bird was missed during that period in the opposition. Premier George Walter was given one term in office, from 1971 to1976. Bird was swept back into power in 1976 and held on to that office successfully, then took Antigua and Barbuda into independence in 1981 to become his nation's first prime minister. During that year, Bird assumed the portfolio of minister of planning, external affairs, defense and energy. In 1982, he was appointed one of Her Majesty the Queen's Privy Councillors.

Perhaps unavoidably, the rumblings of corruption persisted and Bird assigned himself the ministry of finance. The public rivalry and animosity between his two sons, Vere, Jr. and Lester, were notorious. He apparently showed favor for one over the other, but the elder was evidently more qualified and proficient.

In 1984, Prime Minister Bird was invited to the St. John College in Rochester, New York where he was awarded an honorary degree of Doctor of Laws. Four years later, in 1988, he was awarded the Order of the Nation (ON) and, in 1996, the Order of the National Hero (ONH). Doubtless, it was a season of awards for the Antiguan prime minister. The Order of the Caribbean Community (OCC) was bestowed on him in 1998. But to crystallize these generosities to that old Bird, in 1999, he was awarded the Companion of the Most Order of the National Hero (NH).

In retrospect, Vere Bird fortuitously was drawn into the Trade Union Movement as an activist, and from this platform stepped into politics. Agitating and bargaining for workers had taught Bird an invaluable lesson. That was according to him, "Always seem to be a friend who will assist. Even if you fail in the attempt the person with whom you're involved will remember that you gave service to him. And I don't mean to be a liar or hypocrite," he said to me in 1982 in an interview at the La Toc Hotel in Castries.

He was attending a meeting of the Organization of Eastern Caribbean States (OECS). And he was unwell.

The Big Bird was imposing in any company. Intently, he listened with a pair of beady and penetrating eyes on a massive face punctuated with moles. He could be intimidating and often reminded one of a no-nonsense martinet of a primary school. With his long legs extending seemingly a mile away from his body, he smiled without exposing his teeth as though trained in the skill.

I had posed the question, "You are the longest surviving head of any government in the Caribbean. Perhaps only Prime Minister Lynden Pindling of the Bahamas may match your consecutive return to office. Is there a special skill or some work of Jehovah that has sustained you?"

The teeth-hidden smiled broadened. Then he opined, "Refrain from making enemies of people. Don't engage in uncalled-for war with your adversaries. And here I don't mean your political rivals. I mean people generally because people, without them, you can't be a politician. Without them there would be no arena to peddle your politics. If you need people, you must find a way or a strategy to win them on your side. Surely you can't or won't win all but you will win most if it is a sincere strategy."

"I am told by a friend in Antigua that one of your strengths was to remember names," I slipped in.

"Well, I never thought of it like that. Common courtesy alone is one thing, but a politician should give more if he begs for someone's trust. Caring about people is important. You must prove it. I care enough to remember your name. Not, what's your name again? In addition, you're in the business of politics. That's the science of government. This was developed in the hustings. Not polemics. People remember what you say and do, especially if they are unkind: you too should develop the skill to remember the people whom you wish to serve, it reaches people emotionally when you remember their name," he explained.

"Prime Minister Vere Bird, how best will Antiguans remember you, when you will have passed on?" I asked.

This time he released a guttural laugh. "Hawh! Hawh! Hawh!" he retrieved his legs with dexterity for someone aged and unwell. "I see that you remember my name, and it is so easy to remember. But it's good looking too!" We both laughed. I thought, he did have a sense of humor.

He went on to emphasize, "Well, I think I worked harder than Satan, though not with any of his wiles to guide the tourism industry. And perhaps, like the Bahamas, it is vital to us and we take it seriously the tourism industry and government as a business employs the most people in Antigua. We have constructed a deepwater harbor to accommodate cruise and cargo ships. We have a brand new electrification system and a desalination plant to ensure we will never be out of water again. And we do have a small, but a decent, international airport. I think Antiguans are enjoying a lifestyle comparable with any other states in the Caribbean. Our educational and health services are areas in which we could take pride. Our sports stadium allows a stake in the cricket revenue as Barbados, Trinidad, Jamaica and Guyana. In this respect, we in Antigua are ahead of the other less developed states as they are called. We also have a Nelson Yachting facility that is perhaps the very best in the Caribbean. We have done our best with what we earn. We are a small but rich country."

"Prime Minister, is this a novel approach? A reverse psychology? The belief that Antigua is small but a rich country?"

"This has always been my philosophy. We have much to be thankful for in Antigua. There is some aspect of poverty. But not the kind of abject poverty seen in South America and even in America. I have seen some totally depressed communities that I never conceived could exist in America, a huge country, a superpower, touted as being the wealthiest country in the world." He seemed emotional.

"I hope this is not too sensitive a question. But not so long ago you declined to be part of arrangement for the OECS. You indicated that you had worked too hard to take Antigua to its prevailing stage and now to hand it over. The idea, you said, was tantamount to a new form of neo-colonialism? You did incur the displeasure of your Caribbean colleagues."

"I make no apologies for that statement. It is the truth and we know that the truth sometimes offends. I wish them well of course. Antigua is in reasonably good shape. And if that's it, I thank you for coming to see me," he concluded.

Vere Bird, doubtless, was the typical politician, with a different kind of wiles. He had been able to retain the affection of the majority having been out of office only one term since he became chief minister in the early sixties. That is, after he had served as one of the first members of the defunct West Indies Federation legislature.

On July 18, 1982, soon after the OECS meeting here in St. Lucia, the weekly *Star* newspaper carried a report headed: "Bird's Money Problems." The following is an excerpt of this report:

> Faced with mounting debt, some of which dated back to colonial days, Antigua and Barbuda may be forced to ask some of its creditors to reschedule portions of the country's debt. Deputy prime minister Lester Bird, who made the disclosure, said that Antigua's current debt problem was heightened by the recent report of the World Bank to graduate the island state from the bank's soft loan window, the International Development Association.
>
> "We have some problems paying some of our old debts and we are in the process of working with an International Financing Corporation that has now developed a whole new

> program of rescheduling these debts so that we are in a position to pay them," Bird said.
>
> He placed the old debt figure at U.S. $65 million and said that the money was borrowed to build a deep water harbor to facilitate large cruise ships; to introduce a program of electrification when all the lights went out in Antigua in 1968 and to install a desalination plant.
>
> "A contributing factor to the debt problem," he said, "was that all of the projections for the projects didn't quite meet the growth rate that was required to service the loans."
>
> Bird defended the government's action in borrowing the money in the first place, saying that at the time, concessionary financing was not available to Antigua to finance essential infrastructural development schemes.
>
> "We had to borrow money at commercial rates," said the Economic Development Minister, "there was no IDA in those days."
>
> "For example," he pointed out, "Antigua had to borrow U.S. $12 million from the U.S. Export-Import Bank to finance the construction of the deep water harbor."
>
> "As if to make matters worse," the deputy prime minister went on, "the World Bank has declared that because of Antigua's high per capita income, it would no longer be eligible for soft loans from IDA, the window of the bank which is reserved for the world's poorest countries."
>
> "We have just done a five year macroeconomic plan, in which we pointed out the extreme difficulty in which we have found ourselves," he said. "We have been graduated and we cannot access IDA and we have to go to commercial borrowings to do basic infrastructure."

Referring to the criticisms at home about the government mounting debt, Bird described the administration's action as both necessary and a calculated risk.

Meanwhile, Prime Minister Bird had denied that he took EC$250,000 from the treasury for expenses for himself and his entourage for a trip to New York. In a public statement, Bird said that the allegations in an article in the *Outlet* newspaper was an attempt to discredit him at a time "when the government was on an even keel."

It was amazing what the Old Bird considered being on an even keel. First, he claimed that Antigua was rich, though it was heavily indebted to several foreign institutions. And what did Anthony Mark Jones point out in his booklet titled *Caribbean Men*? He said:

> Bird's political philosophy can be considered left of center, but like most Caribbean leaders, his actions have tended to contradict his labor position and policy.

That view of the Old Bird cannot be disputed. And any proposal for political integration of the Eastern Caribbean with Antigua included did not seem likely during his lifetime. This was totally contrary to the earlier view of Caribbean integration. In fact, as I pointed out earlier, Vere Bird was a strong federalist, but he was not at all interested in what the former prime minister of St. Vincent and the Grenadines, Sir James Mitchell, said in a speech in Tortola, British Virgin Islands, in March, 1982. This was extracted from a booklet titled *East Caribbean Unity*, a compilation of two speeches by Sir James Mitchell. This was a salient point:

> If we in the Eastern Caribbean states unite, we will not only have an impact on the entire Caribbean community, but we will be sending tremendous signals to the small states in the rest of the world.
>
> The Americans united 200 years ago. The Germans did it and made a country out of provinces. The Italians did it. So is unity beyond us? Are you telling me that Garibaldi in Italy and Hamilton of America born in Nevis, could all have done centuries ago what we in the tail end of the twentieth century

> can't do? Can't we pull a few villages together! I refuse to believe that we can't. Simon Bolivar created countries out of tribes and so can we. Can't we triumph over the decisive forces in whatever shape or form they come?

These were all valid and nationalistic questions from Sir James. But then, the Big Bird would have no part of the expressions to integrate. In fact, more than ever it revealed Big Bird's obstinacy. He would not be recruited. And I wrote a piece following that OECS meeting here at Hotel La Toc in July, 1987. The piece was titled "The Old Bird Flees the OECS Coop" and published in the *Star* newspaper on July 18, 1987. It read:

> The octogenarian Vere Bird, prime minister of Antigua and Barbuda, would not have missed the recently concluded Heads of Government Summit for anything. He had to be here at all costs, though he was not interested in the sort of proposal being advanced by the Organization of Eastern Caribbean States (OECS). His business in St. Lucia had nothing to do with the OECS, but rather with trade negotiations with the wider Caribbean governments.
>
> Prime Minister Bird could have dispatched his son and deputy Lester to the summit. But the prime minister did not enjoy such a latitude. Moreover, an atmosphere of distrust existed between son and father. Prime Minister Bird had been told that Lester was planning a coup against him. Lester had denied entertaining such a scheme. But Bird was taking no chances. Lester's functions had been limited to his portfolios. Prime Minister Bird came to St. Lucia, listened and left unimpressed. He was not interested in any form of union that removed the twin state of Antigua and Barbuda from his control. He rejected the invitation to be a part of the OECS initiative. By insinuation, he claimed that his prime minister colleagues were neo-colonists. He saw the initiative as a cover for the re-colonization of Antigua and Barbuda!

Technically, Bird was correct, if he were not the prime minister or president of whatever union to emerge out of the current initiative, his twin state would be excluded from the arrangement. He would, in fact, be surrendering his political control and sovereignty to Caribbean neo-colonists. As imminent senility disqualified him as a candidate for the leadership of the OECS; his parochialism rushed up to the fore and seized control of his senses. This was an emotional affair.

At any rate, no one dared accuse the Old Bird of inconsistency. He and John Compton had scuttled Errol Barrow's "Little Eight" initiative in the sixties. Antigua and Barbuda's opposition leader Tim Hector was, as usual, at variance with Prime Minister Bird's decision. He said Bird did not consult Antiguans and Barbudans. Neither did his cabinet agree to take a decision. Bird made and took all decisions alone. Hector pointed out, however, that Bird will have "to talk to the people and with us," and if he saw some semblance of unity on a proper basis he would quite likely join!

Sir Arthur Lewis, who had been the Barbados Prime Minister Errol Barrow's emissary in respect of the political structure of the "Little Eight" had then expressed the view that the Caribbean will only witness a change when the present leaders were removed from the scene. He was correct. Two of that breed remained. One was Vere Bird. The other was John Compton. Since then, the Bird had passed away, but his government had not been free of a seemingly unending chain of problems. First, his sons were said to be jostling for position to succeed him. It was well known that the son Lester, who qualified to be his deputy, was not his first choice. Constantly he had to defend himself against corruption, the inability to meet debt payments and his authoritarianism, among other charges.

Prime Minister Vere Bird did not attend an institution of higher learning to qualify as a philosopher and historian like, for instance, Dr. Eric Williams of Republic of Trinidad and Tobago. His institution was the Salvation Army. Nevertheless, whether he preached but never practiced it, his philosophy was: "Don't ill speak and denigrate others as a pastime. The rest of the world indulges in this behavior. You do not have to, as it is not lifesaving to be unkind to others. This is not saying one must be sacrosanct."

"Just be restrained and thoughtful if not openly kind. Thoughtfulness could be believed is kindness, a scarcity of which is evident almost everywhere in our wicked world today," he admonished.

That was the philosophy of the Big Bird, considered the father of the twin island nation of Antigua and Barbuda. The right Honorable Vere Cornwall Bird, former prime minister of Antigua and Barbuda, passed away on Monday, June 28, 1999. His nation and the rest of the Caribbean mourned his passing as it was like a milestone removed from our Caribbean political highway in life. He was, indeed, literally one huge institution.

CHAPTER 13

Honorable Edward Philip George Seaga
Former Prime Minister of Jamaica

As they headed to test the ballot box again in 1997 to choose a government, we earnestly followed the seeming pattern of the Jamaican electorate and it was presumed with some degree of risk that barring divine intervention, the American-born Jamaican politician Edward Philip George Seaga could again become Jamaica's prime minister. The months succeeded each other to polling day. Now we hasten to admit it. We were wrong. Seaga lost again! Prime Minister Percival James Patterson with his People National Party (PNP) was re-elected to office. Just another setback endemic in politics. That country is the most populous in the English-speaking Caribbean with some 2,000,000 and the most volatile in the region.

Born of Lebanese heritage on May 28, 1930 in Boston, Massachusetts, USA, Edward Seaga's parents had immigrated to Jamaica many years before, where they became an integral part of the business sector. His early formative years in Kingston gave him the opportunity to observe inevitably the cultural landscape that made him supremely knowledgeable on almost every aspect of life in Jamaica, from infancy, childhood and adolescence, then at Wolmers Boys School from 1944 to 1948. Being born an American

was no accident. For his supplemental education, the debonair Seaga entered at Harvard University in 1948.

Education was designed to enhance one's cerebral mechanism such as would allow enquiring minds to explore the unknown dimensions in human growth and development. The exposure to enlightenment at such prestigious institutions as Harvard and Princeton or Oxford and the University of London on the other side of the Atlantic was infinitely more than just privilege. It was more like a phenomenon heard of, but never ever experienced, by most people in the world of educational development.

The young and zealous Seaga graduated with a Bachelor of Arts in sociology, anthropology in 1952. He returned to Jamaica and accepted an attachment at the Institute of Social and Economic Studies at the University of the West Indies (UWI), Mona. This assignment, which was primarily field research, investigated "the development of the child and renewal spirit cults." This exercise demanded enormous patience and tolerance with a capacity to assess and appreciate moods that would lend to appreciating when to pursue or suspend a line of questioning. This job also begged for meekness and compassion. It required the researcher to reside in the homes of subjects being studied in the villages and rural areas. These people were the most indigent of the masses. This was an assignment the young Seaga enjoyed, as it was positively supplemental to his understanding of people and especially the underprivileged. He was experiencing various elements of the sociology and anthropology he had studied at college.

Meeting and living and talking with so many people who were of the view they were ignored, disrespected, neglected and disregarded influenced even inadvertently Seaga's later decision to enter politics. Rather articulate, Seaga made the step and chose politics as a career and, with much enthusiasm, he joined the Jamaica Labor Party (JLP). His power of oral expression did not go unrecognized. Soon he was nominated to the Upper House of the Jamaica

Legislature in 1959. Then, at twenty-nine years of age, Seaga enjoyed the distinction of being the youngest member in the legislature's history.

On his journey to the apex of his new career, he was elected assistant secretary of the JLP in 1960, and secretary in 1962. As a member of parliament and the district representative for Western Kingston, he served as the minister of development and social welfare, an office for which he had prepared himself. A dashing, intelligent young man of fine tastes, it was expected that he would have his pick of the loveliest crop of women in Jamaica. He chose the beautiful Elizabeth Constantine. She had won the title of Miss Jamaica in 1964. On August 22 of that same year, they were married. He was now also the leader of JLP. The island of Jamaica then was an arena of seemingly unending turbulence. The violence was widespread. Supporters of both the JLP and the PNP clashed violently, as though it were a sporting feat in which they had sworn to excel. Though it could be an evil déjà vu, this horrendous posture claimed the lives of over twenty people in July 2001. Of necessity, Prime Minister P. J. Patterson called out the army to restore order. The hooligans of the two political factions were at it again!

Edward Seaga served in the Hugh Shearer regime from 1967 to 1972 when the JLP government lost the elections. Seaga was then officially made the leader of the opposition. During those years it was presumed that the socialist policies of Prime Minister Michael Manley had incurred the displeasure of the U.S. government. Manley empathized with Dr. Fidel Castro of Cuba. In fact, they were next door neighbors and friends. Moreover, the prime minister's constant anti-Imperialist breathings totally alienated the Americans. The vindictive American government declared a ban on all Americans traveling to Jamaica. Tourism was a major industry in Jamaica and the Americans knew where it would hurt. Seaga, it was then reported, had visited Washington on an invitation from the U.S. government.

This American-born Seaga was expected to create an atmosphere in Jamaica that would conduce to cordial relations between the two countries. The USA's reprisal action had affected Jamaica abrasively. Now Seaga and his JLP were expending, it was claimed, "American dollars" as though—according to Dr. Eric Williams—"money is no problem." The 1980 general elections dealt a shattering defeat to Michael Manley's PNP, which was not altogether unexpected. It was charged that many people were paid for their votes. This was not unusual in Jamaica. Seaga became the new prime minister. He struggled, and though reports indicated and persisted that he had been receiving injection of financial aid from the USA, nothing seemed to be working towards improvement in Jamaica. The economy was seemingly comatose.

However, while general elections were constitutional in 1985, Seaga—in a cunning move—called a snap election in 1983. The opposing Manley and his PNP were caught palpably unprepared. He protested to no avail, rather than accept that he was completely out-maneuvered. The result was a clean sweep of the House of Assembly for the JLP. In 1986, general elections were being held throughout the English-speaking Caribbean and regimes were being changed. The *Teller* magazine carried a piece on Jamaica and Seaga then:

> The Jamaica experience since the advent of Edward Seaga's Jamaica Labor Party to power has not been totally free of a series of unending problems. Doubtless, Michael Manley, the present opposition leader, has over-asserted himself in office carrying Jamaica into the Socialist camp close up to communism. Positively a brilliant man, he had formed a close attachment with Fidel Castro of Cuba. Being next door neighbors, economic assistance from Havana was readily available to Kingston. Cuban doctors were then a permanent feature in the life of Jamaica and it appeared then that CARICOM was about to lose a senior member.

The former Jamaica government's repeated pronouncements of American imperialism had alienated the U.S. government and a schism had developed and widened. Over a period of three years, two not insignificant features emerged and worsened namely unemployment and violence. These scampered out of control and Jamaica was totally destabilized. This was the situation that ushered in Edward Seaga and his party into power. Seaga obviously meant well and still does but his policies do not seem to bring about not even some semblance of the panacea for which Jamaica begs. The Jamaica dollar was devalued and had plunged from being the highest dollar in the Caribbean to the lowest currency exchange level in the English-speaking Caribbean. This country now appeared permanently married to the International Monetary Fund (IMF) and has among other problems earned widespread disaffection for the government.

Elections are expected to be called any time in Jamaica despite Prime Minister Edward Seaga's recent statement that he does not plan to go to the polls before it is constitutionally due. Naturally, one can listen to Seaga. Although we believe him, most pre-suppose some doubt as he is essentially a politician operating at his best to stay in power.

Seaga's Jamaica has received more aid dollars from the United States than any other country in the Caribbean, but the gesture seems to little avail. The popularity polls taken in Jamaica have fluctuated, and although the most recent reflected some gain to the incumbent, he is aware that the seeming spectre of losing the next general elections to Michael Manley looms menacingly real.

As it stands, the problems of Jamaica cannot be easily solved in one or two terms, therefore, now or later Seaga must reluctantly give way to Michael Manley. This, as we understand it, represents democracy at work.

Seaga's posture was calculated. It was diametrically opposite to Manley's. This was exploited to ingratiate the U.S. government's goodwill. He rejected the socialism that was sweeping the Caribbean. The Jamaica prime minister projected himself to such a state that he severed relations with Castro and Cuba to become the U.S. President Regan's most trusted friend in the Caribbean. In spite of all these political tactics designed to attract investments and other financing, the economy further declined, the result of factors beyond the government's control at that time. And to exacerbate an already deplorable situation was the continuing political violence. For instance, during the 1980 election campaign, some 850 casualties of that senseless civil war were registered. What pointless sacrifice!

Seaga called the elections in 1989 and lost to Michael Manley's PNP in a landslide. The political struggle still raged on. Significantly, it should be recalled that Seaga was a practicing sociologist, and one of sensitivity who never failed to employ his training by allowing it to permeate his political career. I wrote earlier how his first project for the University of the West Indies had taken him into depressed areas where he had lodged in homes where indigence was stark. Since then, he had always cherished the thought of demolishing every slum area in Jamaica but especially in the capital city of Kingston.

Benevolent Seaga mounted a team of workers and converged on the slum district of West Kingston called "Backadeyard"—translated "at-the-back-of-the-yard." Seaga reconstructed that community and it was now celebrated abroad as the Seaga Project or Scheme, it was renamed Tivoli Gardens. Formerly that slum area was a repository of all the conceivable elements of lawlessness. Violence was endemic and gangs of young men and women merely existed one day at a time. Though life generally was unpredictable, existence in Backadeyard was one of unequal, evil dimensions where grime, tears, guns, drugs, misery, diseases, loss of life were in permanent residence.

As may be imagined, it was not an easy proposition for Seaga and attendants, as the man who was convinced that he was unloved and had nothing to lose and to live for would be a willing candidate for crime and, doubtless, a victim of circumstances. It took some time to convince the community of Backadeyard that their lives were miraculously being transformed; moreover, many had been born and nurtured into this miserable ghetto world and were reluctant to change it. That Herculean task was assailed. This persuasive speaker lectured to them and they listened reluctantly, at first. It penetrated their thinking that a better and more sanitary and tranquil way of life was in the offing. They yielded and gradually accepted the transformation. Schools, skills, home economics, sewing, tailoring, hairdressing and every aspect of cosmetology, mechanics, painting, masonry, plumbing and several other trades and occupations were introduced as supportive elements that attract earnings to sustain community life.

The Seaga vision was realized at a cost of millions of dollars that Seaga later confessed brought him "immense joy." He and his architects had created a brand new world for thousands of destitute, desolate and distressed souls. It was a new lease on life for West Kingston. The residents of Tivoli Gardens expressed their gratitude in a manner that has given cause for concern. That is, they considered themselves Seaga's people. In essence, they would die for him. Not infrequently, gangs from Tivoli Gardens would rally forth to support a Seaga cause against Prime Minister P. J. Patterson's supporters. Recently, there was a spate of violent clashes in which over ten of the rival gangs were killed. Patterson called out the Army to restore law and order. Seaga and Patterson, though, are in harmony relative to the persistent lawlessness and are working together for a common purpose to end the violence. In this respect,

Jamaica is fortunate. The prospects are evident. Seaga is very likely to serve another stint as the prime minister of Jamaica.

A man of probity and sincerity, Edward Philip George Seaga had doubtless left his imprint on Jamaica. One of the most intelligent and charismatic leaders in the Caribbean, his major failing was not unlike that of other brilliant leaders. They were unable to solve the problems of man. Try as they may, this function with its efficacy was way beyond their capacity.

CHAPTER 14

The Right Honorable
Sir John George Melvin Compton
Former Chief Minister, Premier and Prime Minister of St. Lucia

Are we as homosapiens responsible for our birth and the place of birth? Perhaps, if it were possible, some of us may substitute our parents for other humans whom we perceived to be more suitable as parents. This gave an indication of how severely flawed we were as humans. Sir John George Melvin Compton was still being subjected to a deluge of ignorance that emanated, not from the wise or knowledgeable, but from the ignorant. Distressingly, too many people did not know the meaning of ignorant. They deployed it in the context of being stupid. But ignorance was the lack of knowledge of something. The acquisition of nationalism of any country came in two distinct forms: indigenous birth and naturalization or adoption.

Any person who chose to become a citizen of another country should be commended by indigenous citizens who had no choice but to become a citizen through an accident of birth. Perhaps only a negligible few of his vindictive detractors, those who hate as a pastime and enjoy it, will still hold to the view that Sir John was not St. Lucian. My own parents were Antiguans who immigrated to

St. Lucia and here I am, just by accident of birth, a St. Lucian. But then, I immigrated to Canada and became a Canadian citizen.

No one in St. Lucia was more representative of St. Lucia than John George Melvin Compton. He personified St. Lucia. This enchanting "Helen of the West Indies," compared with the rest of the OECS, boasted an infrastructural development that did credit to her beauty. That credit should be given to the vision of the leader.

No one person can be identified as being more culturally St. Lucian than Sir John Compton. He even speaks French Creole more fluently than most St. Lucians.

The attractive Ethel Compton, with her two sisters, visited her two brothers and four cousins in the eastern districts of Dennery and Micoud in St. Lucia in 1913, as a young lady, and then again in 1924 to 1925. Romance entered her lifestyle in 1924 and this resulted in pregnancy. She gave birth to a son at Batula Hall on May 1, 1926. How would Ethel have known that thirty-seven years later that boy would be the esteemed government leader of St. Lucia?

The new mother met someone whom she consented to marry. This marriage did not take them into old age together, and one situation was clear. Ethel's son John was not adopted by her husband. If he had contemplated such a move and acted upon it, Ethel's son's name would have been John G. M. John. As the circumstances would dictate, a mother's love, care and attention could nurture a child that would grow up with or without a biological father. The infant John grew up within the shelter of his mother's family name, Compton. A family name is vital. It anchored a person and, through love and cooperation, members of a family merged on to ensure that a centripetal entity existed. From an early age John displayed signs of being comfortable enjoying his own company. Was this being an introvert? Regarding his primary school days in Canouan, his cousin Julian Compton intimated:

> John was different from all of us. While we played bat and ball or football or rounders or raced on the beach or tried to make it with girls, John was somewhere reading, and reading, and reading, and what was quite noticeable about him again was his attitude. We would walk with our books in our hands swinging. Not John, he would lodge his books under his armpits and walk with his chest out as though going somewhere with a purpose. He left us and went on to the grammar school on the mainland St. Vincent, where he excelled.

I interviewed Ethel Compton John prior to St. Lucia's attainment of independence in 1979. Her son John would be St. Lucia's first prime minister. To commemorate the occasion, I wrote a booklet titled *A Prime Minister's Finest Hour*. She said:

> John was attending the St. Vincent Grammar School. He was twelve years old. He had always been a bright, good, obedient, shy, and honest child. At the grammar school, his teacher Alderman Sutherland, then a young assistant master, but now Doctor Sutherland, once said to me, "Be prepared to spend money on John. He is extraordinarily bright. He will one day be as big as any top man here in Kingstown." That prediction was born out many years later. My brothers and cousins had felt that St. Lucia offered a better life for them. I visited St. Lucia in 1913 as a youngster and then again in 1924 through 1925. My brothers and other relatives were scattered throughout Dennery, Mon Repos and Micoud. I brought John to St. Lucia the day Hitler's war broke out on September 3, 1939. He was thirteen years old.

The Comptons were seafarers and shipwrights. They had established themselves some three generations earlier in the districts of Dennery and Micoud. The roots transplanted from neighboring St. Vincent, only sixty miles south of St. Lucia, had taken place in 1910. Four seafaring cousins and two brothers began building boats, sloops and schooners for domestic and inter-island trade. This was the foundation the young John Compton found when he arrived in St. Lucia. And as was the case with young people who developed later into exceptional leaders, John Compton was noticeably studious. He attended White's Secondary School, Castries Intermediate School and St. Mary's College in Castries.

Reports from his uncle, Mailings Compton stated, that:

> While other children played games and dated and partied, John was reading and he passed his senior Cambridge examination with ease.

Like many young St. Lucians then, John Compton immigrated to the Dutch island of Curacao. Hitler's war had created this opportunity for young West Indians to immigrate and work in the oil refinery overseas. His uncle Mailings explained:

> John should have won the Island Scholarship but it was discovered that he had not lived in St. Lucia for ten years as required. The truth is, he did win the scholarship but the scholarship was awarded to someone else. John wept like a baby when he did not get that scholarship.

Ironically, that person to whom the scholarship was awarded, many years later became Compton's cabinet secretary. The young Compton was in St. Lucia before the scholarship announcement in 1947, and then he returned to Curacao. The next year, 1948, John Compton gave up his job at the refinery and proceeded to Britain to study law. He entered the University College of Wales and earned his LLB in1948 through 1951. He was called to the Bar in 1950 (London). Vital to his aspiration was the discipline of economics. He took an inter-disciplinary BS at the London School of Economics. Now a qualified Barrister at Law, he returned to St. Lucia and was admitted to the Bar. Evidently, plans for his legal practice were all arranged. Compton had agreed to share Chambers with another young lawyer, his friend Maurice Mason. They were successful in several defenses of clients and became quite popular.

The two young lawyers conferred and then chose to enter politics with the view to revolutionize the system. At that time in 1954, St. Lucia was still colonized by Britain. But then, a wave of change was flowing undulatingly throughout the West Indies. Politics was the acceptable route to take to free one's country from the indignity of colonization.

John Compton's strength was the family base already established many years earlier in the rural districts. The British paternalism was being loathed and rejected throughout the British West Indies and British Guiana, though there was little or no coordination. The system was inadequate. The controlled people had no choice but to accept and condone it, as though it were the only means of survival. That was until education enlightened the people.

Remarkably, as this rare wind of change blew heavily throughout the region to effect a movement with some motivation, most prospective politicians seemed to consider the Trade Union Movement as a vehicle into politics. A human resource base had to be established and relied upon, and was a following that offered benefits. Compton entered the movement. Soon general elections were held in 1954 and Compton won his seat as an independent candidate. He had effectively trounced his three competitors as he received 1,442 votes. They received 560, 462 and 361 votes respectively.

Recognition of his talents was not delayed. Soon discussions were held to join St. Lucia Labor Party (SLP), led by popular trade unionist, George F. Charles. As a member and candidate of the SLP, Compton was re-elected to the Legislative Council. He was given the Portfolio of Minister of Trade and Production, and was re-elected in 1957 and 1961. Was there any need to establish another party? Compton found the reasons.

He and the leader of the SLP could not harmonize their views and differences. But this was not unusual; Compton's young, bright and energetic faction was termed the intellectuals. Their perception of development and growth was considered not only novel, but also radical. To assist their cause, they proceeded to arrange the publication of a periodical. They named it the *Clarion.* The pieces were incisive, caustic and provocative. But it seemed then that Compton and two of his colleagues, especially attorney Maurice Mason and medical doctor Vincent Monrose, were the forceful proponents of this change. They were activists and seemingly ubiquitous throughout the areas east, south and west of the city of Castries. The SLP old guard, including its leaders and others, were all traditionalists and perhaps averse to the changes that were inevitable. Compton's faction exerted itself to no avail. It incurred the displeasure of many. The young enthusiasts were in conflict with the barriers being erected to impede their suggestions. Conversely, the old guard themselves resented what they considered pompous dictates of the young upstarts. The conflicts were resolved. Compton, Mason and Monrose were left out of the cabinet after the 1961 expansion of the number of ministries, following general elections.

However, Dr. Vincent Monrose, one of the three musketeers involved, told me recently, "We were left out because we were at variance with the old guard of George Charles, Herman Collymore, Martin (Oleo) Jean Baptiste and others."

This eventually pushed them in the direction of forming their own party after leaving the SLP in December, 1961. The party was established and named National Labor Movement (NLM). The psychology was that the word Labor (Lah-bou-whey in French Creole) must be incorporated to retain and attract the working grass roots.

Understandably, the NLM proceeded to initiate a blistering campaign throughout St. Lucia to steer Labor followers away from the incumbent SLP. It was discovered to be a most difficult proposition. Laborites in St. Lucia were not easily swayed from the belief in the party. Their loyalty was unquestionable, and a most brilliant attorney, Henry Giraudy, gave me this story:

> I had gone to the residence of this farmer. He was one of my clients just outside the town of Vieux Fort. Our relationship was excellent. I was positive that he loved me as a human being of honesty and integrity. I needed his vote to win the constituency. After spending the entire afternoon with him and his family, I could describe the reception and treatment with one word: sumptuous. I was positive that I had won his vote. The decision time arrived when I was preparing to leave them. He took me aside with his hand on my shoulder, he said: "Mr. Giraudy, I don't only like you and what you have been telling me. I Love you, and I trust you. If you wish, you can take any one of my cows or sheep or goats or pigs or hens, I will even permit you to take any one of my three daughters. And if you wish to borrow my wife—and I mean that—I won't deny you. I am going to give you three thousand dollars to help your campaign, as I have no doubt that you will be a good representative, but I can't give you my vote. I am labor and labor I will die." After such an elaborate and truthful explanation, I couldn't help being impressed, and this reflects the views of almost every Laborite.

The National Labor Movement was extremely popular in the Eastern District of Dennery and South Eastern District of Micoud because of the Compton family roots, and its impressing upon followers that it was the same "labor" only a separate faction created because the old labor group would not accept advice and changes for the better. Years before, the sugar workers were experiencing difficult times. They were being treated less like humans and more like beasts of burden. Compton, as a trade unionist, was utterly militant and the legal strength fortified his representation. His following grew considerably, and so did his agitation on behalf of the workers. Methodically, Compton mobilized the farmers of the Mabouya Valley, Dennery, and he initiated a mammoth strike. The cane farmers blocked the roads and caused effective dislocation.

As leader of this disorder, John Compton was arrested and taken to police headquarters in Castries. He was locked away without bail. This turn of events was not accepted; the farmers, as an act of goodwill, gathered together, thousands of them toting cutlasses, machetes, axes, among other weapons, and marched on the police headquarters. It was no secret that when mob rule slipped out of hand, the result never failed to be bloodshed.

To obviate such an occurrence, Compton the prisoner was released. Sometime later, he was convicted and charged at a magistrate's court in Castries on two counts; one under the Trade Unions and Dispute Ordinance for unlawfully besetting the approach to La Caye Estate, and the other for obstructing the use of the public highway to deprive the public of the benefit of using it. We were told that the fine was paid by his cutlass-wielding, cane farming followers.

In 1961, the new party, National Labor Movement (NLM), was launched. But a party is feckless without a membership. The need was urgent to recruit supporters, and the concentration would be the rural folk and the civil service. The government of any country had always been the employer with the largest number of employees. Whenever a civil service became disgruntled or angry with its employer, this employer would have lost substantial support. It was prudent then for any government to ensure as was conceivably possible that its civil service was accommodated within reason.

The rural folk resource would prove no difficulty. It will be remembered that Compton was shot at in the Valley. He had scaled blockades intended to ambush him. Moreover, he was also jailed, however, fleetingly. The Mabouya Valley farmers admired his fearlessness and seeming dedication. Most of all, however, they remembered the Compton men who were a part of the districts of Dennery and Micoud before the twentieth century began.

In the year 1961, Compton and NLM moved a vote of "no confidence" in the George Charles government over the administration's handling of the banana industry. That motion was defeated, but anyone who witnessed that debate would concede that Compton and the rest of NLM team were a spirited and worthy opposition. During the year 1964, Compton was instrumental in arranging negotiations that led to the merger of the other opposition party, the People's Progressive Party (PPP) and the NLM. After the talks were concluded, an agreement was arrived at. The two parties, NLM and PPP, merged formally Easter weekend to give birth to the United Workers Party (UWP), and John G. M. Compton was elected the leader.

That same year, in June 1964, Compton with his young team led the United Workers Party (UWP) to a stunning victory over the St. Lucia Labor Party (SLP). The UWP won six seats in the ten-seat legislature, and these seats were increased by two when the Bousquet brothers, Allan and Joseph, elected as Independents, joined the UWP. Some months after, tragedy befell the UWP and especially Compton. One of the brightest lights within the party, and the founder, passed away. Maurice Mason was also Compton's best friend, perhaps the only friend in whom Compton placed almost implicit trust.

When Compton assumed the leadership of St. Lucia in the early sixties, he was still an eligible bachelor. He gave up that status in 1968, when he married the beautiful Janice, daughter of Sir Frederick Clarke and Lady Clarke. Sir Frederick was the first native governor of St. Lucia. The Comptons later had four children, Sean, Janice, Maya and Nina. Prior to the attainment of independence, John Compton, then the premier of St. Lucia, led many an associated states delegation to overseas meetings. A truly astute politician, he was always prepared to forcefully advance the selective sentiments of the small Eastern Caribbean islands.

Undeniably, Compton was renowned as an articulate negotiator and the *Miami Herald* had quoted a European well acquainted with the region as saying, "There is nobody else around of his stature. He is good. He is well above the rest."

Her Excellency Eileen Donovan was a former American ambassador based in Barbados. She once described him: "Certainly he is one of the most intelligent leaders in the region I have seen and heard."

Again, this writer culled this piece from a documentary I produced and aired on Radio HITS 103.7FM and 91.5FM of St. Vincent and the Grenadines in 1999:

> Fact is, the record will bear witness that when the thirty-eight-year-old John Compton assumed office in 1964, there were only two secondary schools in St. Lucia, St. Mary's College and St. Joseph's Convent. Today, 1999, almost every one of the seventeen districts in the state boasts a high school. St. Lucia then, educationally, was only ahead of tiny Montserrat in the Leeward Islands. When our closest neighbors, Vincentians, were sporting Bata canvas shoes, very many St. Lucians were still walking without shoes. St. Lucia's infrastructural development was the envy of the other East Caribbean states. Its deep water roll-on-roll-off quay, Pointe Seraphine's amazing tourist duty free shopping complex, Rodney Bay Hotel Belt and yachting marina, the Gros Islet Highway, the Compton Highway, the Compton Dam, two excellent airports, and economically St. Lucia is the most vibrant of the East Caribbean states, while tourism in that state matches that of Barbados. The Sans Souci Development, the NIS building complex, the national and commercial banks are all monuments of the Compton legacy. John Compton was St. Lucia's first prime mnister.

His political career has been nothing short of outstanding. St. Lucia—formerly neglected and abandoned by imperial Britain—had gained recognition as a "honeymoon haven" of the world. St. Lucia had become to the Caribbean what Geneva, Switzerland was to the rest of the world—a center where representatives from the various territories gathered for discussion. St. Lucia now commanded the thrust for economic development and stability. Whatever St. Lucia had achieved today, it was by dint of the exhaustive work, intelligence, perception, innovation, decisiveness and ingenuity of Sir John George Melvin Compton, who originated from Butula Hall, Canouan. Sir John had, doubtless, recognized by now that political office was a fleeting career, perhaps more so than any of the leaders of these small states. St. Lucia cannot ever forget the boy—unacquainted with a biological father—who grew into a political giant and statesman. He, more than anyone else, made St. Lucia what it is today. Comparatively, a small progressive nation shifting into top gear as it approached the new millennium.

I wrote that piece in a documentary in the year 2000, and on reflection, I would be reluctant to exchange a word. Rather, I would add that in my humble estimation, Compton, now Sir John Compton, had been one of the most successful Caribbean politicians of our time, and this was measured by the quality and volume of the developmental achievement for his people. Guyana, Jamaica, Trinidad and Tobago, though larger territories with natural resources, had not left St. Lucia wanting. Sir John had nothing to work with, save his vision. His political career, at the time of writing, had spanned nearly fifty years, twenty-nine of these as leader of government and only two years (1979 through 1982) of which he was out of the leader's office. Just prior to that time, I was the Compton government public relations and information director. My function was to articulate government's posture on radio and television and a weekly newsletter and other avenues. I was the government's trouble-shooter. My one brief resentment of the prime minister was that for independence, he brought into St. Lucia an Englishman of dubious sexual persuasion to advise on the public relations. That man spoke with me, often wanting to know how this or that would be done. Then, he took my ideas to Compton, who assumed they were his and he approved them. Compton displayed no faith in me.

In addition, I wrote a booklet that was a biographical portrait of his life. It was titled *A Prime Minister's Finest Hour.* This was widely circulated on Independence Day. He had never acknowledged its publication.

On the eve of general elections in 1979, there was a spate of violence and bombings in the city. The tension could not extend further. Firearms were spirited in from Grenada and Martinique and distributed in Castries. It was a known fact that if Compton's UWP won the general elections of that year, a coup would usurp him. The civil service was against him. He had, what many considered, obtusely declared whimsically that the civil service demands for pay increases could not be met because of the economic circumstances of the country. "You can put a gun to my head but this will not change my position"—words to that effect. By being immovable to such an extreme, the general consensus on his refusal to yield to the demand then appeared to be one of supreme arrogance. But Compton did offer a rational reason, which the civil service and his political opponents chose to ignore. The economy, he said, was in critical shape and the increase percentage being demanded was beyond government's financial capacity to approve. Compton explained, "It was not a question that they were not entitled to an increase. Rather, how could I agree when the income or reserve revenue was not available. To agree to the demand would have been irresponsible. The public service pushed the demand as we were close to independence in addition to the then volatile situation and other factors. They considered the period the opportune time to insist on the increase in wages," he said.

On Election Day, the people voted for the SLP.

We are told that on the eve of the crucial elections, Compton spoke to the members of his cabinet. He told them something like, "We are living in dangerous, dangerous times. Try to be where you are and not where you're supposed to be."

Some days later, though having lost the elections, the UWP consented to hold a "thank you" meeting for its supporters. SLP's foreign affairs minister, George Odlum, who was also deputy prime minister, had issued them a warning. In essence, it seemed more likely an intimidation. It was clear that if the meeting were held, it would be disrupted. The insinuation was that it was too soon after the loss and rejection by the electorate to hold a meeting. That was George Odlum's reasoning! Obviously, this was disregarded by the UWP executive. The meeting would take place as planned on the William Peter Boulevard, in core of the city of Castries.

As usual, John Compton, now opposition leader, arrived after the meeting had started, and his political colleagues on the UWP platform were being bombarded with plastic bags of human excreta. Save for taking one's life, this deluge of excreta was the basest weapon that the mind could invent to tread on the dignity of another human.

Some six men rushed Compton's car. One pushed his hand through the driver's side window to grab hold of Compton, but he had the presence of mind to raise the glass. The hand was almost stuck and amputated. The six assailants were joined by others banging on the car until someone yelled,"Sha-vee-aye! Capsize it! Capsize it!"

John Compton had been in difficult situations before. This moment appeared to be his Armageddon. They were in the process of tilting the vehicle when he accelerated, knocking them aside as the vehicle reversed rapidly, leaving behind a frustrated, violent gang of men, now chasing after the vehicle while resorting to a rain of platitudes. In his desperation, Compton maneuvered the car across the meridian, swerved recklessly, and drove down the wrong southern end of the road and disappeared into the night.

Later that night, almost every show window in the city was shattered with the business houses looted. This was an absolutely tragic episode during the Compton era.

Perhaps the chief architect of military action in Grenada in 1983, it will be recalled, that resulted in the ousting of the Communist-backed regime in that Organization of Eastern Caribbean State (OECS) member state, was the then prime minister of St. Lucia, John George Melvin Compton—invariably in the forefront to express his views when other leaders seem riveted to silence.

It will be recalled that Compton told off the British government in Lancaster House in London in 1966, during discussions on the then associated states status of the Eastern Caribbean States. Then, he called into question the Jamaica government's indiscretion in unilaterally deciding to declare persona non grata Guyanese professor, Dr. Walter Rodney of the University of the West Indies in the early seventies.

Compton also deemed a proposed alliance between the small units of the East Caribbean and Guyana as one reminiscent of a "shark and sardines." He attacked the then premier Eric Gairy's alleged tyranny and his Mongoose Gang, and later spurned Maurice Bishop's coup, and even suggested that the British should take action in the Spice Isle; he was again the leader to speak out when Prime Minister Maurice Bishop was placed under house arrest.

Remarkably, save for that sole period in the opposition, 1979 to 1982, Compton had had the support of the majority of St. Lucians for over four decades. That, in any phase of human politics, was an absolute achievement.

He was an assiduous worker and politician, an industrious farmer and competent attorney. Admirably, he would harvest his fruits and vegetables from his estate at Mahaut and market them himself. He would drive his old cars filled with his produce to the hotels for sale. Then, he would be in his office by 8:00 A.M. to begin his day as the leader of a developing small country. On Saturdays he would be found in his law chambers on the boulevard.

A radical action taken many years ago in the mid-seventies had opened an avenue for a new industry, from which very many St.

Lucians had benefited. Doubtless, we were wallowing in a consumer culture. Most St. Lucians are inordinately materialistic. Compton knew that. They nursed a passion for new cars and large homes with modern appliances. They were fond of displaying themselves to their friends, acquaintances, strangers and enemies. Compton had, for some time, arrested their psychological profile. To aid his construction of schools, he employed practical economics. He increased the price on consumer products, such as cognac and scotch, like Remy Martin and Johnny Walker Black. They were being sold at twenty-eight and twenty-five East Caribbean dollars, respectively. His consumption tax forced the merchants to increase the mark-up price. Today, Remy Martin and Johnny Walker Black are still being bought and consumed at EC$118 and EC$122, respectively.

Similarly, Compton needed feeder roads and to improve those in existence. Cars were being sold at EC$40,000. Rather than beg his Anglo-American counterparts, he earned the money from St. Lucians. He imposed a $21,000 consumption tax on new vehicles. Perhaps it may not have been any consideration for the people at all. It could have been that selfish element native to most people. He cared little about purchasing a new car. If St. Lucians did, then the choice was to pay for them. The price on cars jumped to EC$75,000. Ten years hence, another industry was forced open—USED cars. Most St. Lucians who are enjoying regular employment own one, two or three vehicles. The credit must go to Compton's no-lover-of-new cars vision of economic development. His acumen had taken St. Lucia, closely following a Barbados that had always been way ahead of St. Lucia's socioeconomic and educational development.

While Compton may not ever be as charming a human being as St. Vincent's Ebenezer Joshua, he had been one of the most successful government leaders of our era to have emerged from the Caribbean. Sir John George Melvin Compton announced his retirement from politics in 1996. Since then, he had been utilized by the Organization of American States (OAS) and the Commonwealth of Nations as observer of elections in Africa and Haiti and several other areas in the world. But did he retire from politics? It would seem that just as heavyweight boxers over forty years of age—and once considered over the hill—had made a successful return to the arena, the career of politics seemed no exception. Sir John in September, October, and November 2001 was involved in a National Alliance Movement that was intended to catapult him back into the fray of an occupation the machinations of which one never escaped unscathed. That alliance was shattered disgracefully to the disappointment and wrath of very many St. Lucians. Only Compton knows best his needs for survival. Incidentally, he has resumed his law practice at his Chambers on the William Peter Boulevard, Castries.

Indubitably, Sir John challenged and defied the odds against him. He returned to the political arena. Again, he won the leadership contest for the United Workers Party (UWP).

Not long after, he contested the December 2006 general elections. He won his seat and his UWP defeated the St. Lucia Labor Party (SLP) led by the then Prime Minister Dr. Kenny Anthony. Sir John and his UWP won thirteen of the seventeen seats in parliament.

Eight months later, tragedy visited them. Conflict over China brought about an unfortunate betrayal in Sir John's cabinet. This affected his health. He suffered several strokes from which he did not recover.

Sir John was flown to New York for medical attention to no avail. On his return to St. Lucia, his condition failed to improve. An atmosphere of sheer sorrow permeated the country. Father was gravely ill. On a desperate attempt at remedy, Sir John was flown to the Maynard Hospital in neighboring Martinique. They explored the possibilities, but were unable to assist. He was taken back to Hospital Tapion in Castries, where he passed away several days later.

Considered the father of this bilingual nation of St. Lucia, Sir John George Melvin Compton,who must also be deemed St. Lucia's most valiant and illustrious son, has left a legacy that cannot be erased and will be hard put to replicate. He was truly a cherished Caribbean giant of matchless substance.

CHAPTER 15

The Right Honorable
Errol Walton Barrow
P.c., S.c. B.sc. (Econ.) L.l.d. (Hony.)
Former Prime Minister Of Barbados

If it were put to the vote in Barbados, as it related to the most popular and unquestionably loved political leader of our time, one could hazard a guess that it would be Prime Minister Errol Walton "Dipper" Barrow. But apart from having retained the confidence of the people of Barbados for over twenty years, he led Barbados to attain one of the highest percentages of literacy in the world—over 96 percent. Extraordinarily intelligent and disarming, Errol Barrow's leadership skills had contributed immeasurably to the progressive and orderly socioeconomic and educational growth and development of Barbados. In regard to health care and attendant areas, the United Nations during the eighties survey ranked Barbados ahead of Italy. That was some achievement. Fact was, the tiny, 166-square-mile island of Barbados was fully developed with most of the concomitant services or amenities found in metropolitan states. For many years, Barbados had positioned itself to be the leading tourist destination in the East Caribbean. The government under the leadership for Barrow ensured this realization. He was also considered a modern day sage.

Errol Walton Barrow was born in St. Andrew, Barbados in 1920. His father was the Rev. Reginald Barrow, a retired Anglican clergyman. His mother was Ruth née O'Neil. It was the colonial era when the British controlled and exploited its sugar estates throughout the West Indies. The inhabitants were subjects of Queen Victoria.

Barbados was colonized by the British as far back as the very early 1600s. And that small island's whole character was similar to that of England. The island was sometimes referred to as Little England. During Barrow's early nurturing days, Barbados was infinitely prejudiced. Though some 95 percent of the population was black, these people were regimented. They were people who were offspring of slaves, brought out of Africa. At a period following the emancipation of slavery in August 1838, several groups of undesirables and the indigent from Scotland were forced or influenced into migrating to Barbados. Hitherto, a colony of the descendants of these caucasians still exists at Belmont.

Like the privileged expatriate civil servants, these new Bajans assumed their white pigmentation gave them the license to dominate commerce and the society of the island. Then, throughout the years, an inferiority complex was nurtured by the Blacks that their place was at the back. Upwards to the fifties, Blacks could only enter the Aquatic Club from the back. This was empirical. As a youngster in Barbados working at the *Advocate* newspaper, we reporters were given complimentary tickets to the Aquatic Club Cinema, provided that we entered through the back door and sat at the back, out of sight.

Errol Barrow forcibly changed the system and brought some dignity to black Barbadians. The foreign banks led by the British Barclays Bank then would only employ the white Bajans and then alternatively those of light brown complexion. It was reported that on his return to Barbados, he vigorously initiated the move to revolutionize the work ethic of Barbados. Black himself, Barrow as a boy and then into adolescence suffered multiple indignities. Like many leaders in the Caribbean, education was the liberating force. It jettisoned everyone out of abject poverty and deplorable conditions into an acceptable and comfortable lifestyle.

Errol Barrow progressed from primary school to Harrison College, where he won the island scholarship in 1939. He journeyed to Britain and entered the University of London. He was called to the Bar in 1949, and attained a Bachelor of Science degree in 1950. He also entered the London School of Economics and was awarded an honorary Doctor of Laws degree.

Driven towards a goal, he entered the Lincoln's Inn and read Law. He emerged successfully a full Barrister-at-Law. During that period, England was at war with Germany. Errol Barrow was propelled by patriotism; he joined the Royal Air Force (RAF) and trained as an air pilot and saw combat service. He was an active pilot and the personal navigation officer to the commander in chief of the British Army of the Rhine. Barrow had enlisted in 1940 and was demobilized in 1947. During 1945, he got married to Caroline Peaskett, daughter of Rev. George Peaskett, Anglican clergyman of New Jersey, USA. She was a broadcaster, artist and teacher. They met in Canada and later got married in that country. The marriage produced two children, one son, David, and one daughter, Lesley. During that potentially dangerous period, he also served as a member of the Livery of the City of London. Now fully qualified, the young and bright Barrister returned to his homeland, Barbados. Unquestionably decisive, Barrow needed to rearrange certain social anomalies that influenced his youth.

He joined the Barbados Labor Party (BLP) in 1950 and was elected to the House of Assembly in 1951. Barrow needed to progress, but differences in ideas created conflicts. He reasoned there were too many of them. In the circumstances, he was forced to make a crucial move. Barrow resigned from the BLP, and then proceeded to co-found a new political organization named the Democratic Labor Party (DLP), of which he assumed the chairmanship in 1958. He contested a seat for the federal parliament but lost. However, his DLP won the general elections following independence in 1966, and he became the first prime minister of Barbados.

Undoubtedly, Barrow was a Caribbean man, and even when he was not in office as leader of the Barbados government, he was still in demand as a visiting professor at a Florida university, USA in 1972, and also as a visiting fellow at Yale University, USA. It will be remembered that Barrow assumed the initiative—when the West Indies Federation failed—to conceive the birth of the "Little Eight" integration of the East Caribbean states. The distinguished Sir Arthur Lewis was his emissary. Positively, the prospects seemed glowing for this political grouping, but distressingly it died a stillbirth from sheer want of trust, obstinacy, and supreme self-indulgence by both Antigua and St. Lucia. The failure wounded him personally and he declared that some of the Caribbean leaders were "bandits." Many Barbadians will attest to the fact that the debates in parliament during the Errol Barrow-Tom Adams era were stimulating classics of wonderment as it related to the expression of the English language. The fluency, eloquence and articulation of issues of state were of the very highest standard and comparable with any parliament in developed societies. Bajans were proud of Barrow for the intelligence, benevolence and civility he personified.

Errol Barrow and his Democratic Labor Party had won a smashing victory at the polls in 1971. However, ensuing international events suggested that it was not the ideal period to control a government with a small, open economy dependent on external forces. The major international economies were hugely affected by the Arab oil crisis in the Middle East in 1973. The Arab members of the Organization of Petroleum Exporting Countries (OPEC) had adopted a punitive stand against the United States primarily. This was considered retaliatory for the USA's support of Israel in the Yom Kippur War. They employed oil as a lethal weapon.

The price of oil skyrocketed. It quadrupled almost suddenly from two dollars per barrel. Perhaps the devastating result was not anticipated by the OPEC cartel producers. The small economies like Barbados' were reeling under the unprepared costs for imported oil. Did Barbadians understand Prime Minister Barrow's dilemma? Even if they did, they expected him to have or find a solution! For instance, inflation in Barbados had spiralled to an unprecedented forty percent. This was a nightmare for Barrow when one considered the almost marvellous growth rates of the sixties. He could not respond to this major economic problem that was technically beyond his control. Perhaps then, no prime minister could. That was bad timing in office and, as a result, he lost the elections in 1976.

However, glowing credit is given to Barrow for the improvement and expansion of the Barbados deep water harbor. He hastened this project along when it was discovered that neighboring St. Lucia had constructed an excellent roll-on-roll-off facility and was attracting containerized ships away from the Bridgetown harbor. The competition for economic survival was fierce. He worked ceaselessly to generate some degree of activity in the Barbados economy that had stagnated.

Barrow and his government had been given credit for the Airport West Coast Highway. It is ironic as he had at first vigorously opposed the idea when it was introduced by the then Prime Minister Tom Adams.

Nonetheless, many opposition parliamentarians conceded that Errol Barrow was a pioneering builder as an economic revolutionary, but it is common knowledge that succeeding governments take credit for projects initiated by past administrations.

Errol Barrow had experienced some of life's vicissitudes, but he had hoped that the vision of some semblance of a Caribbean political integration would have been realized in his lifetime. He tried his utmost to no avail. In 1980, Barrow delivered a lecture titled

"Democracy and Development," to celebrate the anniversary of the Academy of Politics, which was established by the Democratic Labor Party (DLP) in August, 1974. The DLP itself as a political entity was celebrating its twenty-fifth anniversary. It was stimulating and inspiring. The lecture began with a definition of democracy, an entity that perhaps the majority of people in this world wanted to enjoy and continued to preach, but failed to practice as required. He posed the question, "What is democracy?" then he proceeded to detail some elements of the word itself being a combination of two Greek words, *Demos*, meaning "people," and *Kraten*, "to rule." In essence, rule by the people directly or by elected representatives. This distinguishes the rule by one "person, a monarch, a king, an emperor, a dictator, an oligarchy or a few people—rule then by the majority." Barrow said he wanted to make his language unambiguous by pointing out that, as most political scientists understood it, democracy was not a philosophy in itself nor a set of thoughts that was totally accepted free of question. He contended that what one would have established was a promise to a method to accept a decision, but not the merit of this decision, nor any conditions that qualified the merit as tenable. Confidently he said:

> The democratic process is supposed to ensure that the decisions ensure to the benefit of the greatest number and there is one substantial support for actions and programs embarked upon in the name of the people. Development is described in the New World Dictionary as economic, social and political progress after emergence into statehood.
>
> The term has been most frequently used internationally with reference to third world countries and specifically we have had the Development Decade and the United Nations conferences on Trade and Development, the International Bank Reconstruction and Development, the Inter-American Development Bank, the Caribbean Development Program and so on and infinitum. The government of Puerto Rico named

> their most successful development institution Formento. Whatever language, in whatever country, in whatever forum we speak, when we say 'development' we immediately stimulate the interest of all classes and races and ideologies, the interest of banker and baker and candlestick maker, the gluttons, the scholars and even the dunces. There is always the promise in development of something for everyone, a little more for some, a little less for other, rich man, poor man, beggar and thief.

Barrow explained that in order to understand the process and objective of development, which he understood to be development, it was necessary to be aware of the antithesis—"underdeveloped" or "undeveloped." He said that economists and sociologists were fond of employing definitions that were primarily concerned with per capita incomes, the strength of industrialization, "Consumption of electricity, number of telephones, television sets and motor vehicles and other particularly North American criteria which are demonstrably irrelevant to the kind of societies that such humanists as Dr. Kenneth Kaunda and Dr. Julius Nyrere are trying to reconstruct in their respective countries," contended Barrow.

Van Der Meid, also a distinguished American political scientist, adumbrated his own view of development. "The average American has built a stereotype of an 'undeveloped' country. According to this stereotype, a state is considered underdeveloped if it cannot be related to a model based upon a Western European or North American polity which is democratic and which has several political parties, widespread literacy, a high standard of living, wide circulation of newspaper and books, a consensus on the fundamentals of government, a long history of peace, and (in some models) a white population."

Barrow noted that another academic, K. H. Pfeffer of the University of the Punjab, wrote in 1960 that:

> The term underdeveloped country is based on the assumption that there exists a commonly accepted standard of development. A person or a group or a nation can only be called underdeveloped when there is a general agreement what a developed or fully developed person, nation or group ought to be like. Thus, the very category underdeveloped should be tested before use, since it is loaded with values and prejudices.

Then, Barrow in winding up his lecture, which gave some degree of insight of thoughts, he referred to the Democratic Labor Party (DLP), of which he was chairman and leader, and what the party had accomplished in fulfilling numerous objectives that impacted propitiously on the lives of the citizens of Barbados. He pointed out that human development had taken place:

> The elimination of the inequalities of the school fees system and text books, the provision of hot meals, introduction of national expansion of job opportunities through the development of tourism and industry, training in the hotel industry and in the Samuel Jackman Prescod Polytechnic, the community college, the provision of free university education, the enactment of trade union legislation and tenantry development and control. All of these and many more too numerous to mention illustrate that our living has not been in vain.

Barrow concluded his lecture on democracy and development, in his terms issuing that since democracy is a system of rule by the people, though not directly but through elected representatives, then the representatives must be told by the people that those who seek to represent them, what their expectations relative to their political and economic system are.

Prime Minister Errol Walton Barrow was a stimulating and immensely perceptive academic and one of the Caribbean's most durable, successful and proficient politicians. He was genuine in his dedication to improving the welfare of the people of Barbados. Barrow achieved enormously in the areas of social welfare, economics, education and health, and towered as the leader who achieved social equity and human rights for Barbados. Leaders of governments generally could do well to emulate Barrow's precept that:

> True personal development cannot take place if the political leaders of a country believe that the masses are there for manipulation. Moreover, to create an atmosphere conducive to the enjoyment of equal opportunities would be an impossibility."

He deserved being applauded thunderously. Prime Minister Errol W. Barrow passed away in 1987. He was survived by his wife, Caroline, son, David, and daughter, Lesley. Caroline passed away at eighty-four in Barbados on Sunday, November 11, 2001. The loss felt by Barbados resonated throughout the Caribbean and beyond. The dashing academic and politician had formed an intimate relationship with the celebrated, black American singer Nina Simone, who enjoyed her holidays in Barbados, where her friend was the leader of government. Simone loved and respected Barrow, like the untold number of people in Barbados, and she memorialized him in song. She wrote and recorded a rather poignant piece, "Little House on the Hill." In essence, it envisioned a little, cozy house on the hill for two, where love permeated to cement the ideal relationship, as it was intended for people who lived and loved as one entity. It is a moving piece of lyrics supported by haunting melody.

The soul Barrow was gone, yet his image still lingered indefinitely with us. His comparatively fleeting period of leadership brilliance still continues to illuminate Barbados and the Caribbean.

CHAPTER 16

Honorable Robert Llewellyn Bradshaw
Former Chief Minister And Premier
St. Kitts and Nevis—Anguilla

Robert Llewellyn Bradshaw nursed a passion for sartorial elegance, and his carefully nurtured moustache seemed animated when expressing his words of wisdom; it completed a sedate character that was now passé in the Caribbean.

Bradshaw cultivated a gentlemanly sort of aristocratic air about him that one could not help but respect and admire or loathe. It took many years to court and perfect, until it became an integral part of his personality. This matched the modulation of his voice as he carefully articulated his sentiments. He was a careful man who was also rather caring.

Premier Bradshaw sat not two feet away from me in his suite at the Holiday Inn Hotel, Reduit, Gros Islet, St. Lucia. The year was 1968. He was in St. Lucia to attend a heads of government meeting of the Associated States of the East Caribbean.

I posed the question: "Premier Bradshaw, what would happen if the other unit of the two-island state of St. Christopher-Nevis decides it wishes to secede like Anguilla? The vocal rumblings want to propose there is a possibility?"

He pondered awhile, then smiled. The moustache predominated the facial expression: "I commend your choice of language. But any question of Nevis seceding from this two-island state is out of the question. We lost Anguilla. We can't now lose Nevis."

"But the reports coming out of Nevis seem ominous. In fact, they are disturbing. They are considering a return like Anguilla to a dependency status with Britain! Should you and your cabinet not be apprehensive?" I persisted.

"We have not arrived at that stage, but we recognize that some areas within the Nevis scenario may have suffered from inattention. We are underdeveloped colonies now struggling for economic survival. We do not have the resources to meet every commitment. We can do so much with a limited budget. But we aim to do our best to give some more attention to the seeming problem. Problems are made to be solved and we are not an unreasonable people. Our intention is to ensure that our St. Christopher-Nevis-Anguilla state will continue the struggle as one nation."

"But doesn't nationhood suggest togetherness? Of a desire to stay together? Through cooperation and understanding? Moreover, the desire to be together as a good family?"

"That, in my view, is the essence. What we are experiencing at this stage is a family squabble. This is found in almost every family. And it little matters if the family is rich or poor. The human behavior allows for misunderstandings, as we do not always share the same point of view or sentiments," he philosophized.

And his gestures when speaking mirrored something of the man himself. He appeared to be enforcing his conviction through his gestures, as though these should convince the sceptic that he was sincere and honest, therefore not as devious as many of his counterparts. We spoke of the just concluded conference that he described as "being useful." The moustache was truly an active force.

"It is merely another of what I do assume will be several initiatives that are intended to eventually integrate the West Indies," he mused. Past fifty, he was a good-looking man and dashing.

"Do you hope to see its realization during your lifetime?" I asked.

"Fervent hope is one thing. Realization is another. I do hope. But my intuition tells me it may not happen. Perhaps it is the Caribbean Sea that literally divides us. My distinguished colleague Errol Barrow of Barbados suggests Sir Arthur Lewis will be calling on us to come to some sort of an understanding and resolution."

He stood up and so did I, and extended my hand in gratitude for his time. And, he was off to attend a dinner engagement; he had squeezed me in for a brief chat. Time was against him. He was admirable.

"Many thanks for these precious moments talking to you," I said.

"The fun was mine; hope I have been of some use to you," he responded. "We must have a longer chat next time."

Robert Llewellyn Bradshaw was born on September 6, 1916 in poverty. But history had proven that this much despised element, poverty, had served as a means to motivate billions of people throughout this universe. First, it taught humility or modesty, though too many of us students had forgotten the deprivation and suffering in youth. Fundamentally, they learned thrift and had to ensure the protection of the welfare of others to benefit themselves. Deprivation and suffering in youth were designed to nurture and strengthen one's sociology. It provided, over a number of years, unlimited guidance that too many conveniently bypass, falling helpless casualties of materialistic greed. The reality appeared to be that many were unable to handle being nouveau riche. They proceeded to erect an opaque, blank screen between them and the invaluable years of struggle. Methodically, they fashioned themselves into a distasteful character unworthy of the molding struggles of former years.

The young Bradshaw attended primary school and then engaged in private study. At the age of fourteen, he found employment at the sugar mills in the engineering division in Basseterre. He functioned as a machinist; it was an ideal source where one could become familiar with the seemingly unlimited problems of not only the machine shop workers, but also the field workers. From this informational platform evolved the matrix that gave birth to the St. Kitts-Nevis Trades and Labor Union. This was, indeed, graphic evidence that our Creator operated in such marvelously mysterious ways! How did one young man transform from being an average boy machinist to dedicated trade unionist to popular politician, chief minister, then premier and government leader of his country?

Bradshaw was driven by agitation and concern for the slave wages and unsuitable working conditions that prevailed then. Significantly, he was appointed a member of the Soulbury Commission of Inquiry into the gravest thirteen-week-old strike action in the sugar industry in 1948. He was then thirty-two years old.

It was obvious that however monstrous the metropolitan sugar estate owners may have been perceived to be, their ruthlessness bore witness that they failed to consider the black man a human being. Rather, he was a beast of burden to be exploited to the limit. They were white scoundrels with no sense of decency and integrity. These English merchants or entrepreneurs were only concerned about an increase in the sugar production. The inhabitants in the British West Indies, though slavery was abolished in 1838, were exploited with inadequate wages as though they were inanimate objects or robots!

The pattern of the trade unionist gravitating to political activist was pervading the Caribbean. Young Bradshaw was complacent. He had entered politics with utter vigor. This was a calling from which he deserved the reward of serving for a purpose, and he was being paid for this duty. The articulate Robert Bradshaw was elected the vice president of the West Indies Federal Labor Party. He was already a member of the St. Kitts Legislative Council. Undoubtedly, he was talented. As a result, he was appointed minister of trade and production during the 1956 and 1957 period of the early struggle for an identity. Bradshaw was also advisor on Caribbean Affairs to the British delegation to Sydney, Australia. Additionally, the Kittitian trade unionist and politician was the leader of a delegation to the International Trade Promotion Conference in Port of Spain, Trinidad. He was also a representative of the Caribbean Tourism Association Conference in Aruba, while being chairman of the eighth meeting of the Regional Economic Conference. Bradshaw was a perfectly rare natural. Fate must have had a choice in shaping his career direction to serve, as he won his elections for the West Indies Federal Parliament in St. Kitts. Duly elected by the people, Bradshaw the shrewd politician was given a senior post as minister of finance in the federal government with head office in Port of Spain, Trinidad.

Later, reports indicated that he performed credibly, but was admired for his unique style of leadership. He was approachable and blessed with a benevolent nature. Not unlike Sir Eric Gairy, the Caribbean's most dapper government leader, Robert L. Bradshaw, dressed impeccably but à la mode the Edwardian era or Old English. He was fond of white shirts, with turned up frontal collars accommodating a tobacco bowtie or fat tie. Bradshaw was the premiere Caribbean Black English gentleman.

Following the breakup of the Federation, Bradshaw faced the polls at home and went on to become the chief minister of St. Christopher-Nevis-Anguilla. His talents beyond his state were not discounted. They were recognized and utilized. Gentleman Bradshaw's origin and concomitant struggle were not free of life's unending vicissitudes and, without doubt, groomed him into the sort of representative he became, totally knowledgeable about the endemic problems that plagued his state. He was an egalitarian with a strong sense of justice. This suggested that he, by his own admission, was of the Socialist persuasion. His policies included free education, improved health and social services, slum clearance, land reform and a radical change for better wages and working conditions.

Bradshaw was a genuine trade unionist. While he had gravitated into political office, that especial affinity to the working man was unshakeable. He was empathetic to the cause of this grouping, whose want of provision in the twilight of their years left them vulnerable and exposed as candidates for charity or social welfare.

St. Christopher-Nevis was devoid of the financial resources to adequately take care of its indigent population, as was done in Britain or the United States of America for instance, or even Cuba. That little nation-state was still underdeveloped. Undaunted Bradshaw initiated the move to introduce the British type National Provident Fund (NPF), which was from employment savings security. Some 5 percent or 10 percent of earnings would be deducted and matched by the worker's employer. This would be remitted to the NPF office until the worker reached retirement age. The concept was introduced and, over the decades, the system of NPF was succeeded by the prevailing Social Security Scheme.

Another project of significance for which Bradshaw will be credited by his people and was introduced into the labor laws of the state was that for Workmen's Compensation. It was designed to ensure the preservation of workers' rights that were constantly being abrogated with impunity. As tourism became a vital industry to the islands of the Caribbean, it was imperative then to establish certain facilities like airports, hotels and infrastructural elements such as electrification, water, and roads. With the generous assistance of the Canadian government, the Bradshaw administration constructed the R. L. Bradshaw Airport that now serves the state.

Incidentally, the home of the Social Security Scheme is named the R. L. Bradshaw building. These memorials reflect the nation's appreciation of that splendid human being described as the father of the nation.

While anyone who knew the character of the man would not accuse him of being racist, he will be found to have been an unshakeably unapologetic advocate of the rights of the black man. For instance, as premier he, a trade unionist, appreciated the need for a periodic increment as shifts in cost of living demand consideration. Bradshaw never fought against an increment for his civil servants as other leaders had done. He instituted an automatic periodic increase in salary and he will always be remembered by the small religions, especially the Jehovah Witnesses. When other governments in the region castigated them, he ensured accommodation was available to them. He treated them with humanity. He was a Christian, who never failed to be considerate to others.

One of the very vocal proponents of the West Indies being taken over and governed by West Indians, it should not be too difficult to conceive how shattered Bradshaw was when the new West Indies Federation—of which he was the government finance minister—was declared defunct. And another incident that severely wounded him was the seceding of Anguilla from tri-state union. Anguilla preferred to return to colonization rather than to be a member of the three-island state; it is still a colony today. There was fecklessness in man from which an illusion of security dulled any desire to struggle independently with integrity to wrestle the future. Some adults with low esteem were loath to face the vagaries of life. They must be forced out by parents who should no longer support them. Anguilla was representative of an insolent, impetuous, spoiled child. The width and depth of the insipidity to secede from St. Kitts-Nevis failed to stand up to examination for rational comprehension.

"Where is the dignity?" Bradshaw begged after Anguilla seceded in 1967 to be a dependency of Britain.

"Colonization is a wicked act imposed on a helpless people. How any group of civilized people volunteer in this twentieth century to be re-colonized is beyond my conceptual grasp. This is unreal," Bradshaw declared. However, in this province of politics the will of the people was paramount. It speaks volumes. It was also well documented that the majority will consist of the stupid, illiterate, subliterate, poor and ignorant. Indications were the Anguillans were playing hard politics with Bradshaw's political opponents. Now the Nevis Reformation Party (NRP) appeared prepared to seriously challenge the Bradshaw government efforts at effectively holding the twin island state together. The agitation had persisted for some years after Bradshaw had passed on.

Premier Robert Bradshaw will be remembered, not just for the superior leadership, but for his probity, integrity, humanity, intelligence, and benevolence. He was an extraordinary human being filled to capacity with love and charity.

This illustrious Kittitian and Caribbean man who held the highest office in his country, and second deputy prime minister of the West Indies Federation was distressed about the quasi-independent status of his country. His aspiration was ultimate freedom and independence for St. Kitts-Nevis. Unfortunately, he passed away in September 1978 before this was attained. Premier Robert Llewellyn Bradshaw will forever be remembered for his contribution to improve the welfare of the people of St. Kitts-Nevis, Anguilla and the rest of the Caribbean. He slipped out of this wicked world an honorable and charismatic leader of the Caribbean.

CHAPTER 17

Honorable Ebenezer Theodore Joshua
Former Chief Minister and Premier of St. Vincent and the Grenadines

Not even remotely was there any attempt to compare the liberation struggles of Ebenezer Theodore Joshua of St. Vincent and the Grenadines with those of Mohandas Karamchand Gandhi of the sub-continent of India. Or, for instance, the biblical Joshua who led the Israelites into the Promised Land. He "was valiant and loyal," and so was his namesake of St. Vincent. But was it not fitting that Gandhi engineered his liberation movement in the British East Indies at a period to lend incentive distances away to Joshua in the British West Indies? There was quite a distance between them. Ebenezer T. Joshua was filled to capacity with confidence and his zeal was reminiscent of someone chosen for a mission to liberate his people. The masses revered him. Eyewitness reports told of one horrendous thunderstorm in St. Vincent, which had battered roads and bridges and other properties. As chief minister, Joshua drove to Mesopotamia by way of Yambou to assess the destruction; hundreds of people were milling about. A landslide had blocked the road. The people recognized Joshua. Someone declared, "It's Pappy's car!"

He told them, "I'm going to Georgetown and Biabou." They responded, "Don't worry, Pappy. You stay where you are." Some forty men proceeded to lift the car with Joshua and companion inside. They carried and deposited the car some ten yards onto a clearing. Such was the veneration for Joshua. They loved and respected him.

Conversely, prior to becoming chief minister, Joshua was twice voted out of the Executive Council and the reason being that "he was a fellow traveler of the Communists and was importing a foreign way of life to the country." Joshua's life was tumultuous. He struggled to improve the welfare of the underprivileged. Not unlike the biblical Joshua, "who defeated thirty-one kings and occupied most of the Promised Land," this Joshua, unbeknownst to him, would have to contend with hostile, disloyal and treacherous Vincentians repeatedly, until they broke his spirit. If Joshua had this premonition, would he have proceeded on his journey to liberate St. Vincent and the Grenadines? It could be hazarded that he would, as his destiny directed him on that journey to elevate and educate his people irrespective of the costs. His sacrifice was an integral part of his survival struggle.

Why would this writer presume there could be some resemblance, if not similarity to the Joshua and Gandhi approach, to the liberation of their peoples from the indignity of British colonization? The link could be that quality—unselfishness. It was rare to find humans who were unselfish! It was the distinguished Scottish economist and philosopher, Adam Smith, who in his book *Wealth of Nations* opined that, "The first law of nature is self-preservation."

Both Joshua and Gandhi seemed to be closely acquainted with the essence of moral sentiments, which argued Smith was empathy and sympathy. Self-preservation though, as Smith intended, was taken out of context. Most people translated this to mean to exclude others to ensure security of self. And this had contributed to the prevailing philosophy, "taking care of number one first." An essential element of survival in this, our grotesque world, was influenced by the pressing need to kill, lie, steal, defraud, burglarize, vandalize, prostitute, and deceive, among other social ills to ensure survival in an extravagant lifestyle.

Significantly, though Gandhi's struggle was within the sphere of politics, he courted no ambition to hold political office—an almost unique characteristic. Relative to Joshua, he already held office as chief minister. About two-thirds of the journey through his political career, he contested the elections and the result was a neck-and-neck finish at the polls with the opposition St. Vincent Labor Party. An independent candidate, James Mitchell from the off-shore island of Bequia, now had the final outcome of the crucial elections to manipulate at will. Ironically, this James Mitchell was expelled from the St. Vincent Labor party, then led by Attorney Milton Cato. It was not likely then that he would be disposed to be reinstated, or would they be inclined to readmit him! But then, politics had been known to extend itself to accommodate strange or obnoxious bed fellows. It would be less hazardous to concentrate on Ebenezer Joshua.

Self-preservation? How will it be employed? Through Joshua or over Joshua? Mitchell held the power of his victorious election seat to usher in either one of the two contesting parties to be the next government of St. Vincent and the Grenadines. Not unexpectedly, advances were made to that independent representative for Bequia. It was an intriguing scenario. He was in no hurry to respond. They needed him. Of course, he needed them more than they needed him, as they could have returned to the polls. He recognized this, but would nonetheless play hard-to-get. If he did not hold that crucial seat, he would have been disregarded. James Mitchell luxuriated in the thrill of being pursued for his attention. We were told that Mitchell, an intelligent man not unfamiliar with the human behavior, took his time to respond to the advances. Unsolicited counsel became numerous, and he was of the seafaring lineage. He got into his boat and went fishing. While fishing to an untold number of people was a livelihood, to others it was a sport that conduced to relaxation. Now the situation was one of, "Soooooo! What's in it for me?"

Well, James Mitchell could demand any ministry save for that of the premiership—all within reason. Though reluctantly, with a little hard bargaining, he would have been accommodated. But what is within reason? Some people scale and cross boundaries daringly and purposefully. Obviously, there would be a constitutional crisis if neither party showed a clear majority. Another election run-off would be of necessity. Now politicians contested elections to win. And winning to most—history had attested to that—was found to be less to serve than it was for the power of office attached. The generous rewards were well known. Under the Westminster system, to which we in the West Indies were bound, there was a job guarantee of five years. There was a government policy, therefore, that when in office, they did not consult the people as a rule. They, totally inexperienced, proceeded to operate as they considered expedient. Did they make many mistakes? But how would the stupid, naïve, illiterate and subliterate majority who voted to be served know when these mistakes occurred?

How could an independent politician with one seat in the House of Assembly be so unscrupulous as to demand being given the premiership and head of government in exchange for his seat? Quid pro quo! Presumably, this was the proposition placed before both parties. Fact was, the demand may be considered outrageous, therefore out of the question! Seemingly it could be deemed unreasonable, therefore unacceptable. The crucial question was, how could a politician without a party machinery to propel him demand to be the head of government because he held the pivotal seat? That politician could be characterized as foolhardy, or obtuse, or a ruthless gambler, or all of the above. Consider also that politicians, as a rule, did not with their own volition relinquish power unless the law demanded that they should. And even then, they resisted vigorously.

A classic example was the prevailing situation with the former presidents of the Philippines, Joseph Estrada and some years before him, President Ferdinand Marcos, and former president of Indonesia, Sukarno. They struggled to hold on to office tenaciously. It is not natural to want to relinquish power to another politician who was not a member of the same party and, moreover, when his demands seemed to be outrageously opportunistic and predatory, which could preclude any possibility of acceptance when perceived by the average power-starved political leader. Fortunately, Joshua, although aggressive, could not be characterized as a power-starved political leader. If he were, he would never have consented to James Mitchell, an independent, assuming the premiership of St. Vincent and the Grenadines. While his decision should be considered unrelated to benevolence or liberality, he yielded to the ultimate demand, as he figured that the government leadership would later be handed over to him. Such a novel concept, though considered by politicians of the same party, was subsequently attempted some years later, but failed to materialize as had been agreed in St. Lucia. It was an intriguing political dimension.

To accept this proposition would demand a Gandhi-like character—one that led and served, and where the preponderance was less on office than on service. "Reach for the sky," we were told. James Mitchell did and accomplished his aim. Why? He met a Gandhi-like modest man, an unselfish man who relinquished the political office but would still be in an influential position to serve his people proceeding gradually on to independence. Joshua accepted the Mitchell proposition. Many still fail to understand why he yielded to Mitchell's self-serving proposal. He would serve under Mitchell, who would be allowed to lead the next government. Mere power to control the lives of his people was not one of Joshua's cherished pastimes. The independent politician's demand to be made head of the government of St. Vincent and the Grenadines, in exchange for his support, could be likened to a long basketball shot from the distant opposite end of the court that netted when no one, not even the shooter himself, had expected it to enter.

James Mitchell was head of the new government in the making. Perhaps this was unprecedented in the history of politics. And as politicians are guilty of the nastiest of behavior, all in an attempt to hold on to power, here we must beg the question: Was it an impulsive, easy, or difficult decision? Why would Joshua yield leadership of his country to someone of unknown quantity, save that he had a degree in agriculture? What motivated him to concede the premiership? First, it spoke volumes of the character of the man, and a rare breed of politician, that was so un-Caribbean! It will be recalled also that in 1953, when the then British Guiana Constitution was suspended by the Winston Churchill British government, only Ebenezer Joshua's People's Political Party (PPP), along with the West Indies Independence Party of Trinidad and Tobago, had protested. He displayed what Adam Smith characterized as the essence of moral sentiment, empathy and sympathy. He refrained from being a part of the sycophantic gang of West Indian leaders who chorused congratulations to the British government on the suspension of the British Guiana Constitution. Joshua possessed rather strong character traits, again, like Gandhi. If he gave a word or made an agreement, he honored it. That was unlike many or most of the other Caribbean leaders. The record will show that Linden Forbes Burnham, former president of the Co-operative Republic of Guyana; Sir John George Melvin Compton, former prime minister of St. Lucia; Vere Cornwall Bird, former prime minister of Antigua and Barbuda; Sir Eric Matthew Gairy, former prime minister of Grenada and Carriacou; Dr. Eric Eustace Williams, former prime minister of Trinidad and Tobago; Sir William Alexander Bustamante, former prime minister of

Jamaica, were all guilty among others. But then, man was free to change his mind as frequently as he wished.

Being the head of government and consecutively being re-elected more than two times were perhaps misread as a license for arrogance. They created an awesome aura that was translated to be God-like, but they were mere impotent pawns of an unreal invincibility. Human beings should never allow themselves to be so misguided. If Joshua and Gandhi succeeded, so could others. Was it believed that Joshua had disadvantaged himself? He gave Mitchell the premiership but he held onto the ministry of finance. But at this period, his invaluable service to his people was nearing its conclusion. So, in retrospect, let us arrest Joshua's political career a distance away in 1931.

Ebenezer Theodore Joshua, or E. T., was born on May 23, 1908. Doubtless, he did not have the premonition that eighty-two years later, he would be a casualty of neglect and malnutrition. How could this have happened? Many are still speculating. The father of the nation, with six biological children, died penury stricken and forgotten, which brings one of Shakespeare's verses to mind:

Blow, blow, thou wintry wind
Thou art not so unkind
As man's ingratitude;

Gandhi's death was more dignified. He was assassinated by a religious fanatic. It was to be presumed that had Joshua known what sort of peaceful end would have been his fate, he would not avoid it. "Whatever will be must be," he once told me. "It is folly to fight against the grain." I considered him perceptive and realistic with honesty. Joshua must have had a religious nurturing, as prayer and God were constantly with him. He was educated at the Anglican School in Kingstown. Later, through correspondence, he graduated from the Chicago School of Science and Physics. A qualified teacher, in 1931, Joshua decided to escape from this survival struggle away from St. Vincent. He journeyed to neighboring Grenada and worked there as a teacher. Sometime later, he again traveled a little further south to Trinidad. In busy Port of Spain, Joshua was recruited within the Trade Union Movement, headed by Uriah Butler. Within that province he acquired the rudiments of militancy. The peoples of the British West Indies then were suppressed in colonialism and had considered it an acceptable way of life as they knew no other.

Joshua learned that there was a more dignified method of survival. It was achievable. But it had to be fought for. It had to be demanded and taken. It would entail struggle, unendingly. He recognized that it would not be an easy proposition. Nevertheless, he was determined to begin the process. He returned to docile St. Vincent where the majority were uneducated, and the so-called educated were still subliterates. Joshua was on a Herculean mission to educate his people. At that period in 1951, while many were fascinated by his brash style of oratory, most were skeptical and feckless. Joshua brought a novel approach to politics. In fact, politics to Vincentians was a new proposition. It was his desire to stir up the political consciousness of Vincentians. He and some friends and colleagues were in the throes of forming a party. Their association was called the Eighth Army of Liberation. In essence, they were the first local political grouping. In fact, this too was the origin of trade unionism in St. Vincent. It was named the United Workers, Peasants and Ratepayers Union (UWPRU). This was born in May 1951. Among the grouping trade unionists were Ebenezer Joshua and George Charles, in addition to several businessmen, such as Julian and Rudolph Baynes, Clive Tannis, Sam Slater, and a farmer and former teacher, Herman Yong.

The green group contested the elections that same year and won eight constituencies. Evidently, this attempt at cooperation was premature. There appeared to be some will and no commitment. The group disbanded in 1952, even before the legislature's term came to an end.

It was through a turning point that ushered Ebenezer Joshua in a new direction to establish his own party. He founded the People's Political Party (PPP); doubtless, it was the party that most intimately identified with the laboring class. However, since its establishment in 1952, the PPP contested every seat in six general elections, that was, from 1954. During 1974, an electoral agreement between PPP and the St. Vincent Labor Party (SVLP) restricted the PPP to fielding only three candidates. But, in 1979, this agreement was abrogated and eleven candidates were nominated. E. T. Joshua had been described as colorful and controversial. Positively, he was the first courageous Vincentian to have started the contention for adult suffrage, and to both chide and abuse the British authorities in the process. Significantly, there was another Vincentian, Carib Chieftain Joseph Chatoyer, many years earlier who had defied the British might and lost his life in the struggle. Inadvertently, Joshua had picked up the struggle for political liberation where the Carib Chief had stalled. His public meetings were provocative and he articulated the issues with refreshing eloquence. Repeatedly he seemed able to mesmerize the people, and according to one press report:

> He ranted and raved about imperialism as usual. At times he attempted to soar to Churchillian eloquence and would then power dive to soapbox oratory, to the delight of the masses.

The British were criminals who convinced themselves that their might gave them the license to invade foreign lands and to colonize them. They were merciless. Joshua did not hesitate to agitate. He was the leading light and he shone brilliantly. Joshua was to discover that one of the major failings of the Vincentian character was a seeming inability to form agreements and keep them. Throughout his political career, he was plagued with the feeble minded who were unable to suffer pressures. Again, he led his faction of the breakaway Eighth Army that evolved into the People's Political Party (PPP), and then into another relationship with the Federated Industrial and Agricultural Workers Union. The other four members stayed with him to form the nucleus of this twin organization. Regrettably, the malaise repeated itself. Some months later, those considered top members slipped away from Joshua's volatile platform. Then, his approach perhaps was considered avant-garde. His colleagues were entrenched colonials who were social climbers. Joshua's modus operandi embraced speaking the truth and this exercise never failed to offend. It was no surprise that his colleagues backed away from him. That early period of the fifties could not have been easy for Joshua, and his success reflected his indomitable courage and strength. It was reminiscent of the early leaders who stayed ahead with sword in hand, leading their army into battle. They were fearless.

Joshua was the man who represented the masses, and the underprivileged never forgot him. One of the remarkable traits of Joshua's personality was one of tolerance. While this uncivil and underdeveloped society embraced the mainstream religions, they were intolerant of other religious persuasions. For example, the Shakers grouping apparently incurred the displeasure of fanatical followers of the main stream Anglican, Methodist and Roman Catholic churches. Joshua was not interested in churches. He was interested in people and the God who created them. This was saying that Joshua was God-fearing, and his addresses were always punctuated with biblical quotations. He also went out of his way to ensure that these religious factions were not abused by those in authority.

Joshua's public meetings were always well attended and invariably they were anti-British and anti-Colonialist. The police, with no difficulty, monitored his sayings and soon arrested, charged and convicted him for public mischief and sedition. Later on, an appeal was taken to the privy council and the charges were dropped.

In a eulogy by columnist Yoen Johny of the *Vincentian* newspaper, he declared:

> Whatever he did, Joshua made sure that he kept in constant touch with the grassroots, taking the pulse of the people and keeping his ear close to the ground. One afternoon he would be at the Bentinck in North Windward pleading the cause of the sugar workers. Next day he would be at Richmond Vale in North Leeward opening an arrowroot field at break of day. He consistently articulated the interests of his consistency on the platform before Commissions of Inquiry such as the Malone Commission on Agriculture and the Jolly Commission on Sugar.

Remarkably, his life generally was consistent with the philosophy of elevating the underprivileged being free of the social pretensions endemic in undeveloped societies. To his economic disadvantage, his life was primarily devoted to giving and helping, not taking as almost every politician did. But then, like Gandhi, that was his mission—to assist the masses and suffer personal deprivation. It will be recalled also that he was a prolific journalist who wrote hard-hitting pieces edited, and not infrequently stenciled and barrelled off the *Voice* information newsletter of the PPP. He rode a bicycle and became a part of the landscape, pedaling his way on his assignments. It was amazing the volume of work he accomplished on behalf of his people, riding or walking from village to village accompanied by his wife, Ivy. In retrospect, very many Vincentians should feel guilty of betrayal and disloyalty. Anent whatever progress was achieved, Joshua was the harbinger and those who followed failed to continue blazing the trail he had set. St. Vincent today is perhaps the most backward of Eastern Caribbean states. The primitive congestion of commuters with superfluous conductors in mini buses is an example. And concrete structures are not necessarily development. This is manipulation. It was the distinguished prime minister of Barbados, Errol Barrow, who advanced that, "True personal development cannot take place if the political leaders of a country believe that the masses are there for manipulation."

When one inquired why the government permitted commuters to drive in such congestion when there was no shortage of buses, the answer never failed to be, "That's how it is!" This only suggested that government leaders had no respect for their people and failed to introduce a better quality of life for them.

The majority sat and jeered and ridiculed as Joshua indefatigably, like a freight train, strained to pull St. Vincent out of that epoch of colonialism. Were there any memorials of him? Just one, as St. Lucians would say, LAPO airstrip. Disgraceful! Unlike the Bahamas where Lynden Pindling had been memorialized on the local currency—coins and paper denominations—a stamp, highways, and a statue in the core of Nassau. And it is relevant to note here that the first chief minister of St. Lucia, George Charles, was in a similar position of destitution after having given all to his people. The John Compton regime remembered Charles' selflessness and free generosity to everyone. They secured the mortgage of his property and extended other generosities to him. Then, the succeeding St. Lucia Labor Party (SLP) named a high school in the Cul-de-Sac Valley and the Vigie Airport Castries in memory of his sterling service to St. Lucia in the forties and fifties. George Charles was pensioned in his retirement, and several years ago received a knighthood from Her Majesty, Queen Elizabeth II. While being a politician was an adventure replete with risks, those who gave to their country and people as totally as Joshua did deserved even a modicum of appreciation.

I spoke to Premier Joshua at the Holiday Inn, Reduit, Gros Islet, St. Lucia in the late sixties, and up to this day fond memories of him lingered. We had spoken of the ill-fated West Indies

Federation, of which he was St. Vincent's representative, having attended most of their meetings.

> But my dear Sir, the Caribbean is quite typical in our short history for talking, as we learned to do that in recent times. Before then, there was no one to talk to. But this failure is not a tragedy in itself. It is a mere set-back. What we need most of all is a commitment to embrace a philosophy and see it to its conclusion.

The voice was deep, guttural yet gentle, and intelligent and believable. I gathered from him through an innuendo that the West Indies grouping begged for maturity and a capacity to re-invent itself.

> The grouping still suffers from the erstwhile colonial mentality.

These were profound and prophetic words, and testimonial of Joshua's discernment. The Caribbean today was still fragmented, and perhaps was fated to be, as no stirrings were in the offing. At home in St. Vincent, the vagaries associated with politics attended Joshua. He had incurred the displeasure of the public service. Why did this come about? It was an ill omen to be at conflict with your public service! Nonetheless, as chief minister in early 1960, he commenced his campaign and he took the PPP on to a six to three electoral victory the following year, 1961.

Joshua's government was beset by several defections, and the closure of the sugar industry compounded the economic situation in the country. It will be recalled that his FIAWU called the several strikes that affected the industry. However, what seemed ineffable was Joshua's public condemnation of socialism. This remained a conundrum. It was never within his nature to be sycophantic. To agree to issues against which his conviction rebelled was uncharacteristic. But this was evidence that, as humans, we lived up to that state of imperfection. This was saying that every one of us was liable to falter. After all, we were humans! This appeared to have been an act of prostitution—totally unlike the Joshua that we had grown to admire and respect.

This, we were told, was done in an effort to appease the private sector. Again, Joshua was not that sort of man to propound a conviction as virtuous, when his thinking was at variance with that conviction. Moreover, he was a student and vigorous advocate of socialism. How could he proceed to repudiate it? Why would he? It must have been beyond his capacity to withstand whatever the persuasion! Knowing the character, we must hesitate the temptation at condemnation. But there was evidence of an obvious flaw. He was also in trouble with the Deep Water Pier issue of "debt entries on the balance sheet." There was also the Public Works Inquiry Report, and a tax waiver allowed to ministers. Joshua appeared to be losing his politically astute power of reason and equilibrium. Despite this, Joshua managed to hold on to a precarious five to four victory in 1966. As though ill fate hounded him mercilessly, within some months a defection occurred and he lost the 1967 elections. It was a humiliating defeat that commenced a visible decline or erosion of his strong political base. This question repeated itself irritatingly. Was it that Joshua remained inflexible and would not recognize that change was inevitable? Joshua and his loyal wife Ivy and a colleague, Roderick Marksman, were in the opposition. But some two years later, Marksman was offered a ministerial portfolio with the labor government. Was he expected to resist the temptation to accept? He bolted and defected from Joshua's PPP and accepted the post. Now, the ruling labor party government consisted of half Joshua's PPP members who had abandoned the party. Was it that the Vincentian politician was depravedly opportunistic, or had Joshua lost touch with reality? Humans did not infrequently fail to lose themselves in delusion.

It was imperative that Joshua should reassess his fortunes, or should it be misfortunes? Did he have the capacity to change his modus operandi? And could he recruit candidates who were defection resistant? Evidently, these were somewhat difficult expectations. Joshua was plagued by the treachery of friends and close associates. Confrontation was the order of the day, and to that level Joshua was no stranger. Statehood was ushered in and it faced the controversy, whether or not it would be preceded by elections. The issue was resolved. Statehood was introduced and elections would follow in 1972. Thirteen were being contested. The PPP captured six and labor six.

Joshua joined an alliance, which was not really an alliance per se, as Mitchell did not have a party as such. He was an independent candidate. Nonetheless, he was made the premier and Joshua was given the ministry of finance portfolio. This association regrettably was ephemeral. Two years later, that relationship ended. But our political genius Joshua seemingly lost us as his behavior appeared to be likened to that of the driftwood. Undaunted, he formed another association with his long-time political adversaries, the St. Vincent Labor Party. It was described a unity government. Milton Cato was the premier and Joshua accepted the appointment as minister of agriculture. He was not averse to playing a subservient role. That coalition of expediency was shattered in 1972 and gave fodder to the claim; this time, the blame—right or wrong—was placed on Joshua, as being unable to get along with anyone if he were not the leader. Perhaps this was correct, as he was gifted with an uncommon generosity of spirit to which the majority could not relate or disposed to comprehend.

Ebenezer Theodore Joshua had struggled from adult suffrage onto independence. This was the ultimate mission. On this journey a plethora of deserving abuse was showered on the British. Gandhi, however, had taken a different route. Independence was achieved, and he savored that accomplishment, unlike Joshua. Obviously he had lost his steam. Perhaps he was derailed! He proceeded to fight, though seemingly blinded and exhausted. But he held on inexorably to his dignity up to the very last. Apparently, Joshua had, along his journey, miscalculated.

He was now fighting, as if unknown, rapacious and greedy animals. The year was 1979. Courageously, he led his PPP into final "conflict" elections and lost ignominiously. This fighter was decimated. He lost his deposit in an area of South Central Windward, where he was once considered invincible. Friends and colleagues had abandoned him. It took immense courage and summoned a strength that was already expended. Now disenchanted, Joshua withdrew what was considered a dynamic leadership from a now visibly bruised, wounded and battered PPP in 1980. Distressingly, in 1982, he retired formally from politics, a valiant giant in his time now pushed into obscurity. Joshua had struggled unendingly for the Promised Land. Now his energy was expended. It was Napoleon who said, "The surest way to remain poor is to be honest." That Joshua was an honest man of integrity was unquestionable. And that he set the tone for Vincentian politics to prosper was again a verity. Single-handedly he cleared away the colonial debris. He was an imperfect being, rather stubborn, contentious, defiant, honest, decent and caring.

Joshua was that wonderful and hugely precious personality to such a degree that the prime minister of St. Vincent and the Grenadines, Dr. Ralph Gonsalzes, earned his doctorate with a dramatic review of Ebenezer T. Joshua's life and times. The man Mitchell he made premier failed to consider him worthy of any honors, save the naming of a serviceable airstrip after him. Pragmatically in this business of politics, politicians were not expected to leave office destitute as Joshua did. Incidentally Joshua and Carib Chief Joseph Chatoyer were now considered national heroes.

That amazing, liberal and benevolent man who began that arduous trek to adult suffrage, to internal self-government, and on to an absolute freedom that independence represented, was now considered as refuse. This brought back, unavoidably, philosopher Marcus Aurelius' gem to mind:

> *Life is a warfare and*
> *a stranger's sojourn,*
> *and after fame is oblivion.*

This was not unlike King Solomon's breathing that all our materialistic efforts were sheer vanity and tantamount to "striving after wind."

At this juncture, Joshua was confined to his home at Mackies Hill. Essentially, this isolation was self-imposed, and his visitors dwindled to a few. That few became nil. Once the most celebrated personality in the nation of St. Vincent and the Grenadines, Joshua was now abandoned and forgotten. Was that utterly charitable man unquestionably improvident? He now lived with his faithful wife in a virtual hovel! Or was it more like a pig's sty? That was the human tragedy! He gave all away and perhaps failed to consider the twilight years. Now he and wife Ivy were left unprotected from the ruthless onslaught of abandonment and neglect. How could such a benevolent soul with six children be so effectively rejected in so short a time, such as to expire from malnutrition? That word means inadequate, faulty or poor nutrition. In other words, not enough food supply!

Joshua died on March 14, 1991 poor, but with integrity and filled to capacity with love. Doubtless, he would have, too late, learned a lesson in human behavior. The Caribbean had lost a "valiant and loyal" son in his passing away.

Ebenezer Theodore Joshua's signature was written indelibly in the annals of the struggle against colonialism in the Caribbean. He was a genuine Vincentian and Caribbean gem and will remain forever treasured.

CHAPTER 18

Right Honorable Sir
Lynden Oscar Pindling
Former Premier and Prime Minister of the Bahamas

Sir Lynden Oscar Pindling passed away on August 26, 2000. He was deluged with delicious encomiums. He was seventy years old. Appropriately, he was described the "Father of the Nation" and the "Modern Day Moses" who led the fight for majority rule in 1967.

Posthumously, honors were similarly being rained upon him. For instance, the incumbent Prime Minister Herbert Ingraham announced that a suitable monument will be erected in honor of Sir Lynden in an appropriate public place of prominence. A commemorative stamp was issued to his honor also. But that was not all. The gesture disputes Russian poet Fyodor Dostoyevsky's claim that "the best definition of man is a creature that walks on two legs and is ungrateful."

More public gratitude was being expressed by so many and in so many ways. This must indicate that though Sir Lynden was not without failings and was the director of several mistakes, these were eclipsed by his monumental performance leading the struggle from adult suffrage and majority rule. It was also proposed by the government of the Bahamas that the "controversial" Discovery

Day be renamed National Heroes' Day, making Sir Lynden one of the first Bahamians to be so honored.

A suggestion was also made that the image of Sir Lynden be placed on a one dollar currency note, as was the case of George Washington of the United States of America. Prospects were the one hundred dollar currency note would also carry his image. According to Prime Minister Ingraham, "Clearly, we wish to have the views of members of the opposition prior to final determination on the note upon which Sir Lynden's image will appear, the site, style and dimension of the monument to be raised in his honor and the month in which National Heroes' Day will be observed."

Sir Lynden had retired from politics after forty-one years of public service piloting the socioeconomic and educational growth and development of the Bahamas through to the end of the twentieth century. Pindling was born on the March 22, 1930 at Nassau, son of Arnold Franklin Pindling, a merchant and his wife Viola Melba. His formative years allowed him to be educated through the primary school system and on to the Western Senior School through to the Government High School. Perhaps he was no young genius, but he was remarkably clever to such a degree, he was admitted to the University of London. Successful in his studies, this Bahamian student who would one day be considered the "father of the nation," was called to the Middle Temple, London. This was establishing that zealous Pindling was now a qualified Barrister-at-Law in 1953.

That year was an especial year for this young attorney. He returned to Nassau and was admitted council attorney of the Supreme Court of the Bahamas in July. Propelled by a powerful career ambition, he joined the Bahamas Progressive Liberal Party (BPLP) that same year in November 1953. Pindling enthusiastically combined his law practice with his political persuasion. He was progressing apace.

Three memorable events occurred to affect Pindling's life and career direction in 1956. He was first elected to the Bahamas House of Assembly as a representative of south central constituency. Shortly after, he was elected parliamentary leader of the Progressive Liberal Party (PLP). And romance had overwhelmed him. He could not conceive of being the leader of the Bahamas without his adorable Marguerite McKenzie beside him and behind him to push him on. He proposed and married her. That marriage later produced two sons, Lynden Obafemi and Leslie Oscar, and a daughter, Michelle Marguerite.

In 1962, his popularity had increased enormously. This was evidenced by his re-election to the House of Assembly. This burning, latent desire to change conditions that effectively enhanced the general welfare of people and country rose to the surface. And it persisted as he continued to articulate his vision for his country. It seemed a daunting exercise, but he persevered. Doubtless, Pindling possessed charisma, intelligence and he was articulate, but he also had a plan. He contested as opposition leader and candidate for the 1967 general election. Incidentally, he was now the representative for Kemp's Bay South Andros. His political campaigns were all stimulating and provocative. And they were all well attended. After the votes were in, Pindling had won his seat in the House of Assembly. He must have been a dynamic and perceptive representative of his constituency, and a sterling political leader of his PLP, as he became the prime minister in 1969.

Evidently, he proved worthy of his commitment to transform a colonial Bahamas to a modern twentieth century self-governing country. He struggled on against his political opponents until he took the Bahamas into full independence in 1973, within the Commonwealth of Nations. In a tribute to his dynamic leader, Bahamian Dr. David A. Bullard, II, who knew Pindling very well, declared fondly that:

> Prime Minister Pindling was instrumental in bringing about the advent of the Bahamian women suffrage during the early years. He was also at the center of the thrust for majority rule. This process of events was called the quiet revolution. I call it the era of Political Autonomy. He mounted the change for independence as the Bahamas marched into nationhood.

Prior to the suffrage campaign, women then were not only marginalized, they were also effectively suppressed. Their primary function then appeared to be that of breeding utilities. The dashing suffragist pledged that he would bring about some positive degree of respectability and dignity to the lives of women to be equal in the process of development and growth in the Bahamas. For this especially, Pindling will be remembered by women who became a major source of his political strength. And the majority rule accomplished was fittingly engineered by this now immensely popular politician with an unswerving commitment to emancipate women. This reflected the man's character.

Moreover, Bahamians and the world had become quite familiar with his protestations against apartheid in South Africa. Repeatedly he demanded majority rule for South Africa. His voice was quite distinguished among international voices appealing for the release of Nelson Mandela. Bullard said, "I declare that he was the ultimate politician. A remarkable statesman and finally the father to the Bahamian Nation."

Was Prime Minister Lynden Oscar Pindling of the Bahamas a Caribbean leader of substance? Probably his wife Marguerite, who fed him and folded him within the security of her arms when he returned home from a harrowing political day of various assaults, had whispered to him the formula for success in office. He was re-elected in 1972, then in 1977, and again in 1982 and 1987. The prodigious leader of the Bahamas, Pindling carefully chose his priorities. He placed emphasis on education and infrastructural development. And it was during his many years in office that the Bahamas became the most popular tourism destination in the Caribbean.

Pindling's government initiated an amazing advertising promotion campaign in the neighboring United States of America, and the Bahamas became synonymous with the vacation or holiday exercise. The Bahamas prospered with the Pindling leadership. He expanded his service orientation to include off-shore banking. Soon, the Bahamas became known as the little Switzerland to secretly store money away. Moreover, it was also known as a tax haven for large corporations.

The USA was perhaps the most ruthless country in the world, as it relates to tax collection. That nation was tax obsessed, which was perhaps why it was considered the most prosperous nation in the world. Large U.S. businesses were banking in the Bahamas to obviate the payment of huge tax impositions. Moreover, as the Colombian drug trade expanded with the USA being its principal consumer, tri-prong agencies of Federal Bureau of Investigation (FBI), the Central Intelligence Agency (CIA) and the Internal Revenue Service (IRS) were convinced that Prime Minister Pindling's government was sheltering and laundering the earnings of drug dealers. Their partial investigation claimed that Prime Minister Pindling himself had accepted millions in bribes along with a couple of his ministers. They accused him of being corrupt!

Pindling vociferously denied the accusation as unfounded and called it an American government designed plot to ruin his reputation and to destabilize the Bahamas as they had done Jamaica with Michael Manley. Nonetheless, Pindling was assessed a millionaire and the argument advanced was that it was virtually impossible to amass such savings on a prime minister's salary. That was unless he misappropriated public funds.

Pindling survived the adverse publicity, and was later knighted by the Queen in London. During this writer's stint as the St. Lucia government public relations and information director, I had the occasion to interview the prime minister at the La Toc Hotel, Castries. He was, in my view, as nice and courteous a human being as I considered Ebenezer Joshua of St. Vincent and the Grenadines, or Robert Bradshaw of St. Kitts-Nevis-Anguilla. I assessed him as an intelligent politician whose primary function in life was to cancel poverty in the Bahamas and to progressively enhance the socioeconomic growth and development of Bahamians. He seemed devoid of the arrogance and bombast associated with Caribbean leaders like President Linden, Burhnam of Guyana, and Prime Minister Dr. Eric Eustace Williams of Trinidad and Tobago.

Distinctly this writer recalled our conversation. I posed a question to him on something that had always intrigued me, the American-like accent of Bahamians: "How did Bahamians acquire their American-like accent? It was the only Caribbean state that seems at variance in expression from other Caribbean territories, each of which had its own peculiar accent."

He smiled and replied, "I've heard this before although I can't accept that it is American-like. I could find one word to answer that question—proximity. But I won't shelter under that. Perhaps it is because many of our early settlers were people who had already settled in the USA then transplanted here. But I don't think it is American-like. It is Bahamian."

He was awaiting a telephone call from Nassau and it arrived. I took my departure from his company to return sometime later, but I was called away.

The Bahamas consisted of 3,000 coral islands and they are located just fifty miles off the east coast of Florida, USA and some 500 miles off Cuba's most eastern point of Guantanamo Bay. Remarkably, as tourism was the major economic product of the Bahamas, very many Bahamians worked in tourism or some business related to tourism. During his infrastructural development drive, priority was given to the construction of cruise ship and merchant ship berths in Nassau, the capital's harbor. He also attracted manufacturing plants, among them being a cement factory, food processing factory, rum distillery, and petroleum refinery. In the area of finance, many foreign banks had established branches in Nassau. The economy was buoyant and the Bahamians were enjoying a lifestyle comparable with that of the average person in advanced metropolitan states. Pindling was the very nearest to the calibre of politician for whom people did not regret having cast their votes.

As was pointed out earlier, plans were well advanced to memorialize him for posterity. This effort should be applauded. Among the many Caribbean and other leaders internationally who recognized and lauded his contribution as a distinguished son of the Bahamas, the Caribbean, and the world, was Commonwealth Secretary General, the Right Honorable Don McKinnon. His tribute to the deceased prime minister appeared in the issue of the *Weekend Voice* of St. Lucia. It stated:

> The Commonwealth Secretary-General Rt. Hon. Don McKinnon, has paid tribute to the former prime minister of the Bahamas, Sir Lynden Pindling, who died on Saturday. In a letter to the prime minister of the Bahamas, the Rt. Hon. Hubert Ingraham, the secretary general said: "It was with a deep sense of loss and sadness that I learnt of the death of former prime minister, the Rt. Hon. Sir Lynden Pindling. With his death, the Bahamas has lost the father of the nation and the Caribbean has lost one of its greatest sons. Sir Lynden Pindling will long be remembered for his charismatic leadership stemming from the time he helped to found the Progressive Liberal Party leading the Bahamas to independence in 1973. The Commonwealth has cause to be grateful for Sir Lynden's role in the association and he will be remembered for his chairmanship of the Nassau CHOGM in 1985 and, more recently, of the Commonwealth Observer Mission to the May 1998 general elections in Lesotho. My sympathies

> and those of the Commonwealth are with you and the people of the Bahamas at this time. I also extend my personal condolences to the family of the late prime minister."

This Bahamian son was also a son of the Caribbean who distinguished himself as a son of the world. Memorials of Sir Lynden Pindling will be instituted and erected and these will serve as symbols of excellence for prospective public personalities to emulate in the service of God and country. His contribution to the orderly growth and development of Bahamas had been immeasurable.

CHAPTER 19

Honorable Roosevelt (Rosie) Douglas
Former Opposition Leader and Prime Minister of the Commonwealth of Dominica

The moving tributes that rained down on a truly illustrious son of the Commonwealth of Dominica and the Caribbean, Prime Minister Rosie Douglas, made needless the research to find the information that would highlight the salient points of his colorful life. The encomiums were, in essence, a celebration of a genuinely golden human being, who passed away in October 2000. He was fifty-nine years old. According to his successor, Dominica Prime Minister Pierre Charles: "Perhaps the most fitting tribute that I have heard in relation to the character of the man Rosie Douglas, was shared by the prime minister of St. Lucia when he said, Rosie has never met a person he did not like or could not get along with;' that I believe sums up the character and personality of the man whose life we are gathered here this evening to celebrate." He proceeded tearfully to say:

"Whether Rosie in Grand Bay, Dominica, or Castries, St. Lucia, St. John's Antigua, Kingstown in St. Vincent, London in Great Britain, Havana in Cuba, Tripoli in Libya, Soweto in South Africa, or any of the hundreds of cities in the world that he visited, Rosie ministered to the ordinary and the dispossessed. Those who knew him well can attest that for the last eight months he lived for nothing else but his people."

And his earlier struggles were numerous. For instance, in the early seventies he was deported in chains from prison in Canada to his place of birth, Dominica, and perceptively, seemingly free of bitterness declared to the officials in Canada, "I will return when I am my country's prime minister."

In a excerpt from the OECS *Advocate,* Rosie's friend, St. Lucia's former minister of foreign affairs and international trade, George Odlum, said it was not always smooth sailing for Rosie:

> He remained for many decades in the political wilderness. A casualty of the Black Power Movement, a casualty of the Civil Rights Movement, a casualty of the Grenada Fiasco. Douglas endured the same political fate as his colleagues in the Caribbean left, like Tim Hector of Antigua, George Odlum of St. Lucia, Ralph Gonsalzes of St. Vincent and Bobby Clarke of Barbados. He had seen it all and endured it all and was slowly developing the empty vacuous store of the small band of believers who had been to the mountain-top and seen the promise of the land. In recent months, his concern had telescoped into the possibility of rescuing Dominica from the deep abyss of underdevelopment. He had started a feverish number of visits to countries he had cultivated during the years that the lotus had eaten.

Positively an activist for the underprivileged, Rosie Douglas had commenced moving in the direction to radically change the character of Dominica. His friend Tim Hector, a politician in Antigua, wrote a tribute to him in the OECS *Advocate* newspaper of October/November 2000.

It declared that Rosie was one of those rare leaders the foundation of whose personal philosophy in the conscious and unconscious believed that he did not derive his authority from any office as such, but rather from the people. He pointed out that, to this end, there was a positive tension between the prerequisites of office and what should be described "the imperatives from people." According to Hector's account, Rosie had indicated to him something anent his life earlier on his father's estate and the ill treatment that was being received by the Caribs. It was not just how they were treated, they were unequivocally exploited and this angered him.

Rosie had a close attachment to the Caribs; Hector explained his role was tantamount to that of "chief servant to the indigenous peoples of the world, be they Caribs in the Caribbean, the original peoples of Latin America, the native Americans of North America, Africans in Africa, Tamils in Sri Lanka, Palestinians in Palestine, Kurds in Iraq, all remained a lifelong commitment."

This was not the end of the tribute to his friend, the fallen prime minister. Hector opined:

> When I saw him last he was moved to fury, unbelievably in silence, because the representative of the Kurds was not given an opportunity to speak at an international conference in which he was assured he would have the right to speak. As a head of government, Rosie could not join the Kurdish leader's lone protest; he felt hamstrung.

Additionally, in Hector's eulogizing of his friend Rosie Douglas, he told of how he and Rosie had lived as brothers together in Montreal in the same apartment in 1973. And their close friendship included the former West Indian cricketer, Alfie Roberts of St. Vincent. As a team that comprised Rosie, Alfie, Franklyn Harvey and himself, they had helped to organize Caribbean conferences that resulted in the founding of the now reputable Black Writers Conferences of 1968. Said Hector:

> Rosie single-handedly befriended the Canadian elite, including former Canadian Prime Minister Pierre Trudeau and Quebec Premier Renè Levesque, who influenced the funding for the Caribbean Conferences. Born out of these activities, he said,

> was that the center of the Caribbean movement for change shifted from England to Canada. And later again it moved to where it ought to be, the Caribbean, and notably one of their vital projects.

Hector, propelled by Rosie and Alfie and supported by them, was the "drive" to encourage every Caribbean person they met in Canada to embrace the study of something. Those people included Haitians and Dominicans, and began a Caribbean nation of language groups of the region that evolved into the Caribbean Nation Bureau. Nonemotional, Hector emphasized that the novel idea of one Caribbean emerged then as distinct from an English-speaking Caribbean grouping. And it was a new departure, he said:

> In 1965 to 1966 after two meetings with Guyana's Burnham in Canada, Rosie, Alfie, Franklyn Harvey and myself put to the then Prime Minister Burnham the idea of CARIFESTA embracing all the French, English, Spanish, Dutch and American territories of the Caribbean.

Hector pointed out that when they had introduced this CARIFESTA (Caribbean Festival of Arts) idea to Burnham, they had proposed also that following the exposition of arts, there ought to be a conference of progressive parties of the Caribbean to set up a sort of a One Caribbean agenda. Evidently, this was not realized. He claimed that to Rosie's dying day, despite his close friendship with President Burnham later, he was always uncomfortable with the version of CARIFESTA Burnham adopted and CARICOM accepted.

Clarifying this statement, Rosie's friend said that Burnham's concept of CARIFESTA on presentation was entirely different from what "our hearts and heads had arranged." He proceeded to explain that "between the idea and the reality fell the shadow." This of course was, doubtless, unacceptable to them. Rosie and the group were resolute in their view that where history, politics and economics divided the people of the region under different colonial rule, the culture, forged as resistance, was in essence representative of a prime vehicle to circumvent any division and disunity that could affect their vision of a "One Caribbean." They were absolutely clear that the political and economic would be indissolubly bound to the cultural. This, he lamented, was not to be and in fact, may not be.

The articulate Tim Hector proceeded to refer to the 1969 incident when Rosie led a group of students in Canada "to resist the racist practices of professors at Sir George Williams, who were ball-curving black students into failure, and to run their lives in some instances."

That incident proved cataclysmic. And when proof of racism was discovered by the Canadian authorities, they hastened to offer "amnesty" to the students. Rosie and other students declined to accept, but chose the penalty of eighteen months in prison. This, of course, reflected the character of the man Rosie. After being held in maximum security, he was deported to his home island Dominica in chains. And as it was meant to be, this shackled man later became the prime minister of his country.

And here it was difficult just to take mere bits of Hector's moving piece on his friend Rosie when the package of the reminiscences was absolutely glowing. Moreover, the intention of this book was to give exposure to the hitherto undisclosed pertinent events that influenced the political direction which, in turn, catapulted them into office as head of government. Hector expressed the view:

> Further, the man, the remarkable person, who stood up against racism in education was slated to be honored with an honorary doctorate by the vote of the student body, years after, of the very university which led to his imprisonment. The rejected student leader was becoming a head corner stone of more than his alma matar. That was some triumph.

It will be remembered that as Rosie's lifetime was charged with unending struggle for change, he was blessed with the good fortune and vitality to write a book titled *Chains or Change.* However, a deliciously defining moment of the Dominica Prime Minister Rosie Douglas' life arrived when he returned home to Dominica in chains, and a group of young men and young women from Grand Bay met to welcome him at the airport. "My faith and love were reinforced. That remained one of my life's treasures," he had lamented.

At this juncture, we could reflect on the ongoing goodwill of Cuba having accepted the role to train the Caribbean. The prospect was that thousands of young people throughout the eastern Caribbean would be university trained. And this project began in the late seventies. One may ask how does this relate to Rosie? According to Hector, it was not inconsistent at all, that this man Rosie who had journeyed across Canada in an attempt to persuade Blacks to "stand up for their rights," and encourage them to pursue some form of educational development, he could be again, in the forefront to initiate a similar project. Hector explained:

> It was not accidental that after the Grenada Revolution, Maurice Bishop, George Odlum, Rosie and I would forge an agreement that Cuban scholarships be granted to those who would not otherwise have access to higher education. This was at the height of the cold war. We were demonised as Communists. And as such, the devils incarnate. It was felt that these students from Antigua and Barbuda, Dominica, St. Lucia, St. Kitts, St. Vincent were being trained in "Cuba as guerrillas," and not as doctors, engineers, veterinarians, agronomists, dentists and economists.

Hector said that they took this demonization as "Communists," with inner pain and outward calm. They knew it was a product of cultivated ignorance, which would pass away. Only when the sweep of history whispered compliance to consign the nonsense and its authors, a permanent residence for posterity—the garbage bin.

Obviously, the Cuban scholarship project for the English-speaking Caribbean had been an enormous success, and Rosie should have taken the credit, but shared it with his friends. As Hector said not unexpectedly, today the governments of the Caribbean region are all rushing in to enjoy the fruits of the scholarships they earlier lampooned. And it was a dialectical and radical turnaround that did not escape Rosie. He luxuriated in the fact that a huge section of this new generation of intellectuals and technocrats would embrace Caribbean development, "not in first world terms, not in cold war terms, but through the clear glass of historic Cuban Revolution."

But there was more to Rosie Douglas than CARIFESTA and making education in the Caribbean healthy. He considered Caribbean development a much more fundamental proposition. Rosie himself, said Hector, was on a first name basis with leaders like Charles Taylor of Liberia, Gerang in the Sudan, and with the leadership opposing both sides in Sierra Leone, while the same is true of Gambia, of Nigeria, of Tanzania, of Zambia and, of course, South Africa with Libya. Proclaimed Hector:

> I mentioned those two last deliberately. It is not so common knowledge that Libya has developed a new International succeeding the four European socialist internationals. It embraces some eighty countries of Africa, the Caribbean, Asia and Latin America, including European countries too.

And at this point of his tribute to his friend Rosie, Hector declared that it would be an understatement to say that, save for Colonel Gaddafi, revolutionary leader of Libya, Rosie Douglas was the best known international leader of this new international. Admittedly, very many in the Caribbean were unaware of this political status that Rosie held so unobtrusively. Some may claim that this placed him in an elevated province, even beyond the considerable efforts of that black activist Marcus Garvey. One, perhaps, could hazard an opinion that Rosie had picked up Garvey's struggle with as little fan-fare as was conceivably possible. Hector advanced the view:

> Once again, those of us who dared to visit Libya, dared to become members of the new International, the first such created in Africa, led by Africans, were demonized. This time not as Communists, but as "terrorists." Rosie scoffed at his critics and ridiculed them with his special brand of comic mockery. "Gorillas," he called them, "and not good-looking either," he guffawed.

But how did Rosie use his eminence in the Mathaba, the African-based International in Libya?

Illustrative of Rosie's effective dynamism, Hector opined that they had visited Libya in the 1980s when South Africa's racist regime was the epicenter of world struggle. The ANC was considered passé as it was established in 1912, therefore suffered from exhaustion caused by the relentless brutality from the regime. Other organizations, such as the Pan-African Congress and the Black Consciousness Movement of Steve Biko (considered more militant), were viewed as being more committed with a dynamism that conduced to the engagement ongoing struggle. Rosie proceeded to argue on behalf of the ANC to no avail. To change what seemed unchangeable appeared then to be Rosie's preoccupation. He then assigned himself a Herculean task to reverse what appeared to be rejection of the ANC perspective. He traveled thousands of miles between Libya, Tanzania, and Zambia, meeting ANC leaders and freedom fighters. He cultivated the friendship of Chris Hani, who later passed on or would have been Mandela's successor. Hani then led South Africa's Liberation Army. Rosie, bold and uncommonly daring, in collaboration with Chris Hani, initiated a scheme that allowed South African fighters to be trained in Libya as Dominicans. Of course, some Dominicans were actually part of this ruse. It was an audacious move that proved effective. The South Africans had so distinguished themselves in training under the aegis of ANC, that the ANC and Libya relented and proceeded to develop an action relationship that Mandela himself had applauded as being decisive in ensuring South Africa's liberation less from racism than from an appalling racist rule. Doubtless, "Rosie was the international catalyst."

Incidentally, the many years of activism will disclose that this unique Dominican Rosie, the Internationalist, was not confined to Africa. He enjoyed a comfortable relationship with the leaders of the countries and parties throughout Europe, and was, as usual, on a first name basis with most.

Relative to Rosie as prime minister of Dominica and his approach to the government of France to enter into a relationship with a similar status of that of Martinique and Guadeloupe, termed departments of France, there was widespread belief that Rosie's mental state had retrogressed. How could he, a militant, a freedom fighter, an intellectual, a progressive, consider neo-colonialism for his country Dominica? The idea was ludicrous. He suffered repeated jeering. Hector explained:

> Even I smelled the rat of re-colonization. When I confronted him, Rosie was working out a strategy through the Socialist International, not only for a special relationship with Dominica, but for the region. And for economic agreements well beyond Lomé, with a very different draw-down economic facility. Rosie dared where others feared to tread, always with the Caribbean and people of African descent foremost.

Here Hector begged the question of what made Rosie a young man from Portsmouth, Dominica, the most prominent Caribbean Internationalist, since George Padmore, C. L. R. James, Frantz Fanon and Walter Rodney? He conceded that Rosie's theoretical contributions were no match with those by James, Fanon and Rodney, but his practical contributions were only equalled by the great Padmore. He said that Rosie's commitment to Dominica embraced Africa and the world. Free of such a commitment to Dominica, his international range and scope would have been restricted. It was within this context that his dynamism touched the universal. Then illustrating a case, he told how a young man was arrested in Halifax, Nova Scotia for organizing Blacks. Rosie got on the phone and called the then conservative prime minister of Canada, John Diefenbaker, and asked him to call the police in Halifax, and post the bail for him. That was influence and Rosie Douglas was unquestionably unique.

On concluding this tribute to Prime Minister Roosevelt Douglas by one of his closest friends, it should be mentioned here that the occasions when such long, eloquent and touching tributes are placed in print after one passed away had been rare.

> Rosie Douglas is in his own right, then, one of the most notable Caribbean Internationalists of this or any time. Long live his spirit to inspire generations unborn. Many great and small, have spoken from the lofty peaks of Soufriere to the plains of Salisbury in tribute to Roosevelt Bernard Douglas, October 13, 1941 to this day of his internment October 14, 2000. Tomorrow would have been his fifty-ninth birthday. It was not to be. Shock at this Titan's sudden fall has given way to calming superlatives and well deserved.

And eulogizing of this immensely popular Dominican prime minister flowed from the people who knew him and loved him dearly. Again, the following was excerpted from the OECS *Advocate* newspaper and the encomiums were from Yvor Nassief. The piece was headed. "Rosie: An Internationalist—A Maverick and a Friend."

It was not possible to carry the full text of the moving sentiments being expressed, but in essence Yvor Nassief, a businessman in Dominica, wrote that the prime minister was a friend and those who knew of the friendship misinterpreted it to one of influence of Rosie. He explained, however, that his friend "did not operate from that level."

Experience had taught that mistranslations of friendships were nothing uncommon. He said that they first met in 1991 when Rosie took him and his father to Cuba to contract the sale of soap, and later the visits were repeated. Opined Nassief:

> I enjoyed his company because he was amazingly candid and open to criticism, which I was not short of. He was genuinely funny and easy to laugh with. Rosie's genius was his uncanny and innate self-confidence, but it was also his weakness. He could walk to the edge of a cliff and have no fear of falling over in the full confidence that he would land on his feet. He was a survivor never falling on his face, but always on his feet with a smile.

Nassief said that Rosie was a maverick. That he resisted and spurned conventional stereotypes, the sort that Dominica's politics suffered for some time. This situation, however, permitted him, like a giant, to straddle the political divide. He did not see nor accept himself of being *Roseau* or "Country" or "little man" or *gros bouy* or some opportunist wanting to enrich himself or looking to advance vested economic interests.

According to Nassief, such a proposition as he represented carried no burden the manner in which he weighed himself, or how others accepted him was a privilege his predecessors failed to enjoy. Candidly, Nassief contended:

> His promise to the region was that he did not come from the same stream as the incestuous clique of UWI political aficionados who now make up the leadership of CARICOM. He distrusted them as much as they misunderstood him. It was he who championed the French Option, despite their protestation and went to Libya against all advice because he was the only one not shackled by conventional wisdom. The people of the region are the losers for Rosie not having sufficient

> time to shake up the body politic of CARICOM and infuse it with new and different thinking. CARICOM will now return to its painful and parochial monotony. Rosie was that Internationalist in the truest sense of the word.

While Rosie Douglas' tenure of office as the prime minister of the Commonwealth of Dominica was only a matter of mere months, from January to October 2000, the measurement of the man and his service encompassed some three decades with a concentration on his unswerving activism on behalf of the oppressed minorities internationally. We have no doubt that his loss represented a huge setback for the Caribbean region. But for the end of his life span with us, he indubitably would have modernized the face of his homeland, Dominica, and make that nation a truly dynamic force to be reckoned with in the east Caribbean and to impact positively on the wider Caribbean. Rosie's contribution as an international activist, intellectual and politician of integrity was recorded as glorious. Titanic, he now rests in a new dimension beyond the disorder of this world.

Bibliography

Adams, Tom. "Interview with Prime Minister Tom Adams of Barbados." *Teller* Magazine 20 July 1983: page 15.

Aurelius, Marcus. *Life's Fame.* New York: Penguin Books, 1986.

Ayers, Ed. "Speech of Change." *Awake* Magazine. New York: Watchtower Bible and Tract Society of New York, Inc., March 2006.

Baptiste, Owen. *Crisis.* Port of Spain, Trinidad: Inprint Paperback Publications, 1976.

Barrow, Errol Walton. *Democracy and Development.* Bridgetown, Barbados: Academy of Politics, Democratic Labor Party. 1980.

Barrow, Errol Walton. *True Personal Development.* Bridgetown, Barbados: Democratic Labor Party, 1980

Beard, Charles A., Mary R. Beard, and William Beard. *Beards' New Basic History of the United States.* New York: Doubleday, 1960.

"Bird's Money Problems." *Star Newspaper of St. Lucia.* 12 July 1982.

Bitt, Bertrand A. "Father of the Nation." *Gulp* Magazine. St. George's, Grenada.

Charles, Ronald A. "GULP Celebrates 50 Years" St. George's, Grenada: RAC Consultants, 1987.

Chambers Biographical Dictionary. 6th Edition. New York: Chambers, 1997.

Churchill, Winston. *History of the English-Speaking Peoples.* London, 1971.

Churchill, Winston. *Memoirs of the Second World War*. Boston: Houghton Mifflin Company, 1959.

Commins, Saxe and Robert N. Linscott. *Man and Men: The Social Philosophers*. New York: Random House, 1947.

Confucius. *Society of Women*. New York: Random House, 1976.

Crankshaw, Edward, *Khrushchev, A Career*. New York: Viking Press, Inc., 1966.

De Gaulle, Charles. "Loving Dogs." New York: Simon & Schuster, 1984.

"Donald Cultross Beattie." *Great Lives Great Deeds*. Pleasantville, NY: Reader's Digest Association, 1964.

Durant, Will and Ariel Durant. *The Age of Voltaire*. New York: Simon & Schuster, 1965.

Grenada's 25th Independence Anniversary. St. George's, Grenada: Grenada Trade Union, 1999.

Hector, Tim. "Rosie, A Friend." OECS *Advocate*. Castries, St. Lucia. October 2001.

Hector, Tim. "Tribute to Rosie." OECS *Advocate*. Castries, St. Lucia. October 2001.

Ingraham, Hugh. "Tribute to Sir Lynden Pindling." *Weekend Voice*. St. Lucia. October 2001.

"Is There a Creator Who Cares About You?" *Awake* Magazine. New York: Watchtower Bible and Tract Society of New York, Inc.

James, C. L. R. *The Black Jacobins*. New York: Random House, 1963.

James, Willie. "A Dictator Passes On." *Teller* Magazine. Castries, St. Lucia: East Caribbean Publishing House, 1983.

James, Willie. "Gairy's So Called Mongoose Gang." *Teller* Magazine. Castries, St. Lucia: East Caribbean Publishing House, August 1984.

James, Willie. "Sir Eric Confuses Grenada." *Teller* Magazine. Castries, St. Lucia: East Caribbean Publishing House, August 1984.

James, Willie. "The Old Bird Flees The OECS Coop." *Star Newspaper.* St. Lucia. 18 July 1987.

Jones, Anthony Mark. *Caribbean Men.* Port of Spain, Trinadad & Tobago: Longman Caribbean, 1981.

Jones, Anthony Mark. *Eustace Eric Williams.* Barataria, Trinidad & Tobago: EDUCO Press, 1983.

Kissinger, Henry. "Tale of Failed Efforts." *Awake* Magazine. New York: Watchtower Bible and Tract Society of New York, Inc.

Mandela, Nelson. *A Long Walk to Freedom.* Boston: Little, Brown and Company, 1994.

Manley, Rachel. *Drumblair: Memories of a Jamaican Childhood.* Kingston, Jamaica: Ian Randle Publishers, 1996.

Mead, Lawrence M. *The New Politics of Poverty.* New York: Basic Books, 1993.

Mitchell, James "Son." *East Caribbean Unity.* Kingstown, St. Vincent of the Grenadines, July 1986.

Moore, Thomas. *Utopia.* Ed. H.V.S. Ogden. New York: Appleton-Century-Crofts, Inc., 1949.

Nascimento, C.A. and R.A. Burrowes. *A Destiny to Mold.* Trinidad & Tobago: Longman Caribbean, 1970.

Nassief, Yvor. "Rosie Internationalist." OECS *Advocate.* Castries, St. Lucia. October 2001.

New World Translation of the Holy Scriptures. New York: Watchtower Bible and Tract Society of New York, Inc., 1984.

Odlum, George. "Rosie the Revolutionary." OECS *Advocate.* Castries, St. Lucia. October 2001.

Perez Vila, Manuel. *Simon Bolivar: His Basic Thoughts: biographical sketch and selection of documents.* Caracas: Academia National de la Historia, 1980.

Pierre, Charles. "Revolutionary." OECS *Advocate.* Castries, St. Lucia. October 2001.

Reagan, Ronald. *An American Life.* New York: Simon & Schuster, 1991.

Rousseau, Jean Jacques. *Du Contrat Social.* Trans. G. D. H. Cole. Franklin Center, PA, 1982.

Schelesinger, Jr., Arthur M. *A Thousand Days: John F. Kennedy in the White House.* Boston: Houghton Mifflin, 1967.

Shakespeare, William. *As You Like It.* Act II, Scene VII.

Smith, Adam. *Wealth of Nations.* Franklin, PA: Franklin Library, 1978.

"Terrorism." *Awake* Magazine. New York: Watchtower Bible and Tract Society of New York, Inc. 22 May 2001:3.

Thatcher, Margaret. *The Downing Street Years.* New York: Harper Collins, 1995.

"The Boy From Batula Hall Canowan" *Dilly Dally with Uncle Willie Show.* HITZ-FM, Dorsetshire Hill, St. Vincent and the Grenadines. 2000. Radio

Theophilus, George. *Management and Development.* n.p. Castries, St. Lucia. 1982. Speech.

Tillinghast, E. "Terrifying Dilemmas." *Awake* Magazine. New York: Watchtower Bible and Tract Society of New York, Inc., May 22, 2001.

Ward, Barbara. *Nationalism and Ideology.* New York: W.W. Newton and Company, Inc., 1966.

Ward, Barbara. *Spaceship Earth.* New York: Columbia University Press, 1966.

Webster New World Dictionary. Ed. David B. Gurainik. New York: Simon & Schuster, 1986.

Wells, H. G. *Short History of the World.* London: Watts and Company, 1933.

Who's Who, Belize. 73rd ed. London: International Who's Who, 2000.

Williams, Dr. Eric Eustice. *Forged from the Love of Liberty: Selected Speeches.* Ed. Dr. Paul K. Sutton. Port of Spain, Trinidad and Tobago: Longman Caribbean, 1981.

Williams, Dr. Eric Eustice. *From Columbus to Castro.* London: A. Deutsch, 1978.

Williams, Dr. Eric Eustice. *History of the People of Trinidad and Tobago.* Barataria, Trinidad & Tobago: EDUCO Press, 1983.

Williams, Dr. Eric Eustice. *Inward Hunger.* Barataria, Trinidad & Tobago: EDUCO Press, 1983.

The World Book Encyclopedia, New York: Scott Fetzer Co., 2010.

Yeltsin, Boris. *Against the Grain.* Trans. Michael Glenny. London: CAPE, 1990.